STOKE
AND I:
THE NINETIES

NEIL JAMES

STOKE AND I:

THE NINETIES

First published by Pitch Publishing, 2018

Pitch Publishing
A2 Yeoman Gate
Yeoman Way
Worthing
Sussex
BN13 3QZ
www.pitchpublishing.co.uk
info@pitchpublishing.co.uk

ISBN 978-1-78531-441-4

Typesetting and origination by Pitch Publishing

Printed and bound in India by Replika Press Pvt. Ltd.

Contents

For Isobel and Daniel
– anything's possible
if you keep trying.

Acknowledgements

WRITING this book has not only realised a long-standing ambition for me, but has also restored my faith in human nature. So many people went out of their way to help, putting me in touch with former players and managers, providing advice and encouragement, allowing me to use material that they'd collected over the years and providing all the necessary support and assistance to get this book out of my head and on to the shelves.

In no particular order, this book could not have been written without: Paul and Jane Camillin at Pitch Publishing; Duncan Olner at Olner Design; Martin Smith and Dave Frith (*The Oatcake* fanzine); Anthony Bunn and Lee Hawthorne (*Duck Magazine*); Pete Smith and Martin Spinks (*The Sentinel*); interviewees Lou Macari, Peter Coates, Ian Cranson, Mike Sheron, Carl Beeston, Wayne Biggins, Shaun Wade, Tim Gallimore, Gareth Thomas, Mick Pinnington and Dave Shenton; Robert Eardley – a great sounding board and co-interviewer; Andrew Wilshaw for the use of the old VCR and finally my family for supporting me in ways too numerous to list.

Introduction

AN invitation dropped through my letterbox yesterday: a 1990s-themed birthday party for my mate's fortieth. They're popping up everywhere now, these '90s nights – the latest carriage on the ever-rolling nostalgia train. Nigh-on 20 years since the decade of Britpop, *The Word* and New Labour ended, the teenage years of my generation have been reduced to teary-eyed reminiscence. Needless to say, it all makes me feel very old.

It seems that two decades is about when it happens – the time when a man starts to grieve for his youth and looks for something to make it better. People will spend time and money on anything that gives them just the merest scent of what it used to be like to live without the burden of responsibility. Believe me, I do exactly the same. Nineties compilation CDs, nostalgia shows on Channel 5, books on Oasis and Blur – I lap them up because they remind me of the last time in my life I felt free. You see, as great as it's been supporting Stoke City in the Premier League as a late 30-something, I'd swap it all just to be 15 years old again, watching a Mark Stein shot arrow through the rain and hit the net at the old Boothen End. That might be why you're reading this book now. It's definitely why I wrote it.

It might seem a pointless exercise to some, but I make no apology for presenting you with what is essentially another dose of '90s nostalgia. Like it or not, there's pleasure to be found in simply remembering and occasionally laughing about the good, the bad and the bloody awful of days gone by, even if all we're doing is distracting ourselves from the present. The 1990s was a fascinating decade though, not least for Stoke City, where extremes of joy and despair sat side by side as the club lurched between a promotion and two relegations, worked its way through nine managers and, at times, had fans rioting in the stands of its new stadium. It's a story that's certainly worth telling.

This isn't, however, just a book about what happened on pieces of turf 20 years ago. It's the stories from the periphery of the sport that give the game its soul; it's the anecdotes from those who played and watched; it's the story of being a football-mad teenager in the last decade before the internet changed the world.

Therefore, if you're someone who's interested in lists of football results and old league tables, you're in the wrong place. Likewise, if you're looking for a thesis on some aspect or other of football culture, you're also probably in the wrong place.

But if I were to borrow the words of one author from the era and say, 'Choose Lou Macari, choose the Autoglass Trophy, choose Potteries derbies played out on the playground, choose Kick Off 2, choose Mark Stein's goal at Rotherham,' and you found yourself nodding along, then you'd be in exactly the *right* place.

Season 1989/90
A New Decade

AT the start of the 2017/18 season, a man stands outside the bet365 Stadium hawking the same pin badges he's been struggling to shift for the last decade. Nobody buys those things anymore. He's branched out though in recent years and diversified his stock a little.

For now, draped across the tired old chipboard displaying the array of tiny enamel club crests is a collection of *the* must-not-have accessory for all true football fans: the much-maligned half-and-half scarf. Fifty per cent of it's woven in the red and white of Stoke, the remainder in the dark blue of Arsenal's latest away kit. Today, the Gunners are in town. Look, there's the date on the scarf. It's a souvenir you see.

My son Daniel, three years old and walking alongside me, tugs on my arm. 'Can I have one, Daddy?' he asks in the same way he asks for anything brightly coloured that catches his eye. How can I explain to him in child-friendly language that only a complete twat would wear one?

'Those scarves aren't very good, mate,' I say, not untruthfully either. 'Give it one wash and it'll fall apart. I'll get you a proper one next time we're in the club shop.'

Thankfully, he's satisfied with this and we carry on walking without the hell of a three-year-old's tantrum being unleashed upon the innocent matchday crowd.

Everybody in Stoke hates Arsenal. Would you wear a scarf that's got 50 per cent of it dedicated to those scumbags? I'd rather use it to strangle myself, thanks. Just make sure it's not left anywhere near my dead body afterwards.

Unsurprisingly, the scarves aren't shifting. Maybe it's just us – Stoke fans are old-fashioned types for the most part, not a bunch of tourists here on a day trip. Nobody's buying half-and-half scarves and nobody's stood in front of the ground taking selfies. It's just another Saturday at the match, the way it always used to be, right? 'A proper football club,' as our old manager Tony Pulis was so fond of saying.

Anyway, this Arsenal thing. It started when Arsene Wenger, bitter as always after a 2-1 defeat, called us a rugby team, and then it escalated when the press turned on our captain, Ryan Shawcross, for mistiming a tackle on Aaron Ramsey. Ever since that day there's been bad blood and ill feeling always bubbling under the surface of this fixture. You could call it a rivalry I suppose, even though that would suggest a level of parity that we know doesn't really exist. Arsenal don't like us though, and we absolutely *hate* them. This isn't a place for half-and-half scarves. This is old-school.

Yet look around you, because outside the ground, a few blokes in Arsenal gear are walking around freely, talking in loud, brash London voices, there's a family by the club shop – the kids all sporting shirts with 'Fly Emirates' across their chests. Nobody's bothering them and Stoke fans are milling around too out here, plenty of us, mostly wearing club colours, laughing, shouting, full of pre-match optimism as a new season begins in the late afternoon sunshine. In 20 minutes' time there'll be no one left outside, we'll all be in the ground in our seats awaiting the kick-off, a few of the stragglers left on the concourse watching the televisions showing Sky Sports News.

Ours is the second game of the weekend to be televised and we've only reached Saturday teatime. There'll be another two matches on tomorrow and maybe one on Monday night. Football's everywhere – the people who love it watch game after game, but those who don't are still always aware of it.

When I get to work on a Monday everyone knows whether Stoke won or lost and it's the first thing they mention. Football's mainstream.

Travel back in time 30 years or thereabouts and this scene would have been very different. We were in another ground for starters – one that didn't have 30,000 shiny plastic seats and two electronic scoreboards, but crumbling terraces, leaky roofs and weeds growing up through the cracks in the concrete. Any Arsenal fans would be running for cover by now, probably being chased up the street by casuals or, in the case of the family, at home in north London, not even here, not even interested. A day at the football, Mum and Dad? Take the kids? No thanks, we'd rather not all go home in an ambulance if it's all the same to you.

The police would be all over the street too. I can't see a single one out here, just a few stewards carrying out body searches and directing a few confused non-regulars to the correct turnstiles. Policemen aren't really needed out here, not like in the old days when there'd be a riot van parked up and coppers on horses in the middle of the road.

I didn't exactly see it go off very often back then – Dad knew how to keep us out of trouble. We'd park up in the same place every week, the corner of Sturgess Street, then wander down past the old library, follow the road round past the police station, round the corner where the old Victoria Hotel once stood and the ground would be there before we could even complain our feet were tired.

The Boothen Stand was our destination – a monolithic block of 1960s architecture rising above the terraced rat runs that surrounded it. These streets were safe territory, relatively at least, as the away fans would be herded into the Butler Street Paddock on the other side of the ground or in the Town End behind large spiked railings. The train station was in the opposite direction too, so it was mainly just Stoke fans here stepping through piles of horse shit and getting barked at by moody-looking Alsatians.

Most of the away followings were sparse in the old Second Division. A couple of hundred here, a couple of hundred there, only swelling into a threat when the big sides were in town: Leeds, Chelsea, Manchester City, Liverpool in the cup that time. Dad used to avoid taking me to those games. He'd seen what used to happen in the 1970s when those bastards were around and he'd rather not take the risk.

I'd seen the fighting on the news as well – fans on the pitch, tearing the place up. Millwall fans at Luton, smashing Kenilworth Road to pieces. Nan told me about how one man had his ear bitten off – it was in the paper, she said. The Heysel disaster was beamed live into our living room when I was seven. English hooligans running amok, the cameras catching more of the violence than they'd dare to film now, Barry Davies registering his disgust at the missiles being thrown into crowds of innocent spectators. Thirty-nine people dead at the end of it.

The fire at Bradford was another tragedy – an entire stand going up in flames. Fifty-six died that time, including that poor man, that poor, poor man we saw on the news, his hair and clothes ablaze, desperately trying to escape the most horrific death imaginable.

And Hillsborough. The FA Cup semi-final. Mum came out into the garden and told me something had happened at the football. It didn't register at first, only later when I saw the television pictures and people were lying dead or dying right there on the pitch. Ninety-six people killed at a football match like the ones Dad and I went to. One of them, Jon-Paul Gilhooley, was ten years old, a year younger than me.

These were the shadows cast across the game. Death, violence and neglect. Eleven-year-old boys don't understand the times they're living in – can't really grasp the answers that adults give them when they question why people are dying at football games. Sometimes the adults giving the answers don't understand what they're seeing either, they just read the newspapers and listen to the man on the television telling them it's all mindless violence and that football fans are the scum of the earth.

And when you look back as an adult and think about the lines of steely-eyed policemen with their horses and dogs at the games you went to, and the old death trap stands and terraces, the news footage of another disaster or another riot, the spiteful disdain in the voice of Colin Moynihan as he condemned football fans, and the lies and the cover-ups that went on for years and years after Hillsborough, only then do you understand the contempt in which supporters were held by the establishment and what the game you loved was truly like.

Fans were seen as nothing but a bloody inconvenience – a mindless, drink-fuelled mob that needed to be controlled by any means necessary. Herded into pens in squalid stadiums, assaulted with batons and tear-gassed simply for being in a certain place at a certain time. This was the culture of football in the late 1980s – far removed from the stickers in the playground or posters in *Match* that piqued the interest of boys like me, who'd beg their dads to take them to matches, enthusiasm overriding the risk that entailed.

Sure, Dad could keep us as safe as he could, knowing which streets to avoid, or getting tickets for the seats not the terraces, but no one could truly guarantee safety at a match at that time because it turns out that nobody in authority was that bothered about keeping *any* of us safe. No one cared if we were injured or even if we died. If you went to a match and didn't come home then it was your own fault for being a dirty, horrible football fan wasn't it?

Many people outside Stoke-on-Trent won't be aware of this, but on 31 January 1989, Stoke played an FA Cup replay at Barnsley's Oakwell ground. Those who attended said that traffic congestion on the motorway caused thousands of Stoke fans to arrive late – this being a time when FA Cup ties were far more high profile than they are now.

Outside the ground a crush developed and a sense of panic began to ripple through the crowd as so many bodies pushed towards the turnstiles to gain entrance. The initial response from South Yorkshire Police was to send a mounted officer charging forward through the melee, only adding to the chaos and fear. Eventually, in a bid to ease the congestion, the police opened one of the huge exit gates, allowing the crowd to pour into the ground without tickets. This was the same response the same police force used two months later at Hillsborough. Had there been more Stoke supporters on the away terrace that night then we could have suffered a similar disaster and the same lies and cover-ups that Liverpool fans had to suffer for 30 shameful years. It really could have been us. It could have been *any* of us.

I don't think twice about taking my own children to the game now. They both attended their first matches at much younger ages than I was before my dad took me, and no one raises an eyebrow or judges me when I say I'm taking my kids to the football. It's entertainment, and we can 'hate' the other team in that pantomime way we do and still stay safe as we walk home among the opposition fans who, minutes before, we were jeering at.

Maybe something has been lost along the way in the 30 years separating then from now, maybe the game has been sanitised a bit too much, and it's definitely too bloody expensive. But look around at the people smiling and chatting, walking freely in whichever direction they wish to. I'm giving my little lad a piggy back, he's enjoyed his day out and no one's looking nervously over their shoulders for flying bricks. Yes, something has been lost, but you can't help but realise that something's been gained too.

But 1989: it seems like a lifetime away.

What Went Before

The 1989/90 campaign was the first season when I attended the Victoria Ground properly. I'd been an occasional visitor during the previous three seasons, but only on Saturdays when Dad wasn't working and we were facing opposition he considered to be low risk. This year though, we attended pretty much every home game, usually managing to secure the same seats in the Boothen Stand.

At this time, Stoke were becoming used to their role as Second Division also-rans. Manager Mick Mills had been a breath of fresh air at first, but by 1989/90 things had gone stale and boredom was creeping in.

We really need to start the story though by jumping back to the calamitous relegation of 1984/85 – a footballing famine of three wins in a season and a record low points total of 17. At that time, the Stoke support held a genuine fear that their team was about to plummet all the way through the divisions. The squad that had relegated us was painfully incapable of competing at the highest level – a bunch of kids who hadn't started shaving yet and a handful of ageing pros with dodgy joints. There was nothing there for anyone to work with.

Mick Mills, 36, a former England full-back with 42 caps, was given the task of stabilising a ship that was looking more like a submarine: a demanding task for someone with no managerial experience as the team could only be described as crap. Not crap in the casual way we might describe a bad performance to everyone in the pub either, but crap as in 'breaking all known records for being crap'.

Mills kept his boots on for the first 12 months. He was getting on as a player, but we were short on numbers. Putting faith in the same youngsters who'd pretty much burst into tears every week in the unforgiving environs of the top flight wasn't a choice he *made*, it was the only option he had. Unsurprisingly, the season started badly, but the players grew a bit of hair on their chests, began to find a little confidence and Mills guided his team of damaged fledglings to a respectable tenth place.

Winger Phil Heath was one such youngster. He remembers Mills as having a hugely positive impact on his own career and lifting a demoralised squad. 'When Mick Mills arrived he did a great job in steadying the ship under extreme financial pressures,' he recalls. 'Mick came in at left-back and instantly gave my game a great lift with his vision and experience. It was this two-year period where I played my best football for Stoke. Mick gave me the confidence and belief that I could become a top player.'

Using the money brought in from a few player sales, Mills added well to his squad in the summer of 1986. The likes of Lee Dixon and Tony Ford arrived – good signings for small fees. A blistering run in the middle of the 1986/87 campaign, which included 7-2 and 5-2 home wins over Leeds and Sheffield United, saw Stoke go unbeaten for 11 games to put themselves in contention for the promotion play-offs, which were newly introduced that season.

Alas, it wasn't to be. A collapse in form towards the end of the season saw the challenge peter out. Nevertheless, Mills had improved Stoke's standing from the previous year and an eighth-place finish hinted that he was somehow panning gold from the septic tank of a squad he'd inherited.

Where did things go wrong? Well, 1987/88 simply never got going for Stoke. The side spluttered along in mid-table for the whole season, eventually finishing 11th – a long way from the play-offs.

The following year was worse still. Stoke finished 13th but ended with a customary collapse in form that, worryingly, seemed more pronounced than in previous seasons. From March onwards, Stoke won only one of their final 14 games. We were even beaten 3-0 at home by already-relegated Walsall. Stoke looked for all the world like a side that had gone beyond stagnation and had started to rot from within.

It was clear that Mills had long since run out of ideas. The number of flops in the transfer market became more noticeable with every passing year, and he failed to adequately replace some of the key departures from his squad. Stoke were going nowhere but backwards and supporters had been campaigning for change for quite some time. 'Mills out' was a regular chant at games and became an iconic piece of graffiti in Stoke-on-Trent. Spray painted on to a wall clearly visible from the A500, the message remained in place for years and years after the departure of its subject!

However, Peter Coates and the rest of the Stoke board were clearly in no mood to acquiesce to the demands of supporters who'd lost patience. They handed Mills a new contract as well as a transfer kitty of £1m with which to overhaul the squad.

'We had about seven directors at the time,' recalls Coates, 'and although I was on the board, I didn't own the club, so we had a collective viewpoint that prevailed. Mick Mills had been good for us up to this point so we decided to make this money available and try to push on.'

This was a real statement of intent from a board that would normally have made Ebenezer Scrooge seem profligate in his spending, a seven-figure sum being a significant amount of money at that time. Whether Coates and company were panicked into doing so by the abject form shown by the team at the end of the 1988/89 campaign, or genuinely worried by the presence of local rivals Port Vale following the Valiants' promotion is unclear. However, fresh optimism surged through the supporter base, many of whom saw the gesture as a likely catalyst for promotion.

Mills Builds His Squad

There were, however, those who remained concerned that Mills had completely lost his mind in the transfer market, recklessly buying any old tat as soon as he had money to spend. The manager always seemed to have more success when shopping in the bargain basement. Give him money and he couldn't wait to flush it down the toilet.

The most disappointing of all his signings, and a contender for the worst player to ever wear the red and white stripes, was Dave Bamber. The striker had cost somewhere north of £100,000 and arrived with a goals record that could generously be described as 'modest'.

Quite what possessed Mills to sign him, I have no idea, but it soon became clear that the gangly target man was out of his depth in the Second Division. No sitter seemed too easy to miss, no ball too difficult to mis-control; Bamber's ability to fuck up almost any situation was legendary, and soon had Stoke fans pulling their hair out in frustration as the striker ambled apologetically around the pitch with the sadness of an enfeebled old horse put out to pasture.

Somehow, Bamber had managed to notch six goals in 23 appearances during 1988/89, a fairly poor record that still flattered him in comparison to the abject level of his general play. Yet Mills didn't see a problem with Bamber's contribution. In fact all he felt was needed was a partner for the ex-Blackpool man, so in came the tanned form of Wayne Biggins for a fee of £250,000 from Manchester City. A quarter of Mills's war chest was spent, but at least Biggins had some pedigree, having previously played in the top flight for Norwich City.

'Manchester City had just signed Clive Allen from Tottenham,' recalls Biggins. 'And to be fair to Mel Machin, he told me that I'd be third choice and that Stoke had come in for me. I've always had a soft spot for Stoke since I was a kid, even though I've always been a Sheffield Wednesday fan. I remember watching the cup final in '72 and since then, for some reason, I'd always kept an eye out for Stoke's results. As soon as I met Mick Mills and looked around the ground, I knew it'd be a great move for me.'

On paper, the new strike force should have had a plentiful supply of chances given that Mills operated with two wide men in the form of Gary Hackett on the right and the sublime Peter Beagrie on the left. Hackett was competent but unspectacular while Beagrie's dazzling dribbling skills had a number of top-flight clubs sniffing around for his signature.

In the middle of the pitch was the combative Chris Kamara, now more famous for his on-screen buffoonery for Sky Sports, but back then a tough-tackling hard man who would probably last no longer than five minutes before being sent off, or even arrested, if his somewhat 'loose' challenges were to be refereed under modern rules.

Thinking that Kamara perhaps needed a cool head alongside him, Mills plumped for another Manchester City player in the shape of Ian Scott, a 22-year-old midfielder who'd broken through into the first team at Maine Road during the previous campaign. The £175,000 that Mills spent on Scott was supposed to add genuine competition for places in the midfield, where the risk of Kamara being suspended meant that an extra body would be needed fairly often.

The other midfielder who Mills had to call on was local-born crowd favourite Carl Beeston, an England under-21 international who'd risen through the ranks of Stoke's youth academy, but had suffered a luckless spell with injuries. Beeston had lost an entire year of his career to glandular fever and missed countless games with a persistent ankle injury. Any game that Beeston could appear in was a bonus as his fitness could never be relied on.

Where Mills spent the majority of his kitty was in defence, smashing Stoke's transfer record by bringing in centre-half Ian Cranson from First Division Sheffield Wednesday for £480,000. Cranson was 25 years old and had played the majority of his career in the top flight, promising experience and class that he would surely need given that he was to partner the popular but sometimes erratic George Berry.

'I turned the move down initially,' remembers Cranson. 'I wasn't sure about dropping down a division, so I started the pre-season with Sheffield Wednesday. But I had another chat with Ron Atkinson, who was manager at Wednesday at that time, and as the club had just bought Peter Shirtliff back from Charlton and already had Nigel Pearson, it seemed like I was going to be the odd one out. Ron said he didn't want to force me out, but he wanted to balance the books and he'd still got the offer from Stoke on the table. I spoke to Mick Mills again and he confirmed he was still interested so I said I'd join.'

More First Division experience was added in the form of Derek Statham, who arrived for what looked like a bargain £75,000 given that the 30-year-old left-back had amassed over 350 First Division appearances for West Brom and Southampton. With Statham operating on the opposite side to the dependable John Butler, Mills was convinced that he'd now assembled a rearguard to offer some protection to goalkeeper Peter Fox, the diminutive but agile stopper who'd already given 11 years' service to Stoke and who would end the season with the captain's armband.

Despite obvious areas of weakness, as the 1989/90 season approached, most fans considered the team to be an improvement on the one that had finished the previous campaign. A pre-season tour of Sweden, where Stoke rattled in 32 goals in only six games, also contributed to the expectation level being raised higher than it had been for some time, despite the fact that we'd been playing a bunch of Scandinavian postmen!

The Season Begins

There's always a special atmosphere to the opening day of a new football season. The sun always seems to be out, the crowd is always bigger and optimism hangs in the air. Until we see them play and the disappointment inevitably kicks in, new signings promise to be the missing piece to the puzzle and the deficiencies of the players we already know about are viewed in a softer focus. In early August, anything's possible and whatever disappointments we suffered during the previous campaign will have long been forgotten.

Saturday, 19 August 1989 was no different. West Ham were the visitors and 16,058 people, a much bigger crowd than usual, packed into a sun-drenched Victoria Ground to watch Mills's new-look side kick off the season.

'We are going up!' was the chant from the Boothen End before a ball had even been kicked. Never has optimism been more misplaced. Yet the start to the season wasn't bad at all. West Ham were strong opponents, fancied by many for promotion, and although the visitors took the lead, Biggins headed in an equaliser on his debut to earn Stoke a point.

However, the game will probably be remembered more for the post-match reaction of West Ham striker Frank McAvennie following a tackle from, surprise, surprise, Chris Kamara. McAvennie went off injured after the challenge, which was firm but fair, and tests revealed that he'd actually broken his ankle. Rather than accept this as a risk inherent to the game, and perhaps swayed by Kamara's reputation as a 'dirty' player, McAvennie threatened to take legal action against the Stoke midfielder.

'It's a shame because there have been so many lies and false recollections of that incident,' Kamara told *FourFourTwo* in 2010. 'Basically, it was an innocuous challenge and if you don't believe me, it's on YouTube and you can make up your own mind. It was one of those things that you see from time to time where a perfectly good tackle injures someone. Poor old Frank got a bad injury but nobody knew at the time just how bad it was. I certainly didn't know and the other players on the pitch didn't know.'

To be honest, the only person that the blond-mullet-sporting McAvennie should have been suing was his barber. Thankfully, these threats were nothing but hot air and the storm blew over fairly quickly.

Stoke's start was tricky, but given the levels of pre-season optimism, to only have four points on the board after six games was undoubtedly a huge disappointment. These points had been gained through draws, the first win remaining elusive. By the time that Oldham came to town on 16 September and returned to Lancashire with a 2-1 win, it was clear from the attendance of just over 10,000 that the Stoke crowd had realised they were going to be served more of the same old mid-table fare. That was the best-case scenario too, as already the bottom three was looking worryingly close. In the short term though, the following Saturday, local rivals Port Vale would be the visitors for the first league meeting between the sides in 32 years. Defeat in this game was unthinkable, yet given the start to the season, very much a possibility.

Following their promotion from the Third Division, under the stewardship of the canny John Rudge, Port Vale were in the ascendancy, and with a talented side containing the likes of Robbie Earle, Darren Beckford and Ray Walker, our Burslem-based rivals weren't to be taken lightly.

The atmosphere in the ground and the atmosphere around the city in the weeks beforehand was crackling with the buzz of anticipation for this fixture. There was a pretty even split between Stoke and Vale fans in our class (I'd only just moved up to high school) and the banter flying back and forth made the prospect of defeat something that I didn't even dare to acknowledge.

My friend Lee Leighton reckoned that Vale's left-back, Darren Hughes, was so good that he should be capped by England. Wildean wit that I was, I told him that Peter Beagrie would turn Hughes inside out so often that he'd be pissing out of his backside by full-time.

Even the players were feeling the pressure. Carl Beeston recalls receiving numerous phone calls from friends in the days leading up to the game. 'Yeah, the phone kept ringing the week before and people would be saying, "You'd better not lose this game, Beest, we know where you live." And these were supposed to be my mates!' There was a lot at stake here for all concerned.

Even 28 years later, I still have some vivid memories of that day; the sharpest being the moment that Port Vale took the lead, and the sea of black, white and yellow erupting on the old Stoke End in delirious celebration. It sounds awful to say this, and I'll blame my immature mind for such a terrible sentiment, but at that moment in time all I could think of was, 'Die, you fuckers.' I've probably thought that every other time I've seen Vale fans celebrating a goal against us as well, the difference being that as an adult I've never mean it literally. Probably not anyway.

It was the dread of facing my mates on Monday should Vale have beaten us, you see. The gloating and mockery, especially from Lee Leighton, would have been relentless and I knew it. I might have cried had we lost, so I still feel grateful to the long-forgotten midfield nobody Leigh Palin for scoring an equaliser that day.

Well done, Leigh, you bog-standard, journeyman midfielder who most fans will probably have forgotten even existed. You might have only had a career that took in the likes of Bradford

City and Hull, you'll have made nobody's 'Best XI' list, and nobody will ever be searching the internet wondering what happened to you (apart from me, a few seconds ago) but on 23 September 1989, to me you were more important than Gordon Banks, Denis Smith and Stanley Matthews all rolled into one.

A 1-1 draw saved us the embarrassment of losing to our local rivals (the ignominy of seeing them with two more points than us in the league was bad enough!) but we were still faced with the situation of being winless seven games into the season. That wasn't a position that was going to get better for a while yet, either.

By the time the full-time whistle blew following a disappointing 1-1 draw at home to Hull City on 14 October 1989, Stoke had gone a scarcely believable 11 games without a victory. Mick Mills was known for slow starts to the season but this was taking the piss even by his dilatory standards. At this point, we all knew that the longed-for promotion was not going to happen and we hadn't even got to Halloween.

Another horror that we dared not speak of was looming large though, the spectre of a relegation battle, which would mean Stoke playing in the third tier for the first time in over 70 years. We had to get a victory on the board at some point, surely, and that moment of blessed relief came in the very next game, a 2-1 win over West Brom thanks to goals from Gary Hackett and Wayne Biggins.

It was a welcome result but sadly proved to be a false dawn as Stoke went on to lose the next four games and firmly ensconce themselves in the bottom three, a run which ended with an embarrassing 6-0 thrashing at Swindon Town. How did the Stoke fans in the away end respond to this performance? By doing a conga in the rain of course, then indulging in ironic celebrations for the home side's final two goals – not the usual response to seeing your team annihilated, but typical of the black humour that most fans were adopting in order to get through what was starting to look like a miserable season.

Nothing was going right for Stoke. There had been many moments when luck had simply deserted us, but it's not unlucky teams that lose games 6-0, it's very, very bad teams. We were certainly looking like one of those. Something had to change and the board finally acted by terminating the contract of Mills – a contract he should never have been awarded in the first place.

Peter Coates still thinks fondly though of Mills as a person, and describes him as decent, intelligent and a good judge of a player. 'I never enjoy sacking managers,' he states, 'but sometimes events happen that leave you no choice but to take action. My theory now, looking back, is that we put Mick under pressure to spend the £1m rather than let him do it in his own time, in his own way. I used to get my colleagues ringing me up saying, "Have we bought anybody yet? What's he doing?" and I think perhaps our impatience contributed to the situation. It's a lesson learnt really.'

Two years of slow decline had finally reached an inevitable conclusion. Although the pressure from the board might have been a contributory factor, really Mills only had himself to blame – he kept faith with the frankly awful Bamber until the bitter end of his reign, stubbornly refusing to acknowledge his mistake in signing such a misfit.

Other mistakes were also becoming apparent – Ian Scott had barely featured and had looked poor when he did, while Derek Statham looked unfit and disinterested for the most part, eventually losing his place to the man he'd been bought to replace – Cliff Carr, nicknamed 'the Lego Man' as he was probably the smallest full-back ever to grace a football pitch!

There was also the infamous incident when Mills went to watch future England captain David Platt at Crewe and turned down the chance to sign him because he didn't believe him to be as good as either Carl Saunders or Graham Shaw, both of whom were on our books at the time. Being generous, you could say that everyone makes mistakes.

Realising their £1m gamble had failed, yet perhaps failing to realise the very real danger the club was in, the board followed the decision to sack Mills with the sale of star man Peter Beagrie for £750,000 to Everton, recouping most of their summer outlay in one hit.

I was upset at Stoke losing games to teams like Swindon by six goals to nil and I was upset at my team being below Port Vale and in the relegation zone, but nothing upset me like seeing my beloved Beagrie depart the Victoria Ground.

An Ode to Peter Beagrie

The seeds of my Beagrie obsession were first sown after I watched our wide man torment Newcastle Town's motley bunch of plasterers, bus drivers and bricklayers in a meaningless preseason game at the start of the 1988/89 campaign. It was all very well showboating against men to whom football was just a supplement to the rest of the week's working and drinking, but come the season's arrival Beagrie's brilliance was still apparent even among his fellow professionals.

This new and exciting capture from Sheffield United would be described in the world of tired football clichés as an old-fashioned winger, whose only mission in life was to take possession of a football and dribble with it until his arse bled. Once he'd run out of opponents to beat, he'd gain greater pleasure in turning round and skipping past them again just for a laugh rather than actually parting with ball. At times he was nothing more than a self-indulgent, greedy show-off, but Christ I loved him for it.

Another endearing trait was that, in addition to being the new Stanley Matthews, Beagrie transformed into an Olympic gymnast whenever he got on to the scoresheet, back-flipping and somersaulting his way around the Victoria Ground turf in acrobatic displays of joy.

Embarrassingly, I so longed to *be* Peter Beagrie that I decided to tell the other kids at school that I *too* could do a back-flip, naively failing to anticipate that an outlandish claim such as this would have to be backed up with physical proof. Being as my natural athletic prowess was somewhere between that of a pissed-up sloth and a Christmas pudding, the exact mechanics of how I would accomplish this gymnastic feat had clearly not been calculated by my pre-pubescent brain.

At first, I laughed off these sceptical requests to perform my new and entirely fabricated party piece, but did foolishly promise that I would display this new talent the next time I scored a goal during a PE lesson.

Soon after, in a move that could kindly be described as 'ambitious' but more accurately labelled as 'a fuck-witted act of self-delusion', I confidently declared to the PE teacher, Mr Eckersley that I was the flying left-winger he was looking for in the high school football trials. Recommending that he should cast aside his arbitrary rule of excluding kids who hadn't played football for their junior school in order to give me the chance to perform some magic, my sure-footed confidence seemed to win the teacher over.

Nobody wants to be the guy who turned down The Beatles and whether old Eckers was fearful of overlooking an undiscovered gem or just relishing the chance to watch this cocky little shit embarrass himself, I'm not sure. All that mattered was that Mr Eckersley had cast me as Peter Beagrie in Team A and the stage was now mine to illuminate.

It was only as I was warming up, doing some purposeless stretches that I'd seen the professionals perform on the telly, that I started to wonder exactly what I should be doing as a left-winger. I'd always played in defence before and knew vaguely where to position myself at the back, even though I was usually too slow to get there in time. However, this left-wing business was uncharted territory, so I figured that just getting my head down and running for the corner flag was the best course of action.

My initial concerns were alleviated somewhat when I first laid eyes on Team B's right-back. He was a squat little fat lad who looked like he'd be more suited to appearing in the school production of Snow White than coping with the slinkiness of my wing skills. Not for a moment did I think I was being overconfident as, after all, if Peter Beagrie could terrorise a hung-over milkman at full-back, I'd absolutely marmalise this four-foot human dumpling. Infused with confidence from dribbling around my Grandma's concrete bird bath several times at the weekend, I awaited the moment when Mr Eckersley would sound the whistle and a new back-flipping wing wizard would be born.

It only took a few seconds for the ball to be spread out wide, and I immediately set off at a less-than-blistering pace towards my dumpy opposite number.

Figuring that a flashy, showy move early in the game would have Mr Eckersley marking a tick next to my name on his team sheet, I decided that I was going to cut inside on to my right foot, only to then trick fatty with a Cruyff turn to the left. This would leave him statuesque, just like Gran's bird bath had unsurprisingly been, and I'd be nutmegging the centre-half before the applause had even abated.

The next thing I recall is being hit with the force of an articulated lorry, which was, in reality, the feeling of being slide-challenged by an overweight child. 'Good tackle Jones!' hollered Mr Eckersley as I lay in the mud, groaning like some sort of dying cow, wondering why fatty hadn't stood there open-mouthed at my attempted manoeuvre.

This theme recurred throughout the afternoon: me devising increasingly elaborate moves to confound my marker, but fatty reading each pathetic, telegraphed attempt with ease, enabling him to thunder his way into one successful tackle after another. I'd like to tell you now that this young lad overcame his Humpty Dumpty-like build to become an unlikely defensive colossus, and went on to not only represent the school at football, but progressed on to a selection at county level, where he was spotted and signed by Stoke City. I'd like to tell you that this kid's name was Andrew Griffin.

But it wasn't.

He was just some random fat kid playing in a school trial match. A fat kid who must have thought that all his birthday cakes had arrived at once when he realised the opposition left-winger was a big, clumsy carthorse who was even slower than he was, and for the next 90 minutes would be making him look like a decent player.

'James, isn't it?' said Mr Eckersley, jogging over to me as I lay prostrate on the ground for about the fifth time that afternoon. 'Yes sir,' I weakly replied.

'Okay,' he smiled, turning back to the game and writing something on his team sheet. He probably just put a cross through my name, but it wouldn't have been unfair if he'd written the word 'wank' next to it as well, just to emphasise the point.

Needless to say, I didn't make the school team, but it didn't stop me worshipping Peter Beagrie as he was continually the shining beacon of brilliance in what was, it has to be said, a very poor Stoke team.

There were countless sparkling granules of solo Beagrie genius sprinkled throughout the 1988/89 and 89/90 seasons, and if only hormones would have permitted it, I'd have grown myself a fetching moustache in homage to my new hairy-lipped hero. As it happened, I couldn't even grow pubic hair on my bollocks at this point, so had to settle for scrawling 'Peter Beagrie is ace, OK' on my pencil case instead.

Predictably, my idolisation of Beagrie quickly waned once he was no longer adorned in the precious red and white stripes and I quickly came to terms with his departure, as well as my failure to transform into a mercurial, twinkle-toed winger. My humiliation at the hands of a chubby dwarf on the school games field had seen to the death of that dream, but there were still the backflips … the backflips that I'd told everybody I could do. Ridiculously, I still maintained that I could perform them. My excuse was that I just needed the right setting, and the middle of a Maths lesson wasn't it, so people would just have to wait until that moment arose. Needless to say, I hoped it never would.

Inevitably, that time did arrive the following summer during a game of rounders, another game that I was hopeless at. The usual routine of me arriving on strike would involve some precociously developed kid with a hairy arse hurling the ball at 90 miles per hour, its intended target being my face. On rare occasions of sporting bravado, my response would be a tokenistic limp-wristed waft with the bat, but the usual reaction was an act of self-preservation, namely ducking out of the way and ambling towards first base. Cordially accepting a meek run-out in exchange for the conservation of my facial features seemed a fair deal to me, so that was how events usually panned out.

It would restore some of my damaged self-esteem to state that on this single occasion, I'd decided that enough was enough, and instead of passively accepting my dismissal from proceedings, I slammed the hairy-arsed kid's delivery into next week like a vengeful Babe Ruth. However, what actually happened was that I performed the usual Quentin Crisp wrist action in the general direction of the ball and somehow the delivery connected straight on to the sweet spot of the bat.

This, to general amazement, meant that the ball pinged over the astonished heads of the outfield and a rising panic as to what I should actually do next. I opted for a leaden-footed jog around the bases, still giving the fielding team plenty of opportunity to avoid the ignominy of conceding a rounder to such a half-arsed opponent. However, a couple of misfields by players who were probably as disinterested in the whole charade as I was meant that I now faced the prospect of only having to travel home from third base to score a point.

The anticipation of lapping up some rare glory soon dissipated when the collection of malevolent scallywags that constituted our team began to chant 'Beagrie! Beagrie! Beagrie!' in my direction. Adopting the flawed mental approach of 'if I want it to happen then it will' that I'd developed during the dreadful left-winger experiment, I put my head down, my hands on the ground and hoped for the best.

I can only imagine what the resultant attempt at acrobatics would have looked like, but I suppose that the sight of a dead baboon being hurled from a motorway bridge wouldn't be too far away from the actual result. Raucous, mocking laughter ensued, and a cacophony of harsh playground insults filled the air as once again I lay on the ground wishing that I'd never laid eyes on Peter bloody Beagrie.

Alan Ball's Red and White Army

Ask any Stoke fan of a certain age who the club's worst ever manager is and it'd be a fair bet that the name of Alan Ball would be prominent in their thoughts. Ball had been appointed as assistant to Mick Mills two weeks before the former was sacked, the board making the obvious move to offer him the job following the 6-0 mauling at Swindon. Ball breezed into the manager's chair, effervescent and hopeful, bringing with him a surge of squeaky-voiced positivity and predictions of a turnaround in the club's fortunes.

As a World Cup winner and a friendly, bubbly presence, the fans instantly warmed to Ball, enthused by his honesty in stating straight away that the squad he'd inherited was not good enough. He brought with him a promotion on his managerial CV, achieved in his previous role at Portsmouth, and the feeling was that Ball would be the ideal man to rescue the club from what looked like impending doom. How wrong that would prove to be.

Initially though, Ball's positivity spread to the players, who delivered their best performance of the season in beating Brighton 3-2. Carl Beeston opened the scoring in the first minute, with Dave Bamber and Chris Kamara adding two more goals within the first half an hour. Stoke were forced to hang on for the win by the end of the game, but in typical bullish fashion, Ball declared, 'Don't write us off for the play-offs!' – a statement so wildly optimistic that it bordered on manic delusion. However, at the time we lapped it up, even though it was business as usual the week after as Stoke went down to Bournemouth and lost 2-1.

'I was never sure that it was the right decision to appoint Alan,' recalls Peter Coates. 'I wasn't against it, but it was a collective decision by the board that I was never convinced by. I'm not being wise after the event, as I did say at the time that I wasn't sure it was the right appointment. What it came down to was that Alan was a really nice guy, very enthusiastic, but football's a tough environment. Really, I think he was a little bit *too* nice.'

Despite Coates's reservations, the board realised that they'd need to back their man in the transfer market, and promptly handed Ball a sizeable chunk of the Beagrie money, the majority of which he effectively flushed down the toilet. The sum of Ball's transfer activity was basically bringing in a few old Portsmouth players who, rather than improving a poor team, somehow seemed to make it worse.

The exception to the rule was Lee Sandford, a 22-year-old defender who followed his old boss to the Victoria Ground for a fee of £140,000 and would go on to prove himself an excellent investment. Less successful were Vince Hilaire, a 31-year-old winger who looked long past his best by the time he arrived at Stoke, and Noel Blake, a centre-half whose defending was as unreliable as it was uncompromising. To his credit, Ball quickly seemed to realise that Dave Bamber was about as useful as tits on a fish so sold him to Hull. The only problem was that Bamber's replacement was Tony Ellis, who cost £200,000 from Preston and brought with him very little other than a neat moustache and a lorry-load of hair gel.

The arrivals didn't stop there though, and Ball took a £20,000 gamble on acquiring the services of winger Tony Kelly from St

Albans City. Kelly certainly had a bit of pace, but could have feasibly been the inspiration for Forrest Gump as on the rare occasions he did get past a man he would usually keep running in a straight line until he either dribbled the ball out of play or trod on it.

With players having to depart in order to make way for the new arrivals, it was something of a surprise to see Ball dispense with the services of Chris Kamara, who seemed like the ideal character to have in a relegation battle (perhaps not as a manager though!) and a few of Mick Mills's reliable old troopers such as Gary Hackett, Nicky Morgan and Carl Saunders. To be fair to Ball, the Kamara situation may have been out of his control. As he later revealed in his autobiography *Playing Extra Time*, the alleged reason for Kamara's departure was a financial situation the player had allowed himself to get into, and he desperately needed the signing on fee to clear a significant personal debt.

Kamara joined Leeds for £150,000 and his place was taken by Dave Kevan, a youngster from Notts County, who Ball signed along with team-mate Paul Barnes.

At first, Ball's changes seemed to have a positive effect. A rousing 2-1 victory over Newcastle United on Boxing Day, with Carl Beeston scoring a dramatic last-minute winner, promised a turnaround in fortunes.

Beeston, a lifelong Stoke fan himself, laughs as he remembers the goal. 'It was ace! I didn't score a lot of goals because I was crap at shooting, but I just came to the edge of the box and leathered it one. It went straight into the top corner. With it being Christmas it was absolutely rammed everywhere. It was the first time I'd ran up to the Boothen End – if I could have jumped in there I would have done!'

This unexpected result was followed by a respectable 2-2 draw at home to Watford and a shock 1-0 win at Middlesbrough. For a brief moment it seemed like Alan Ball's bluster might not be hot air after all and a rescue mission could be on the cards.

The Taylor Report

As an 11-year-old, the politics of football unsurprisingly tended to pass me by. I read the back pages in the superficial way that children do, scanning the papers for match reports of games I was interested in – hoping to find something good about Stoke in the dailies (they all had more important things to write about than us).

The Taylor Report wasn't something that would have registered with me at the time, and the prospect of Stoke being legally required to replace the Victoria Ground's terracing with seating post-Hillsborough would have caused more ripples of panic in the Stoke boardroom than it did with me as I sat in Maths writing odes to Peter Beagrie on my pencil case.

However, the Taylor Report stipulated that any club playing in the top two divisions of English football would need to comply with the report's recommendation of all-seater stadiums by the 1994/95 season. Clubs in the bottom two divisions would be given an extra three years following promotion to the second tier to provide seating for all spectators, and every Football League club would need to be all-seater by 1999/2000. Whichever way they looked at it, the Stoke board would need to get their act together on this sooner or later.

'We knew straight away we'd got quite a job ahead of us,' recalls Peter Coates. 'That either way it would be costly, and the more we looked at it and considered it, we soon came to the view that a move would be the right thing to do.'

It would be a few years before what would become the Britannia Stadium began to crystallise in the minds of all involved, but even as far back as 1990, it seemed like the Victoria Ground's days were numbered. In the short term though, there were immediate changes that needed to be made.

The report also called for the removal of spikes on fencing, and the provision of clearly identifiable gates within any fences that were retained. Stoke removed all fencing around the Boothen End and Boothen Paddocks at the end of the 1989/90 campaign, choosing to keep fencing up at the Stoke End (the away end), but with the necessary modifications of a few bright yellow gates being fitted at strategic intervals.

Those were the headline changes, but there are many other aspects of modern stadiums that we take for granted now, buried deeper within the 76 main recommendations of the document. The report also stipulated changes on policing, police communications, access and egress for emergency vehicles, the responsibilities of stewards within and outside the ground, as well as changes to the provision of disabled facilities within stadiums.

The improvements to the nation's football grounds would not come cheap, and Thatcher's government wasn't exactly rushing to throw money at football clubs to enable them to make the necessary alterations. A total of £130m from the public purse was set aside for various stadium grants, but football clubs would need to become smarter commercially in order to raise enough revenue to meet the inevitable shortfall. Ticket prices being raised would be a start, followed by the hunt for an improved deal on television rights. With the new satellite broadcasting company BSkyB looking for ways to increase its market share, the economic circumstances that led to the formation of the Premier League were beginning to unfold.

As well as delivering his findings on the physical environments that hosted football, Taylor's report also addressed the government's panic over hooliganism. During the 1980s, the language of the press and those in power implied that all people misbehaving at football matches were scum-of-the-earth criminals who just needed tagging or locking up and the problem would be solved. The Conservatives' answer to the problem was an ID card scheme for all football supporters, and the proposal was to introduce the plan by the start of the 1989/90 season. Taylor effectively quashed this, causing an embarrassing U-turn for Thatcher, by stating in his report, 'I have grave doubts whether the scheme will achieve its object of eliminating hooligans from inside the ground. I have even stronger doubts as to whether it will achieve its further object of ending football hooliganism outside grounds. Indeed, I do not think it will. I fear that, in the short term at least, it may actually increase trouble outside grounds.'

Taylor's report also took a sardonic swipe at the other draconian action that the government was considering, and which Luton Town had already implemented: a total ban on away supporters.

'To exclude away supporters from Luton is one thing,' stated Taylor. 'Those excluded can at least go at present to any other match instead. But to exclude all away supporters from all matches and especially to exclude them from "local derby" matches or matches in large cities could cause serious disorder. If Manchester City supporters could not go to Old Trafford when their team plays there, or Chelsea supporters follow their team to Highbury or to their neighbours Queen's Park Rangers, trouble could result. There would be attempts and devices to defeat the scheme and get into the ground in defiance of it. There could well be disorder outside grounds. The more fanatical supporters and the hooligans would be unlikely to stay home and play patience.'

So much of the content of Taylor's report centred on the government's bogeyman – football hooligans – but took a more measured approach than the reactionary agenda pushed by Thatcher: that hooligans were not really normal people like the rest of us but a kind of subspecies that needed eradicating. Yet most of the people who were getting involved in trouble weren't monsters, they were just blokes with a few beers inside them, swept along by what felt normal in the settings and circumstances they were given. In short, provide people with shit stadiums and shit conditions, treat them like animals, and that's exactly how they'll behave.

Taylor knew this, and the thrust of his report was that measures should be put in place to deal with and penalise genuine troublemakers without impinging on the civil liberties of others, while at the same time providing fans with better, safer venues for football.

After listing the various court orders that could be used to ban the genuine hardcore troublemakers from attending, Taylor noted, 'Put together with progress towards all-seating, improved accommodation, better facilities, improved arrangements for crowd control and better training of police and stewards to achieve it, I believe these measures would give the best chance of eliminating or minimising football hooliganism.'

It wasn't all good though. Have you ever found yourself in a long queue at the ticket office as the staff ask everyone for reams of personal information so that it can be fed into Stoke City's computer system? That's the report's recommendation 39.

A Dismal Slide to Relegation

In some ways, Alan Ball had positioned himself in a no-lose scenario. So bad had the team been when he took over, and so clear did he make it how poor his inherited squad was, that most people were willing to accept that it would take a herculean effort to turn things around. For the last two and a half years we'd resembled a Second Division version of the *Titanic*, heading slowly towards the iceberg with a doomed inertia, a course that hadn't been plotted by Ball and one which it would be unfair to blame him for.

On the other hand though, the squad changes he had made were definitely the equivalent of re-arranging the proverbial deckchairs on board. The faces were different but the style of play the same – incompetent and uninspiring – and there was little to suggest that a concerted revival was ever likely.

A 0-0 draw away at Port Vale in the return leg of the Potteries derby was a rare ray of sunshine among a run of defeats, the goalless stalemate qualifying as a positive only because it was a fixture that we were all convinced would end in an embarrassing loss. Vale had taken to this higher division like ducks to water, were comfortably sat in mid-table and revelling in their new-found status as top dogs of the Potteries while Stoke floundered pathetically in the relegation zone. Laughably, many Vale supporters claimed the result of the game was fixed by the local police, so convinced had they been that their team would rub Stoke's noses in it on the day!

It seemed that Stoke were only prepared to turn up for derby games, as a 2-0 win over Wolverhampton Wanderers a fortnight later gave another flicker of hope that they weren't quite dead yet. However, despite these fleeting moments of joy, most fans were already considering what Third Division football would feel like.

The side had given off a distinct whiff of relegation for some time, had lost its best player (Ian Cranson) to a long-term knee injury and had found goals extremely hard to come by all year. After following up the Wolves game with a 2-1 defeat at Leicester, the team went five games without scoring a goal. The only positive in this was that they weren't conceding either, as four of these matches ended 0-0, but single points weren't going to be enough to drag Stoke out of the relegation zone.

With each passing week, safety seemed to be slipping further and further over the horizon. Following a run of one victory (the aforementioned 2-0 win over Wolves) in 17 games, Stoke travelled to St James' Park on 16 April 1990 to face Newcastle United knowing that defeat would see them relegated and playing in the third tier for the first time since 1927.

Stoke's resistance was token at best and the team were soon behind, outfought, outmanoeuvred and outclassed by a home team chasing promotion. The score ended 3-0, could have been a lot more, and by the end of the afternoon everyone was relieved that we'd finally been put out of our misery. With four games left to play, Stoke City were officially relegated.

'We looked woefully short of the required standard out there,' admitted a dejected Ball following a game in which *Sentinel* reporter Ian Bayley had described Stoke as 'resembling sacrificial lambs'.

'Going down could be the best thing to happen to us,' argued Ball. 'It will give us the chance to regroup and rebuild.' For some reason, everyone believed him, and the following away game would see fans return to the same kind of mindset that had seen them doing the conga at Swindon.

The Brighton Relegation Celebration

Adopting gallows humour when necessary is one of the prerequisites to following a football team, and there was plenty of it about as Stoke visited Brighton & Hove Albion for a meaningless fixture at the end of what had been a miserable campaign. Stoke fans decided that beachwear was the theme for the day, and a huge following journeyed down to the south coast wearing shorts and sunglasses, armed with an array of inflatables.

Bizarrely, the team decided to put on a bit of a show for their long-suffering supporters, scoring four goals in the second half and returning to the Potteries with a 4-1 victory. Where on earth had this result come from? The team had only scored 31 goals all season, the strikers couldn't hit a cow's arse with a banjo, yet they'd gone goal crazy when it was far too late to matter. None of this frustration seemed to register on the day though, and supporters cheered the goals as if each and every one were a last-minute promotion clincher.

Supporter Mick Pinnington, a fan of Stoke for over 40 years, remembers the carnival atmosphere well, and how one fan's trip summed up the carefree nature of the day.

'Six of us arrived at Stoke station to catch the 6.30am train to Brighton,' he recalls, 'and there was this bloke, Frank from Bentilee, who we all knew, just sort of hanging around at the station. We asked him if he was going and he said, "No, I've only got £2 on me." Anyway, he ended up jumping the train there and back. He was only questioned once by the guard who said, "Fuck it, good luck mate!" I bought him his breakfast, we all bought him his beers for the day and then he rounded it off by blagging his way into the ground as well!'

Mick reflects on how the atmosphere differed to that at a usual away game, 'We went drinking in the city centre and it was rammed with Stoke, but there wasn't a hint of trouble in sight. Believe me, in those days that was extremely rare.'

The scenes at Brighton epitomise what football support is about. As much as we all want to win trophies and watch glorious, memorable games against top sides, for most clubs outside the elite few there'll be periods of history when we're faced with watching wretched sides full of awful players going through the motions on bad pitches in grounds that belong in the non-league. Support is sticking with your club through these periods, not necessarily happy-clapping along to every dismal defeat, but being there and suffering alongside the other people who share this mad passion.

That was what Brighton was about. It was a celebration of support itself, of having come through a lamentable season, of only seeing six wins, of having dreams of promotion turned into the nightmare of relegation, of knowing that the glory years of the 1970s were now further away than ever and yet despite all this, still being there on the terraces come three o'clock on Saturday.

Somehow, optimism *was* still present. People were still willing to back the manager, laying the blame more at the door of Mick Mills and the board than Ball, despite his equally horrendous moves in the transfer market. The mistaken and arrogant belief that a lot of bigger clubs hold when relegated was also present: that we were simply too big a club for the Third Division and would therefore only have to turn up to sweep aside the sort of minnows we would be facing each week.

Sure, Stoke were going down, but it'd be a chance to visit new grounds we hadn't seen before as we regrouped and inevitably came back stronger. You can laugh now about the delusional state of mind we adopted, but sometimes as football fans, hope really is all we have.

The Moment Football Changed

The summer of 1990 offered fans the chance to set aside the day-to-day disappointments associated with supporting a rotten club side and instead focus on the disappointment of supporting a rotten national team. Bobby Robson's much-maligned England were going to Italy for the World Cup, and while the back pages savaged the dismal displays in friendlies leading up to the tournament, the front pages saved their ire for the fans who followed them.

English club sides were still banned from European competition following Heysel and it seemed like no one, including sections of our own press, wanted the national team anywhere near foreign shores either. While the England followers were certainly no angels, there were also many examples of heavy-handed policing contributing to the combustible atmosphere that accompanied English supporters wherever they went.

In the lead-up to the tournament, hundreds of English fans were deported from Sardinia (where England would play their group games) simply for being in the wrong place at the wrong time. Flashpoints occurred, but at the time the gutter press carried one-sided reports of hooligans running amok through foreign streets like a barbaric invading army, intent on nothing but mindless destruction. Colin Moynihan, Thatcher's Minister for Sport, was at the forefront of the condemnation, fully supportive of the Italian police in these deportations.

'I am grateful to the police for their swift and decisive attitude which defused the situation, avoiding serious violence and confrontation between English and Dutch supporters,' said Moynihan, barely able to disguise the venom in his voice as he went on to call the English supporters 'animals' and 'a criminally-motivated group of thugs'.

As time went by though, a second side to the story emerged – of police charging at groups of law-abiding people whose only crime was to be enjoying a drink and a good-natured sing-song outside a bar, of tabloid journalists actively trying to spark trouble in order to source themselves another chapter in the long-running saga of English hooliganism and, disgracefully, the Italian authorities indiscriminately rounding up enough Englishmen to fill a 246-seater jumbo jet and deporting them back to Britain.

This was the kind of behaviour that football fans had become accustomed to at home, but now it was being played out on the international stage. Police forces being allowed to operate with impunity and no one in government advocating for the civil rights of its citizens. The message was clear – if you're a football fan then you're fair game for whatever we want to do to you. You are scum with no civil rights whatsoever and we'd rather you didn't exist at all.

It didn't help that England got off to a slow start, drawing 1-1 with Ireland in the first match in an atrocious game. The press were merciless and cruel in their attacks on Bobby Robson – a decent man, fatherly and approachable, but savaged by journalists determined to fill column inches with hateful bile. As far as the tabloids were concerned, English football – its players, its fans, its teams – were all in the gutter together and deserved nothing but scorn.

Something happened though that started to change things. First of all, the team improved. A change in tactics prompted a rousing display against Holland, albeit in a 0-0 draw. Then, in the final group game, a 1-0 win over Egypt enabled England to qualify as group winners. After a dramatic last-minute goal in extra time saw England beat Belgium 1-0 in the second round, the mood of the press turned and the stories about hooligans and riots started to reduce. Robson, the man who only weeks before had been 'Bungler Bobby', was hailed as a master tactician. For the first time in the tournament, the question started to be asked in earnest: could England go all the way and win it?

A dramatic and slightly fortuitous 3-2 win over Cameroon, the tournament's surprise package, followed in the last eight and a state of delirium took hold as England faced Germany in the semi-finals. As kick-off approached, the nation's street were empty: Piccadilly Circus, Trafalgar Square, not a soul around other than the odd latecomer dashing home or towards somewhere there was a television set.

That was the day when football changed. It wasn't merely the heroic performance on the night, or the romantic narrative of England being gallant and tragically inevitable losers, but the disconsolate tears of one man – Paul Gascoigne. Gazza's display of emotion when he was booked (meaning he would have missed the final should England have got there) was the point in time that football tipped over from being of exclusive interest to angry young men who'd claimed the sport for themselves, to capturing the attention of the wider population.

Gazza's moment was a classic Greek tragedy playing out on 20 million television screens – the excitable man-child who'd won the hearts of a nation, suddenly plunged into despair by his own over-exuberance and impulsive immaturity. He looked so pained and vulnerable in those seconds after the card had been shown – not a professional athlete anymore but a tearful schoolboy unable to cope with the frustrated anguish of an unjust punishment.

Gary Lineker, even then a personification of maturity and dependability, was straight over to him, assessing the situation, trying to see what was going on behind the eyes of his distressed young team-mate. Then that look over to Robson on the bench, the pained expression, pointing to his own eyes as if to say 'watch him, gaffer – his head's gone'. This wasn't a football match anymore, it was melodrama. Everybody was hooked, unable to take their eyes off what was playing out in front of them.

I don't need to tell you how it ended, but the game had attracted a record TV audience and the England players were treated like heroes on their return to the UK. A country that had turned its back on its own national game for the last decade suddenly fell in love all over again.

Paul Gascoigne described in his autobiography *Gazza: My Story* the moment he realised his own life, and with it the status of football, had changed, when he walked into a Burger King on the way home to Newcastle immediately following the squad's return from Italy. Even though nobody knew Gascoigne was going to turn up in that particular place at that particular time, within seconds of getting out of his car, he was mobbed by well-wishers wanting to shake his hand or get an autograph.

In a matter of weeks, culminating in that iconic moment in Turin, the general public no longer wanted to read about hooligans, they wanted to watch Paul Gascoigne play football, to go through the turnstiles again and reclaim the sport they had once loved. It wasn't all sunshine and skittles overnight, but the tide had definitely turned. Following the World Cup, English club sides were re-admitted into European competition, domestic attendances rose to a ten-year high and football became marketable to the masses.

In 1990, the seeds of the modern game were sown.

Season 1990/91
The Piece of Cake

'**D**ON'T worry about promotion,' Alan Ball confidently told the supporters at a meet-the-manager event prior to the start of the 1990/91 season. 'It'll be a piece of cake.'

Thinking back to those days following our relegation to the third tier, Ball's chutzpah almost brings a smile to my face. We actually believed him too! Nowadays, bitter experience and common sense has taught most of us that relegated clubs don't tend to storm back in a blaze of glory, due to the main handicap that got them relegated in the first place – namely, being absolutely shite. Back then though, the third tier was an alien landscape of which we had no experience.

We didn't know how good or bad any of the teams would be (these were the days before Sky televised lower league games for the entire population to ignore) so we all assumed that the Third Division was comparable to one of the North Staffordshire Sunday leagues. Even Tony Ellis would look good, we thought.

If Ball did believe his own hyperbolic bombast, then he must have watched the previous six months of football under the influence of some powerful hallucinogenic because the disorganised rabble he'd led to relegation wouldn't have found doing *anything* a piece of cake.

Even eating a piece of *actual* cake in a competent fashion would have probably been beyond them, so utterly useless had they been the previous season.

But we went along with it. We believed Ball the flat-capped messiah, squeaking out his call-to-arms and a healthy crowd of 12,700 turned up for an opening day fixture bathed in sunshine. An opening day fixture against Rotherham United. Welcome to the Third Division, Stoke.

Ball's confidence that his troops would be up to the task was exemplified by the minimal transfer activity that he conducted that summer. The only fee spent was on midfielder Mick Kennedy, another of Ball's old Portsmouth troopers, who came with a reputation as a hard man following red card-littered spells at Luton, Middlesbrough and Bradford, among others.

From what we saw of Kennedy, I'm not sure 'hard' would be the adjective I'd use to describe him. Certainly not 'hard' in the sense that Stoke legends such as Denis Smith or, in later years, Robert Huth were 'hard'. Those two were human walls of granite who attackers would physically bounce off, and who could instil fear into opponents simply by fixing them with a cold, blue-eyed stare.

Kennedy came across as more cynical: a bloke likely to stick a stray boot in when the referee wasn't looking – more of a walking red card than someone whose physicality could be used to unsettle the opposition or inspire those around him.

Partnering him in midfield would be Mickey Thomas, a former Stoke player of the early 1980s, who was still going strong at 37 after being released from Leeds (just to clarify, I'm talking about the team there, not the prison). Despite his reputation as being a bit dodgy, Mickey was a popular character due to his wholehearted approach and amazing fitness levels, which were quite staggering given his age and rumoured antics off the field.

Thomas's shady dealings did eventually catch up with him, but not until 1993 when he was jailed for 18 months for his part in a money-laundering scam ('Roy Keane's on £50,000 a week at Manchester United, and so was I until the police found my printing machine,' was his favourite quip on the after-dinner circuit for years after!).

And so it was that Ball's motley bunch of Portsmouth cast-offs and general football misfits lined up against the mighty Rotherham, ill-equipped to deliver the outcome their manager had so confidently claimed they would achieve with ease. I was actually on holiday in Scotland for the opening two games of the campaign, and twice forced my entire family to sit through 90 minutes of Ceefax pages so I could follow the scores. Next time you're complaining about your internet stream buffering or Jeff Stelling not providing us with enough reports from Stoke's game, please think about what I've just said – an hour and a half of staring at text on a black screen. That's dedication and it's also very, very sad.

There was something undeniably special about the simplicity of it though. Every division would have three or four Ceefax pages dedicated to the latest scores, each carrying updates from three games.

If Stoke were on page four, the anticipation would build when page three came up as you knew that in a few seconds' time, Stoke's score would be there in front of you.

No fanfare, no 'GOAL!' written in red letters, no flashing text, just the dry, factual reality of a football score. More often than not, it would be unchanged. Oh, it's still 0-0 you'd say, and the anticipation would fizzle away to nothing as you waited for the cycle to repeat itself and the exciting page three to page four transition to come around once again. Occasionally though, the news would be positive. There before you, as page four flashed up, would be glory itself in text form.

If I close my eyes, I can remember it clearly. It's there now on my auntie's TV, the screen's black, the text is green:

Stoke 1-0 Rotherham
Blake 15

The cake's out of the oven! Ball the master baker's mixed the ingredients and big Noel Blake's just come along and iced the bastard. Fifteen minutes in and we're sweeping the rest of the division away! I try to imagine how the goal has come about – such details being impossible to find, 400 miles away in the Scottish Highlands. It's probably a header from a corner, Blakey crashing through a stunned Rotherham rearguard unable to cope with these beasts from a higher division, athletic specimens the likes of which they have never encountered before in their sheltered Third Division lives.

The pages roll on throughout the afternoon and by five o'clock, page four contains the scoreline of 3-1 to Stoke, Mick Kennedy and Mickey Thomas adding goals either side of half-time to lay down a marker for the rest of the division. Read it and weep, Third Division underlings – your lords and masters, Stoke City, have arrived.

The glory continues the following Friday, evening kick-offs being standard for our hosts, Tranmere Rovers. They're regular promotion chasers at this level and have a chap called Ian Muir up front who seems handy. Muir's obviously not read Bally's cake recipe and impudently puts his team 1-0 up from the penalty spot. Ceefax carries the bad news. With no other games going on, there's no page-turning excitement either, just one screen, one scoreline and the dreaded 'flicker' telling us when something's changed.

Losing on Ceefax is worse than losing at the game, no doubt. When you're there and the action's happening in front of you, delusional as it might be, you still feel that you can somehow affect the result. Even if it's just hollering encouragement, you're there in the moment and you can often sense which way a result's going to go based on the balance of play.

Ceefax is a void though – a blank, desolate void. Losing on Ceefax is pure helplessness, like pacing up and down the waiting room as a loved one lies in theatre – anything could be going on in there and you just have no idea. Are we peppering the goal with shots? Are we looking like we're getting back into it? Tell me for God's sake, what's happening out there!? Nothing. Just emotionless green text on a blank screen.

Losing 1-0, until the page flickers again, which it will surely do – but perhaps only to add HT or FT next to the scoreline. Sit and stare, you fool. Willing it to change won't help, either. You should listen to your mother, rationally explaining that spending 90 minutes staring at a blank screen won't affect the result either way, and that it's not reasonable to expect the entire family to forego Friday night viewing to sit through an hour and a half of watching one football score on a screen. She's right, but perhaps if you just concentrate that bit harder, the screen will flicker again and it'll happen.

Tranmere 1-1 Stoke
Muir 12   Ellis 36

I dance around my auntie's lounge, punching the air, leaping about in unbridled joy. Mum isn't happy – I almost knock the drinks over as I flail excitedly around the room. Dad's probably pleased, but retains a sense of perspective that equalisers in the Third Division aren't worth trashing your sister-in-law's living room for. He remains seated and scowls at me, looking like he's about to dish out a bollocking.

Tranmere are among the promotion favourites. If we can get one more goal, get three points at their place then we'll be top of the league – even if only for a few hours. Then we can find the league table page on Ceefax and look at that for a while, what about it Mum?

But first we have to score. We will though, surely? We're Stoke City, League Cup winners 1972, Matthews, Greenhoff, Hudson. Gods from up on high. Tranmere might be a tough place to go, but this is the Third Division and we're too good for it. Even seeing the name 'Stoke City' will surely scare the opposition into submission, right? Come on lads, sort it out for Christ's sake.

And then it happens. I make it happen through the power of thought. I'm convinced of it.

Tranmere 1-2 Stoke
Muir 12   Ellis 36
**   Kennedy 43 (pen)**

I'm up again, off the settee and considering another attempt at a Beagrie backflip. I'm not alone this time – the rest of the family might not get excited about equalisers, but a winner to send us top of the table? Mum loses her shit, has chucked the peanuts over and is gleefully stamping them into the carpet; Dad's jumping up and down on the furniture, screaming and beating his chest like a caveman; Nana's risen from the armchair and is sliding across the carpet face first, Jurgen Klinsmann-style; Grandad's ripped his shirt off and is sprinting round the room, turning bookcases over and shouting, 'Micky Fuckin' Kennedy! Get in you fucker!'

Even my auntie and uncle, who don't follow football that closely, are swept away in celebration and immediately fetch champagne from the kitchen before spraying it triumphantly around the lounge like Lewis Hamilton.

'We are top of the league! We are top of the league!' we all chant, knowing that Bally's leading us back to the Promised Land.

I think that's how it happened anyway. Or I might have celebrated on my own again, a bit too exuberantly, knocked some lemonade over and the TV was turned off to teach me a lesson. Some of the finer details of that evening have been lost to time.

A Different Kind of Game

I'd love to say that I stood on the Victoria Ground terraces in the bad old days against Chester, Rotherham and Exeter, suffering the ignominy of lower league home defeats and general Third Division atrocities. In the days of Premier League football and comparative glory that we've experienced in recent times, being there for the bad times can be worn as a badge of honour.

Call me a Johnny Come Lately? A plastic fan? I was there at Wigan mate, knee-deep in mud, eating dog shit and watching Billy fucking Whitehurst etc. Well I was there for the bad old days – some of the time, at least. How I spent the majority of my Saturdays in the harrowing 1990/91 season, however, is a complete embarrassment.

There's an old Harry Enfield sketch where the comedian's infamous Kevin character instantly transforms from a normal, polite 12-year-old boy full of 'pleases' and 'thank yous' into an ungrateful, truculent pain in the arse the very second that he turns 13. My 13th birthday arrived in the middle of the 1990/91 season, and while my personality might not have changed quite as dramatically as Enfield's character's did, in August I was a fresh-faced 12-year-old Stoke fanatic in a catalogue tracksuit with posters of Wayne Biggins on his bedroom wall; by May I was a grunting acne explosion with greasy hair and a Faith No More t-shirt.

Thirteen's certainly an awkward age to be. Neither a child nor an adult, you're too old to go and play 'tick' outside with your mates, but too young to attempt to get served in the off-licence or sneak into a nightclub with fake ID. Your body's changing, your hormones are all over the place and your once peach-smooth cheeks now resemble a pizza with pubic hair randomly sprouting from it. For me, it all added up to a serious identity crisis.

After the blistering start to the season I'd watched via Ceefax, Stoke maintained their position in and around the early-season promotion picture. Although a defeat at home to Birmingham and a couple of tame draws followed the brace of victories, we then thrashed early pacesetters Southend 4-0 and were dreaming of the dominant promotion campaign that our manager had predicted.

However, during the next home game, I think I had my first real 'Kevin' moment. It was just too much to take, getting all worked up about an instant return to the Second Division, only to then sit through a pitiful 3-1 defeat against Shrewsbury. With about ten minutes left I got up and asked my dad if we could leave. When he grumpily told me to sit down and watch the rest of the game, I decided to storm off instead with the intention of waiting for him by the car.

Obviously not wanting to have to face the wrath of my mum if I'd somehow managed to get beaten up by hooligans or trampled by a police horse or something outside, the old man followed me out in a foul temper and told me that following my display of defiant pique, he wasn't taking me to any more Stoke games. For him it was probably a convenient way of getting out of watching any more of Ball's drivel as he'd probably had enough as well by that point. I just shrugged my shoulders and said 'not bovvered' in my best Kevin voice. So that was it. I didn't care about those losers anymore. I'd just find something else to do on Saturdays.

Another 'fun' part of being 13 is that whereas 12 months ago, girls were just an annoying species that got in the way of your playground football match, it now only took a glimpse of page three in *The Sun* and you'd be bouncing around the place with a hard-on. The problem was that while spending half your waking hours with an erection might sound like fun, when you've got a sea of festering pimples adorning your forehead, a pair of jam-jar glasses, and your idea of sophisticated humour is giggling at a cock and balls spray-painted on to a bus shelter, the chances are that no female is going to let you near them. So what did I do for sexual kicks? I went out on my bike with my equally sad mate every Saturday and looked for discarded pornographic magazines in hedges. Yes, you have read that correctly.

To a generation growing up with a world of enticing filth only a convenient mouse-click away, rooting through foliage for an hour just for a peak at a crumpled vagina might seem a bizarre way to spend an afternoon. You did feel a sense of pride and achievement though when you found some filthy treasure in the shape of an old *Razzle*, I can't deny that. I would like to make it clear at this point, that although we might have had a good flick through the magazines, and perhaps even taken one home in triumph if it was clean enough (oh God, please stop me typing this) we did NOT actually sink as low as to masturbate in bushes.

This exciting and wholesome new hobby meant that although I was keeping tabs on the Potters via the old Ceefax and Radio Stoke, I wasn't missing them that much. I do remember having a mental around my grandparents' living room when Mickey Thomas netted a late winner at Bradford, and it was my grandad who took pity on me around Christmas time when he defied my dad's ban on Stoke games and took me to see a 2-2 draw against Brentford. All in all though, my statement following the Shrewsbury game was proving to be correct – I really wasn't all that bothered.

People who stop attending games often say how easy it is to get out of the habit once you make that initial break, and I certainly knew that I was losing the bug. It was one of my Christmas presents from my mum that really saw my interest in Stoke dip to a new low. It was *Readers Wives Go Hardcore – The Annual*. Only kidding, it was a role-playing game called Hero Quest, which was one of the Dungeons and Dragons-type games very popular at the time. They were played with dice and little painted men, mainly by socially inadequate virgins in sweat-soaked heavy metal t-shirts and (just like porn in hedges) their popularity has inversely waned as computer technology has advanced.

As my Wayne Biggins posters were now being displaced by pictures of heavy metal bands, this was a dangerous path to be on. Every Saturday would now be spent with a few mates piling round to push wizards, dwarves and elves around a board and cast imaginary spells on each other. Before long I wasn't even checking half-time scores on the radio as I was too immersed in the Tolkien-esque world of goblins and orcs to care about how Stoke were getting on away at Preston.

I think the moment of realisation arrived during a visit to a particular shop in Hanley, where all the serious dice-throwing sad acts used to hang out. All I remember is the smell of body odour hitting me as a few sweaty men with goatees and ill-fitting black t-shirts talked gobbledegook at each other and moved pieces around a board.

'What a bunch of nerds!' I said to myself, before noticing that my own appearance resembled a junior version of the men I was sneering at. Both are embarrassing activities, but on the Grand Richter Scale of Sadness, a 25-year-old IT engineer spending his Saturday afternoons pretending to be a warlock probably measures higher than a 13-year-old leering at some tits in a hedge. Realising that this was where I could be heading, I knew it was time to get myself back on track.

Who was I kidding anyway with this new grunge-nerd persona? My voice might have broken, and a few straggly hairs had sprouted out of my ball sack, but I was still a daft little kid at heart: a kid who still wanted to keep those cardboard league ladders up to date and read *Roy of the Rovers* like the football-loving fool that I'd always been.

Perhaps sensing that his son was losing his way a bit, my dad forgave me the Shrewsbury incident and said he'd take me to games again. (It wasn't until I hit 14 that I was allowed to go on my own, and I couldn't have afforded to pay for myself anyway as I was still too idle to get a paper round.) There was only one caveat to that. We weren't going again until Alan Ball left. That wouldn't be too long given how things were going on the pitch.

What I Missed (Not Much)

So what had actually been happening on the pitch during my absence? Not a lot, to tell you the truth. Looking at Stoke's results during that spell from October to February, I have no memory of any of it. I wasn't going, was only occasionally listening to the radio and for the most part, had pretty much lost interest in Stoke City.

It's getting on for 30 years now since the days of Mick Mills, but I still remember the tiniest of details from the season before (1989/90) and every season since. Of course, games tend to blend together a bit and I probably couldn't tell you every score off the top of my head anymore, but looking through the list of results, I have memories of pretty much every game – even the ones I didn't attend.

Sometimes it's a mental image of reading the match report in the *Green 'Un* that Saturday night (the *Green 'Un* was the football paper printed on a Saturday evening featuring hurriedly written football reports from that afternoon and printed, unsurprisingly, on green paper), other times it's a memory of listening to the game in a particular location – whether it be my bedroom, the lounge, my dad's car or round at a mate's house.

Sometimes I remember seeing the goals on *Central News* at five o'clock, just as I was waiting for my weekly fix of Pamela Anderson in *Baywatch* (I'll never forget *her*!). Whatever it was though, there's still something there, lurking in a dark enclave of my brain – a tiny morsel of a memory that I still retain all this time later. Saturday, March 1990, home to Sheffield United, lost 1-0. Do I remember the goal? No. Do I remember the fluorescent away kit that Sheffield United wore – a yellow so dazzling it looked like 11 stewards had taken to the pitch? Yes.

A 2-1 loss at Sunderland the week after I associate with playing football in the street. My mate Dazzer and I were booting the ball at his gates; the metallic clattering used to drive the neighbours potty as we crashed shots against them. Dazzer's mum popped her head out of the window to tell us that Stoke had scored. That's it – one second in time from decades ago, one of many random events that stick in my head from a time when I was living and breathing Stoke City. But that 'lost' period during 1990/91 gives me virtually nothing. It's just a list of teams, names and numbers. Games that I wouldn't know had ever even happened if it were not for the record books telling me they did.

Those records don't make for particularly happy reading though. They tell of a team that started well, perhaps buoyed by their manager's optimism, but lacked ability, and as soon as things started to go against them, collapsed very easily into long winless runs. By the time winter came, Stoke were hanging on to the play-off positions by their fingernails, that good early-season form providing a bank of points that, week by week, was being eaten into by teams below them. By the time that Stoke inevitably did get dragged out of those top six spots, a team in such dire form had no chance of returning to those precious play-off positions.

The one memory I do have of this 'lost' period is a 3-2 home defeat to Chester in February. Fucking Chester. I don't think we'd even played them in a league match before that season, but they arrived at the Victoria Ground and stormed into a three-goal lead, the cheeky bastards. I paid attention to this match only because I had to write a match report on it as part of an IT project at school, and as I sat there the following Monday, painstakingly typing the words, one-finger-style, on to a computer the size of a bin lorry, my teacher came up behind me and looked over my shoulder at the screen. 'Mark Devlin came off the bench to make his debut and played well in the second half,' he read aloud. 'Who's he then, a new signing?'

'I think he's from the youth team,' I said.

'Oh. I remember watching Alan Hudson's debut against Liverpool. Brilliant day that was.' And with that he moved on to the other kids, probably checking that none of them were typing swear words. I think *I* should have been allowed a few profanities though, given the subject matter.

That was my dad's problem too. He remembered Hudson's debut against Liverpool. He remembered watching Jimmy Greenhoff and John Ritchie combine up front. He remembered Stoke playing Ajax in Europe. He remembered Stanley Matthews's return and 35,000 packing into the Victoria Ground. Mark Devlin coming off the bench and playing well in a 3-2 defeat to Chester wasn't even the same sport as the things he'd watched as a young man. He'd lost interest in it a while ago and as long as Alan Ball was manager, he'd given up on the good times ever coming back.

Those who were still going had turned on Ball too at this point, his pre-season 'piece of cake' comments coming back to haunt him more with every miserable defeat. The nadir was Wigan away on 23 February 1991. Maybe not the most embarrassing defeat in

Stoke's history, given some of the horrors we've endured since, but still probably up there in the top ten.

The Horror of Springfield Park

Springfield Park is now a long-forgotten football stadium, demolished in the last century as Wigan moved to the all-seater JJB Stadium thanks to the investment of multi-millionaire owner Dave Whelan. Back in the early 1990s though, it was considered one of the worst football grounds in the whole country, featuring a grass bank for an away end with a corrugated cow shed at the back, complete with leaking roof.

If Old Trafford is the theatre of dreams, this place was the shit-hole of nightmares – a suitable place for Alan Ball's reign to come to a grisly end.

On the day Stoke arrived, out of form, out of sorts and rapidly dropping out of the play-off picture, the heavens opened. From start to finish it pissed it down. People who were there all talk about 'the sliders' – unfortunate souls who lost their footing on an away end that rapidly turned into a mudslide and were sent careering down on their backsides, occasionally taking out other supporters on their way like a game of human skittles. This wasn't good old-fashioned away-day drunken fun though, the mood was as ugly as the weather and people were chanting for Ball's head before the game had even kicked off.

Wigan were no better than Stoke, on paper. They were a team going nowhere, mid-table also-rans who'd looked poor when Stoke had beaten them 2-0 earlier in the season. However, on this cold, wet and thoroughly depressing day, Stoke contrived to make them look like world-beaters. The misery started just after the half-hour when Phil Daley stepped in front of an inexplicably static Lee Fowler to comfortably head past Peter Fox.

Daley doubled the home team's advantage just after the break. Bryan Griffiths – a tricky winger who always seemed to cause problems for Stoke – went on a jinking run and drew the entire defence to him. Daley was left with the freedom of Greater Manchester and had the simple task of chipping the ball over Fox's despairing dive to give Stoke a bigger uphill task than the fans lying in the mud at the bottom of the away end.

The mood on the away end was venomous, and things got worse as Wigan added a third and a fourth from unchallenged headers. In truth the score could have been even worse had it not been for several smart saves from Peter Fox and a late shot hitting the woodwork.

Stoke had already lost plenty of games in the season that was supposedly going to be 'a piece of cake' but this was different. This was a thrashing handed out by the sort of team that many couldn't even believe we were playing let alone being totally outclassed by. The arrogance with which we'd gone into the season was now well and truly trampled into the mud by the reality that even by Third Division standards we were a very poor team.

Ball was angered by his team's lack of effort, but even more so by the Stoke fans' response to his team's failings. His autobiography describes the unsavoury scenes at Springfield Park as fans spat, threw things and yelled abuse at him. Ball claimed that when he went out to look at the pitch, a Stoke fan, a young lad of about nine or ten years of age, spat at him. Understandably, Ball decided that being spat at by a child was the indicator that he should go.

Ball claimed that he resigned immediately after the final whistle, but would certainly have been sacked anyway. Peter Coates admits that following that result he did something that he'd never done before or since, 'Usually I never make a decision after a match, but we were so bad that I asked the Wigan chairman if there was a room available where I could speak to Alan. I don't think I'd do that again – you can get very worked up watching football and it's better to take a bit of time to compose yourself before you make a decision like that.'

In truth though, the decision to remove Ball wasn't one that required much consideration. Somehow, he'd made a poor team even worse, following Mick Mills's disappointing reign with 12 months of staggering incompetence.

Of course, Ball blamed everyone but himself, claiming that Coates had appeared to be more concerned with his personal business interests than the team. That might have won him some sympathy with the fans, none of whom had much love for the chairman throughout the '90s, but the background of boardroom unrest that Ball alleged undermined his tenure couldn't possibly account for the sheer ineptitude of the performances that Ball oversaw. If it wasn't the board's fault it was the players' ('their hearts were not in it') or the fans' ('there was neither willingness nor patience when things began to dip'). It couldn't possibly have been Alan Ball's fault though for being a dreadful football manager, oh no.

The level we'd sunk to was too much for some Stoke fans. The personal abuse directed at Ball was hateful and undoubtedly went too far. As well as the flak he took against Wigan, 12 months later Ball had hot drinks thrown at him while managing his next club, Exeter. Ball might have been a terrible manager, but he wasn't really a bad human being. People who met him spoke about him in glowing terms – a friendlier man you couldn't wish to meet was the consensus of opinion. Even Peter Coates, despite what Ball had said about him in his autobiography, still describes Ball as 'someone you couldn't fail to like'.

And although results had been poor, some of the players still thought highly of Ball. 'I'll never understand why Alan Ball didn't work out at Stoke,' Peter Fox told author Simon Lowe in *Match of my Life* (Pitch Publishing, 2012). 'He brought so much passion to his work and that's what Stokies like to see. I liked his methods of getting you wound up before games, but some of the lads didn't. They thought it was too intense. But it got the best out of me.'

Carl Beeston agrees that Ball was a fantastic personality: 'Bally was a brilliant bloke Coaching was brilliant, everything was top drawer The problem was that we weren't good enough for him really We couldn't do half the things he wanted us to do in training He was a legend as a footballer, a legend as a person – I loved him to death He just loved football It was a shame what happened to him really as I can honestly say that he did genuinely love Stoke He cried when he left – honestly, he was in tears '

If Ball was so popular with the players, I wondered why the team hadn't performed better for him in order to keep him in a job. Beeston offers one explanation, 'I think he tried to be one of us a bit too much, he wasn't as strict as say, Lou was, which probably wasn't the best thing to do really. Whatever we were doing he wanted to be involved as well. He liked getting us together and seeing if that'd work, but it didn't, it just made us worse to be honest!'

All things considered, Ball was also one of only 11 men who have won a World Cup Final for England. Although some of the decisions he made at Stoke were poorly judged, it was the behaviour of the supporters that was the real embarrassment. Ball had to go – he was a poor football manager at Stoke and at other clubs too, but even if I live to be a hundred years old, I hope I never witness personal abuse on the scale that Alan Ball suffered during his time here.

The Oatcake

The first game my dad took me to following Ball's departure was a 1-0 home win over Crewe Alexandra (another reminder of how low we'd now sunk). The winner was scored in the last minute by Mark Devlin, hero of my school match report in IT, and one of the few bright spots in what were, indeed, the darkest of days. It wasn't the goal or the game that I particularly remember about this night though, it was buying *The Oatcake* for the first time.

I'd heard about this publication when someone brought one into class and a bunch of lads gathered around as if it was some kind of illicit material, laughing at the cartoons taking the piss out of Port Vale and reading aloud from the text pretty much any sentences with swear words in. What was this, I thought. I was still reading *Match* and *Shoot* at the time, and hadn't even heard of fanzines. I had a few programmes from games I'd attended, but none of them were as entertaining to read as this was. I can't remember the exact words that were written on that cheap-quality paper, just that it was absolutely hilarious and never before had I read such honest, biting prose about football, especially my team. It looked like it was put together using a typewriter and a photocopier (it was) but in a world of glossy poster magazines and anodyne player interviews in the matchday programme, this thing seemed edgy and dangerous. Needless to say, I was hooked, and every home game I attended, my pocket money would be spent on the latest edition of *The Oatcake*.

The fanzine was the brainchild of Martin Smith and Dave Frith, two Stoke fans who'd been inspired by the student 'rag mags' that sprung up during this time. Rag mags were cheaply produced magazines that were basically full of jokes of questionable taste, and I remember seeing a few knocking around school at the time – all clearly influenced by *Viz*, another alternative magazine/comic that was popular in the early 1990s and is still being produced today.

The first issue of *The Oatcake* was published during the 1988/89 season at the height of supporters' frustration with Mick Mills and consisted of a handful of crudely photocopied pages stapled together.

Only 400 were printed and went on sale at the home game against Swindon Town. They sold out in minutes.

Martin laughs as he looks back on that first issue. 'We'd heard about these fanzines,' he told Bear Pit TV, 'and one of the lads, Rob Ledgar, sent off for copies of an Arsenal one and a Celtic one. By then we'd done our first issue – this really rubbish eight-page thing – and then these super-glossy 48-page things arrived in the post!

'We decided there and then that *The Oatcake* can't just be about jokes, we wanted to give Stoke fans a voice.'

At this time of course, before the internet, fanzines provided a unique platform for people to speak from the heart about football. While the letters pages of the local press also offered that opportunity, nervy editors were often wary about printing anything too controversial and would heavily edit letters to the point where the material that had originally been submitted was barely recognisable.

Fanzines were different though – they didn't really play by the rules and (within reason) it was a case of anything goes. People relished the opportunity to read the views of other fans, to contribute to the discussion through letters and articles, and within a couple of years, *The Oatcake* had rapidly grown from a one-off experiment to a full-time job for its editors.

'By issue six we were up to 1,500 copies,' recalls Smith. 'By issue ten we were selling 3,000. At its height, we were shifting 5,000 copies. But back then there was no internet and no social media. We used to have four pages of letters and even that wasn't enough to fit them all in.'

Three decades on and it's sad that many clubs' fanzines have now died a death – unable to maintain viable sales figures in a world where so much free content is instantly available online. Some still survive: *Fly Me to the Moon* (Middlesbrough) is still going, as is *The Gooner* (Arsenal) and *The Square Ball* (Leeds), but many, many more have fallen by the wayside. The national fanzine that inspired a lot of the individual club versions, *When Saturday Comes*, is still around but is a very different animal now than when it first started.

I'm a little bit too young to have read other fanzines in the early days of the mid-to-late 1980s, but back then, in the shadow of Bradford and Hillsborough, there was something for fans to rally against. It truly was the people versus the establishment, and that gave early fanzines an anger that fuelled much of the writing. One of the most famous covers of *WSC*, post-Hillsborough, featured Graham Kelly, the police and Margaret Thatcher all stating, 'It wasn't our fault,' followed by a shot of football supporters saying, 'Oh well, it must be our fault again then.' Make no mistake, football fans truly were shit on back then, and the written word was a method of rallying people to fight back and refuse to tolerate the treatment they received from the authorities.

Nowadays, there are still campaigns to be run and issues to be challenged, but by and large the average fan's matchday experience is a comfortable one – raging against the pies being a bit too expensive or your kick-off time being moved to a Sunday just doesn't quite convince as much as the political battles of yesteryear.

This applies to *The Oatcake* as well, I suppose. What have we truly got to complain about in the modern era when you compare it to the miserable years we endured under Brian Little, Alan Ball and Chris Kamara? Nothing. And when people complain that *The Oatcake* is not as good as it used to be, I think what they really mean is that it's not as angry or as new as it used to be. Speaking as a reader, rather than a contributor, I feel the standard of written content is much higher than the old days, but when there's nothing to fight against, it does become harder and harder to generate the kind of hard-hitting, urgent material that people associate with fanzines.

Looking back at the issues from the early '90s now, some of the content is a bit naïve, the layout is badly put together, but none of that mattered at the time because it was the punk ethos that made fanzines what they were. As a long-standing contributor to *The Oatcake*, in a world where many fanzines gave gone online, become glossy magazine-style publications full of adverts, or (in most cases) disappeared completely, I'd like to think that our club's publication still retains much of its original spirit. It's amazing that a paper fanzine is still selling a healthy number of copies in the digital age, almost 700 issues in, and that's testament to the high esteem in which it's held by so many Stoke fans and the dedication that Martin and Dave have put into keeping it going.

Nevertheless, like all print media, the editors of *The Oatcake* feel that the end for the fanzine may be on the horizon. 'I think we're still just about relevant,' says Smith, 'but I think we're clinging on by our fingernails now. It's just the way things are heading. All print media's struggling. If you look at the offices *The Sentinel* used to have, and no one covers Stoke more than them, they're struggling; they moved into smaller offices and had to move their content online, it's sad.'

The direction of travel for fan publications is all too clear, and there's very much a sense that the fanzines that do still exist are the last wave of that original generation of alternative voices. One day we'll have nothing in the written form providing a coherent rhetoric, just the incessant babble of a million Twitter users, hovering over us every waking moment, constantly firing off barbed soundbites like a swarm of angry wasps. Shards of opinion and fragments of argument. Noise that we can't really hear.

From Bad to Graham Paddon

With Alan Ball gone, the board decided that with Stoke in mid-table, far enough away from either end of the table to have a chance of going up or down, handing the reins to his assistant Graham Paddon was an acceptable way of seeing out the season. There were also the financial implications to consider, and even if Ball's resignation had saved them the money that would have been needed to pay up his contract, the cash that Ball had wasted in the transfer market, as well as the losses associated with last season's relegation, meant there was no money to pay compensation should Stoke wish to appoint a man contracted to another club.

Paddon is now very much the forgotten man of Stoke City, overseeing the period of limbo between his erstwhile boss being sacked and the inevitability of his own departure once the board could appoint a new man in the summer. As caretaker periods go though, it was quite a long run, 18 games in all, but it was just as poor as the rest of the season had been – understandably so given that most of the squad, and Paddon himself, knew they were just marking time until their contracts were up.

So who was Paddon, this poor sod with a moustache who looked a little bit too much like Mick Mills for comfort? Making his name as a player at Norwich, Paddon's playing career had also taken in a spell at West Ham before he returned to Norwich for a second time in the early 1980s. Following a brief period in non-league and the announcement of his retirement, he joined Ball's coaching staff at Portsmouth in 1985. Paddon followed Ball to Stoke after the latter's appointment as manager in 1989, this time working as his assistant. With a manager as high-profile as Alan Ball, it was understandable that Paddon was happy to be in the background, and that's where he seemed to be. Personally, I must admit that the first time I'd even heard his name was when he was handed the job as caretaker!

Initially, the squad seemed to respond well to Ball's departure and put together a run of decent results. One defeat in eight games, a run which included a completely unexpected 4-0 away win at Brentford, hinted at an unlikely revival as Stoke crept back into the top half of the table. Mathematically, the play-offs would still be possible if the team went on a blistering run.

Paddon wasn't holding his breath though. When asked by *The Sentinel* if he would allow himself a look at the league table that night, he replied, 'Well, I haven't bothered recently.' That's the spirit, Graham!

However, Paddon's apparent pessimism was entirely justified because regardless of who the manager was, the team were still as bad as they always had been.

It didn't take them long to return to type either and a run of six straight defeats followed. A 2-1 win against Bradford briefly ended the misery, but things got even more depressing a week later when Grimsby were the visitors and Stoke fans invaded the pitch. The game was held up for 15 minutes as the police struggled to get control of the situation. This was an ugly incident that had occurred primarily as a revenge attack for the trouble that had flared up at Grimsby's Blundell Park earlier in the season, but one which could also be seen as evidence of the frustration and anger that the supporters felt towards those running the club.

While talk in the top flight was of a Premier League forming and a TV deal that would bring new money into the game, Stoke fans were rioting in the middle of a 0-0 draw with Grimsby. We'd finally reached the lowest point in our history by any definition of the words.

Statistically, 14th place in the Third Division *was* the lowest we'd ever finished in the Football League and remains so to this day. We'd only ever played one season in the third tier before (1922/23) and had finished as champions, so we were probably destined to finish 1990/91 with that dubious 'honour' regardless. However, it was still a shocking outcome for a club of Stoke's stature and everyone was glad to see the back of a campaign that had proven extremely hard to digest.

As for Paddon, our caretaker manager unsurprisingly never had another management job in England. After being released from his contract in the summer of 1991, he returned to Portsmouth, this time assisting Jim Smith. Following the latter's sacking from Pompey, Paddon moved on to Derby in 1995 – again to work with Smith – this time as a scout, a role he also performed for Liverpool and Leicester in later years.

Sadly, Paddon passed away in November 2007 aged just 57. It speaks volumes that I can't remember reading or hearing about Paddon's passing at the time, and while I'm sure that the club acknowledged it, it perhaps goes to illustrate how much the tail end of 1990/91 has been airbrushed from our memories. Of course, Alan Ball also passed away in the same year, aged just 61, which did prompt a number of tributes from Stoke fans, including some who perhaps felt a bit guilty about how they'd treated our former manager at the end of his time here.

The words of one supporter, Doz, who was lucky enough to meet Ball and obviously *did* respect him, provide a wonderful description of our former manager as the warm person he was, and not the cruel caricature of a flat-capped idiot that others created to legitimise their abuse of him:

'I know that I risk the wrath of many supporters but, to me, Alan was a brilliant football man who, unfortunately, didn't turn out to be a very good manager. I can't defend his time at Stoke in terms of the poor performances we were forced to endure, but I have to stick up for the bloke when it comes to his passion and desire to succeed. He always had so much time to stop and talk and was prepared to discuss almost anything to do with football with anyone who asked him.

'On one occasion he spent almost two hours in conversation with me and my brother-in-law and his clear passion for the game was wonderful. Stoke were very poor under him and his departure was inevitable after the shame of Wigan away but I loved the bloke as a football man and was disgusted with the abuse he endured from some Stoke fans.

'After they had thrown coffee all over him during our game at Exeter, I wrote to him to express my disgust and received a wonderful hand-written reply from him which basically forgave them. He was a proper football man, a fantastic player and a man who I will always retain fond memories of. On top of all of that, he was man of the match when England lifted the World Cup.

'Football is much poorer without Alan Ball.'

Season 1991/92
A Time for Heroes

THEY say the darkest hour is the one before dawn, and never mind an hour, we'd suffered an entire season of darkness in 1990/91. It's dangerous to assume that you're at your lowest ebb when supporting Stoke because experience has taught us that no matter how bad things get, it's impossible to guarantee that it won't get even worse in the future. With the club and the squad in disarray following years of mismanagement on and off the pitch, we needed a hero – a talisman to lift us and give us hope. But we didn't just get one. We got four.

The first man through the door was arguably the most important – the guy tasked with the job of sorting out the complete dog's dinner of a squad. Lou Macari had just left Birmingham City following a dispute with the club's owners, the Kumar brothers, and arrived at Stoke with a history of controversy and courtroom battles following his spell as the manager of Swindon Town.

Macari took over at the County Ground in 1984/85, was sacked by his first chairman, Harry Gregg, but then re-instated six days later following supporter protests. He led Swindon to the Division Four title in 1985/86, amassing a record 102 points, and followed that with another promotion in 1986/87 via the play-offs. Macari almost made it a hat-trick of promotions in 1987/88 when Swindon reached another play-off final, only to lose to Crystal Palace.

The achievement of taking Swindon to within a whisker of the top flight was amazing considering the meagre resources Macari had at his disposal. His success was built on countless hours spent travelling the length and breadth of the country to watch reserve team games, where Macari would spot players unwanted by other clubs, sign them for negligible transfer fees and then train them to within an inch of their lives. His sides were always the fittest in whichever division they were playing and relied on a basic, no frills 4-4-2 system in which every player knew his role. It was a simple formula that was effective time and time again.

'So many people overcomplicate football,' Macari tells me. 'It's not about managers plotting, or formations and tactics. It's about the players and their attitude.' It's a philosophy that might seem outdated now, but Macari's track record speaks suggests there might just be something in it.

Macari's talents caught the eye of West Ham, who'd just parted company with John Lyall following their relegation to the Second Division, and the promise of a healthy transfer budget and a higher prestige job saw Macari switch allegiance to the Hammers at the start of the 1989/90 campaign. Things turned sour though as the past came back to haunt Macari following newspaper allegations of wrongdoing during his time at his former club.

Swindon were found guilty by the FA of making illegal payments to players and immediately demoted to the Third Division. Macari felt that Swindon were being made an example of – punished for something that was quite commonplace in the lower divisions, where players' wages were still pretty much in line with what the average man in the street would earn. There was also the matter of new chairman Brian Hillier and Macari being charged with betting on their own team to lose an FA Cup match at Newcastle, their explanation being that if the team *had* got through to the next round, they would have made more money than had been staked on the defeat; the chairman was effectively hedging his bets to cover travel costs at a time when money was tight for the club.

The allegations didn't end there though, and Macari was also dragged into allegations of a tax fraud conspiracy alongside the board members at his former club (he would eventually be found not guilty). With his problems mounting, Macari thought it best to resign from his position at West Ham after just seven months in charge.

So while Stoke weren't getting a man who anyone could describe as having a whiter-than-white image within the game, what they were getting was someone with a fantastic track record of taking under-performing teams and turning them around without needing to spend money. Stoke being flat broke at the time, the board decided to take the gamble that Macari would be exonerated of the tax fraud charges that still hung over him at the start of the 1991/92 season and handed him the job.

Macari would be the first manager to be appointed by Peter Coates as the outright owner of the club following a share issue that saw Coates and Keith Humphreys purchase a controlling stake. 'I'd just been impressed by what he'd achieved,' remembers Coates. 'His Swindon team had beaten us 6-0 and I hadn't forgotten about that! He was very different, very quirky, but I thought, we've cracked it here. This man will do well for us.'

The former Swindon man got straight to work, presenting his squad with a punishing pre-season fitness regime, the likes of which they'd never seen before under the relaxed stewardship of Alan Ball.

'There were a lot of experienced players in the Stoke side,' Macari recalls. 'Without being critical, some of the boys in that squad had been in the game a while, had been there and done it, but for whatever reason, had stopped doing it. It's always going to be difficult to convince players like that where they've gone wrong, but when you turn things around and start winning football matches, that does tend to convince them.'

The fiercely teetotal Macari set about wiping out the drinking culture in the dressing room and players who refused to toe the line were removed from the first team at the earliest opportunity.

'There were little things I changed: no drink on the team bus. Before, there were people drinking on the bus then getting back to Stoke and getting in their cars, and I said no, you're not doing that anymore – I don't want to be responsible for anything happening to you. Overall, we overcame that hurdle, because I've seen so many team loading their crates of lager on the team bus and I'd think, fucking hell, where are the priorities here?'

'Lou used to meet us by the door on Monday morning,' laughs Wayne Biggins, a player who was known to enjoy a rather active social life! 'And if he thought you'd been out for a drink at the weekend he'd send you out on a run down by the canal while other people did five-a-side. Most of us ended up down by the canal!'

Carl Beeston still looks slightly traumatised as he recalls the horror of a Lou Macari training session, 'Every single day he'd have us running laps around the track. It was more of a test from him to see what we were made of. That's where he was brilliant – man-management and working out what you were about. I remember one day we got in the bus and all the balls were on – we didn't know where we were going for training.

'Anyway, we stopped next to Parkhall. I said to the lads, "There's some frigging hills around here, we're running!" Sure enough, the balls stayed on the bus, we got off and he said to us, "Right lads, your training session today is get back to the ground, that's it." His actual test was to see whether you'd run back, walk back or get in a taxi! Afterwards, he'd suss everybody out and work out what you'd done. You'd be there shitting yourself, saying, "He knows we got a taxi – he's going to run us even more now!" He used to scare me to death!'

Macari needed time to build a squad in his image, and for the first half of the campaign at least, had to make the best of what he'd inherited from Ball. Getting this rag-tag bunch fitter than they'd ever been in their lives and organising them on the pitch was a starting point, if nothing else.

As well as signing the young Australian goalkeeper Jason Kearton on loan, Macari moved quickly to sign his former captain at Birmingham City, Vince Overson, for a fee of £55,000. I mentioned four heroes in one season, well, here was the second.

To this day, I have no idea what Birmingham were playing at in selling Overson to us for such a paltry fee, but it soon became apparent that we'd got ourselves an absolute bargain. At 29 years old, Overson had the experience, know-how and charisma to organise and lead a defence. He wasn't quick, but he was built like a brick shit-house and immediately set about barking orders to the rest of the backline.

I've always thought that certain types of players suit certain types of clubs, and while fans of more pretentious clubs than Stoke go weak at the knees for flighty number tens with their array of back-heels and flicks, give Stoke fans a big, hairy-arsed centre-back and they're happy as pigs in shit. Denis Smith was probably the archetype for this. The local boy from Meir (believe me, that makes him hard already) was before my time but is still spoken of in revered tones by those who watched him play through injuries that would have hospitalised lesser men, striking fear into the hearts of attackers mainly by, well, kicking them up in the air all afternoon.

Overson was of similar ilk. From the minute he first set foot on the pitch for us we could see that he was big, he was hard and he took no prisoners. We liked him already.

Peter Fox also remembered the impact Overson had, writing, 'Vince was a great signing. Yes he was arrogant but that was all part of him. I mean, before the game if there was a mirror around you wouldn't be able to get in front of it because Vince would be there sorting his hair out! But if there was a cross coming into the area, he'd put his head on it, no mistake.'

Our third hero was not a new arrival, but a man already at the club. Since signing for Stoke two years earlier, Biggins had notched 22 goals in 73 appearances; a reasonable return but nothing to write home about. Whether it was a case of benefitting from the extra fitness work or having his confidence boosted by the charismatic Macari, who knows, but whatever it was, it transformed Biggins from a journeyman forward into one of the hottest strikers outside the top flight. In the first 13 games of the season, Biggins chalked up 12 goals. It wasn't just his finishing that was impressive either, his all-round game suddenly looked a class above the level he was playing at.

'Before I met Lou I'd played three years at Norwich and a year at Manchester City and scored about ten goals each season,' admits Biggins. 'Lou comes along and I had the best season of my career – 28 goals. It was entirely down to him that I did that.'

However, despite Biggins's hot streak in front of goal and Overson's organisational skills at the back, the results didn't immediately roll in for Macari and his Stoke team. It took four games for us to record our first victory – a hard-fought 1-0 win over Shrewsbury – and an infuriating habit of letting two-goal leads slip meant that we were hovering just outside the play-off positions by the time that September drew to a close.

It was the arrival of our fourth hero that kick-started things, although he too would take a while to get going. When Mark Stein signed on loan from Oxford United, no one was expecting too much from him. He was a once-promising forward who'd long since lost his way. Always in the shadow of his more famous brother Brian at Luton, doing little of note at QPR then losing his place at Oxford United. A glittering CV it wasn't, but Macari had seen something in the little man, and when Lou spotted something we tended to trust his judgement. Stein was a typical Macari signing in many ways.

'The way the game was back then, you'd finish training, jump on a train, watch a reserve game in London at two, go and watch another at seven then get back home,' Macari states. 'That was the only way you could see what was out there. Teams had big squads and some players used to miss out on a Saturday, so you'd see first-team players who'd been injured or dropped playing in the reserves.'

Macari certainly saw something in Stein, 'I went to watch Luton play Oxford one night and Steiny was up front for Oxford. He looked a bit out of shape but I thought there was something there – an eye for goal.'

An eye for goal is exactly what Stein possessed. Once he was match fit, there was no stopping him.

An Amazing Night at Anfield

How long does an average football career last? Fifteen years? Twenty years? Whatever the answer, for some players, two decades can be distilled down to a single moment. For two former Stoke players, the word 'Liverpool' would bring about entirely contrasting memories.

The previous time that Stoke had drawn the Reds in a cup competition during the 1988/89 season, striker Graham Shaw had missed a last-minute chance for glory. With the scores locked at 0-0, Shaw went through on goal and panicked at the crucial moment. His shot cannoned off the legs of goalkeeper Mike Hooper, and in that single second of action, Stoke's chance of a giant-killing was gone, while, unbeknownst to him at the time, Shaw's entire playing career contracted to one frantic kick of a football.

Shaw's long-retired now; he's actually a qualified solicitor and, by all accounts, an affable and intelligent man who's still more than happy to talk about his time as a professional footballer playing for his hometown club. People who meet him still mention it – the miss. He must get sick of talking about it. It'd be enough to darken the mind of many an individual, I'm sure, being remembered for a moment that, in the harshest of lights, could be classed as failure to do your job properly: the moment you let everyone down.

Poor Graham Shaw. Your other 134 appearances have mostly been forgotten, the memories of your 25 goals are hazy, but that moment, the time when, as a raw 20-year-old, your composure understandably let you down is still crystal clear in the minds of everyone who saw it. Football's unfair like that.

Because all things considered, Shaw was a good player for Stoke – a rare bright spot in the dark days of the late 1980s and a valuable member of the 1992/93 promotion-winning team. But no one who meets him these days thinks of that. They just see a ball hitting Mike Hooper's legs on a muddy Victoria Ground pitch and hear the collective groan all over again.

It's different for Tony Kelly though. Now there's a man whose life hasn't turned out quite as well, but who would probably allow himself a smile if you were talking 'Liverpool' to him. Kelly wasn't a good player for Stoke – he was poor in fact, possibly even one of the worst players we've ever had – but everyone who was around in 1991 will know the moment we now associate him with.

Few people gave Stoke a chance of getting a result at Anfield in the first leg of the League Cup (then going under the moniker of the Rumbelows Cup) as even though Liverpool's decline had started under the management of Graeme Souness, they still retained something of an invincible aura following two decades of domestic domination, not to mention the numerous nights of European glory under the Anfield floodlights. It would take a few more years before the reality of Liverpool as yesterday's team would set in. As far as we were concerned though, we'd been drawn against *the* glamour team in the country and had the chance to once again see our team face up to one of the game's true giants.

Stoke sold 6,000 tickets for the first leg at Anfield, most fans travelling more in hope than expectation, but given the improvement in their league performances under Lou Macari, and the feeling that under his stewardship we could go anywhere in the country and give anyone a game, there were an optimistic few who didn't see defeat as a foregone conclusion.

I didn't make it to the game despite my pleading to be allowed to go. I was only 13 at the time, I had school the next day, and there was no chance Mum was going to allow me to board a coach to Liverpool by myself. I was stuck with the radio and the velvet tones of Nigel Johnson, the BBC's commentator for all Stoke City games since time began.

Stoke lined up on the night with a five-man defence which featured four of the players who'd go on to form the formidable rearguard on which our subsequent promotion season would be based. Vince Overson, Ian Cranson and Lee Sandford formed a trio of no-nonsense centre-backs, with the always-dependable John Butler at right-back and the not-so-dependable Lee Fowler on the left. Behind them was the veteran goalkeeper Peter Fox, who had allegedly fallen out with Lou Macari and was ostracised as a result. However, with on-loan goalkeeper Jason Kearton being refused permission to play by his parent club Everton, Macari had no choice but to reluctantly turn to Fox for cup games.

Another key player whose services we were denied on the night was Stein, still on loan from Oxford at this point, and so another whose club refused to allow us to pick their man and cup-tie him in the process. This meant a recall for misfit Tony Ellis, who partnered star man Wayne Biggins up front ahead of a midfield trio of Ian Scott, Mick Kennedy and Carl Beeston.

This being a time before managers saw the League Cup as an unwanted distraction and a chance to give half the youth team, a couple of reserves and the tea lady a start, Liverpool's team looked pretty formidable. The likes of Bruce Grobbelaar, Ian Rush and

Steve McMahon might have all been the wrong side of 30, but they were still household names. Supported by the likes of Steve Nicol, Mark Walters and big-money signing Dean Saunders, as well as a young Steve McManaman, it seemed like a thrashing might be on the cards.

It didn't take Liverpool long to score. Sixteen minutes to be exact, and it had to be Ian Rush, didn't it? I hated Ian Rush. It all went back to the days when, as a young football fan, I disgracefully picked one of the glamour teams to support rather than my local side. It made perfect sense at the time – Stoke seemed to lose every week and my dad kept moaning about them and telling me how bad they were. Therefore, I picked Everton – mainly because a couple of my mates at primary school 'supported' them, but also because they were top of the league and had my hero, Gary Lineker, playing for them. What a glory-hunting little shit I was.

I wasn't alone though. In the mid-1980s, our entire playground was divided between Liverpool and Everton, with arguments raging as to who were the better team as well as who had the better striker. During playground kick-arounds, the Everton fans all pretended they were Lineker while the Liverpool lot were all Rush. At the end of my first year at junior school, the two Merseyside giants faced off in the 1986 FA Cup Final and when Lineker gave Everton the lead I couldn't wait to get to school on Monday and proclaim 'my' team's greatness. It didn't last long though. Rush bagged a brace in the second half, Craig Johnston added another, Liverpool won 3-1 and I was heartbroken.

Thankfully, my dad realised that he was bringing up a glory-hunter, took action and dragged me along to my first Stoke game. Everton were quickly forgotten, but I still retained a residual dislike of Ian Rush. And here he was again, the big-nosed bastard, tormenting me by scoring goals against *my* team.

Twelve minutes later though, the unexpected happened. A Stoke corner swung in and there was Ian Cranson, towering above the Liverpool defence and thumping a header past Grobbelaar to level the scores. The roar on the radio told me what had happened even before Nigel Johnson could describe it. We'd equalised against Liverpool. Liverpool, who beat absolutely everyone;

Liverpool, whose foily badge Panini sticker was more sought after on the playground than a Willy Wonka golden ticket; Liverpool, winners of 18 league titles – we'd scored against them. Little old us, who did things like lose 3-2 at home to Chester and get drubbed 4-0 on rainy days at Wigan. How could it even be possible?

'I've not got many happy memories of playing at Liverpool,' Cranson admits. 'I've been on the end of a few drubbings there as a player, but we really showed our resilience that night. From a personal point of view, to be able to say that you've scored at the Kop End is something special.'

But not only did we equalise, we then took the game to them and could have scored again. Actually we could have scored three. A header from Tony Ellis looped agonisingly over the bar, a shot from Lee Fowler was blocked – Stoke were on top and everyone started to dream that something special was about to happen.

Of course, it couldn't last. A shot from Nicky Tanner crashed off our crossbar and bounced back into the danger area. I don't need to tell you who was there to gobble up the rebound. Why was that git even there? If he hadn't been so crap during his time in Italy playing for Juventus he wouldn't have had to come back to Liverpool with his tail between his legs and he wouldn't be scoring undeserved goals to shit all over our dreams of a giant-killing. ('It was like a foreign country out there!' he hilariously informed the press on his return to England.)

Cometh the hour, cometh the man. With time running out, Macari played his wild card and on came Tony Kelly. I don't know what the thinking was: perhaps that Kelly's raw pace would work against tired legs, maybe that the Liverpool defence would be so busy laughing at Kelly tripping over his own feet that they might be distracted, perhaps just pure, out-and-out desperation?

Whatever it was, it was a last throw of the dice and on 88 minutes, these dice rolled a double six jackpot. Gary Ablett fluffed a clearance and it was Kelly who capitalised, going through one-on-one against Grobbelaar. Even listening at home, time stood still at that moment. It was Graham Shaw all over again, this, a chance for glory falling to the wrong man, someone without the composure to make himself a hero and write himself into the record books.

Kelly bore down on goal and side-footed his shot straight at the goalkeeper, whose legs were wide open. Grobbelaar collapsed on to the ground as the ball rolled underneath him and over the line, setting off scenes of wild celebration in the away end.

Nigel Johnson couldn't believe it. I couldn't believe it. I cried. Honestly, I did. It was a 2-2 draw, we hadn't even won, but all I'd known up to this point was a team who'd let us down at every turn in the road. Whenever we threatened to go on a run and rise into the play-offs, we'd lose and go plummeting down the league; whenever we played a big team in the cup we'd miss last-minute chances or just get thrashed; whenever we came close to doing anything at all remotely good, we'd find a way of fucking it up and disappointing everybody.

It might have only been one game, and Liverpool might have been a poor side by the standards of the past, but Kelly's equaliser was about more than one mildly surprising result. It was about a club that suddenly seemed to believe in itself again, when success no longer seemed to be a distant dream – something that only happened to other fans. The last few years had been a waking nightmare, but now we were daring to dream. If we could go to Anfield and refuse to give in, to come back twice and fight tooth and nail for every ball, then we might be able to turn it all around and get back to where we all felt we belonged.

The highlights were on TV that night – *Central Sports Special*. Even though the show was on late and I had school in the morning, I stayed up and watched it (perhaps Mum did feel a bit guilty about not letting me go to Anfield after all). I also set the video to 'record' too and watched it again and again over the next few days. That's how starved of success we'd been. A 2-2 draw in the second round of the League Cup and it felt like we'd been crowned champions of Europe.

Of course, Tony Kelly being Tony Kelly, there had to be a postscript. He couldn't even manage to write himself a happy ending following his own glorious chapter because in the second leg at Stoke, it was Kelly who played the most inexplicable back-pass I've ever had the misfortune to witness – presenting a gift to Dean Saunders, who duly obliged and put Liverpool 2-0 up on the night. This being Macari's Stoke, we came back, scrapping and kicking and harrying, but it wasn't quite enough. We lost the game 3-2, meaning an aggregate loss of 5-4, so all the late drama at Anfield had ultimately been for nothing. We'd lost the tie and were out.

As disappointing as it was, none of that really matters now. I can barely remember the second leg at the Victoria Ground, even though I was there. What sticks in the memory is that moment in the first leg – Kelly's 'moment'.

Poor Tony Kelly. He was released from Stoke the following year and spent a few years in the lower leagues before drifting back into non-league. In a time when lower league footballers earned modest wages, Kelly reportedly ran up debts of £300,000. Kelly was a gambling addict – his story can be read in his book *Red Card*, which chronicles his playing career, but mainly the effects of his problem gambling.

Now rehabilitated, he set up the Red Card Foundation, an organisation raising awareness of gambling addiction and offering support to those affected by it. He's not had an easy time of it over the last 25 years. Scoring an equaliser at Anfield was probably as good as it got during his modest career, but if it gives him any comfort whatsoever, the sight of him running away to the celebrating Stoke fans will stay in the minds of everyone who was there and even some, like me, who weren't.

The Big Games Return

I don't know how far Stoke City goes back in my family lineage. My dad has always supported them – his dad, my grandpa, took him as a child – first team one week, reserves the next. My maternal grandfather had a season ticket for years, almost right up to the end of his life, and he was first taken by *his* grandfather in 1935. That's a lot of history, and a lot of stories, and Stoke hadn't *always* been so bad.

My grandad used to talk *a lot* about the 1946/47 side that came within a whisker of winning the league championship. Stoke were probably the finest team in the country as World War II broke out, but a team packed with talent such as Stanley Matthews, Neil Franklin and Freddie Steele lost its best years to the war and finished in an all-time high of fourth place as league football resumed.

Every time we lost or did something bloody awful like lose to Telford in the FA Cup (only a few weeks after our performance at Anfield. How? How was it even possible?) I would be regaled with stories about this great team we'd once had. I loved my grandad, I still miss him now, five years after his death, but Christ almighty, he used to bore me stupid with endless stories about Freddie Steele.

My dad is old enough to remember Matthews, albeit at the end of his career, but his youth was spent watching our second great era – the 1970s side led by Tony Waddington. Again, a team that went close to winning the league, finishing fifth twice and bringing home our only major trophy to date – the 1972 League Cup. Forty-five years later and we're still going on about that one and having open-top bus parades on every tenth anniversary of it: that's how desperate for glory we are! He didn't bang on about the '70s team as much as my grandad did about the 1940s, but having seen a genuinely good team grace the turf at the Victoria Ground, my old man couldn't help but judge what he was now watching by the standards of the past.

I'd heard so much about the big games and the big nights enjoyed by previous generations that I was desperate to experience something similar. Just something I could tell my kids about in future years and tell them I was there. It might have only been the third tier, but as Stoke began to gain momentum and the wins started to rack up, we found ourselves in a promotion battle with a number of other sides.

The West Brom game in December was when a return to the big time first seemed tangible. It was a Wednesday night under the floodlights, and a win would send us top of the table and above the visitors. The game really captured the imagination of the supporters, who'd had a taste of glamour again when Liverpool had come to town earlier in the season, and they clearly wanted more of it.

The clamour for tickets took everyone by surprise. On the night there were at least 2,000 people locked out and the Boothen End swayed and pulsed with anticipation – bodies packed in to the old terrace. You never experience it anymore, but people who are old enough to have watched football matches before the days of all-seater grounds and smoking bans will remember the smell. It was a unique thing – intoxicating in its own strange way, a cocktail of odours, each unremarkable or downright unpleasant on its own, but together they created something wonderful.

What did it smell like, football? It smelt like the cigarette smoke and beery breath of a thousand swearing men, drifting on the breeze and giving 13-year-old boys like me an alluring impression of adulthood. Deep voices barking obscenities through a fug of smoke and stale beer. It smelt like cheap, processed meat frying on griddles, plastic cups of scorching hot Bovril and flasks of coffee laced with whisky or rum. At Christmas you could add the smell of several different aftershaves, new leather gloves and yesterday's sprouts in gas form. Lovely.

This top-of-the-table clash against the Baggies had it all. The floodlights, the packed stadium, that familiar football smell. I lived for it, truly I did. The whole day would be spent in anticipation of the game itself, sometimes the whole week. After every full-time whistle, walking back to the car in the dark, toes frozen in my shoes, trying not to tread in puddles or piles of horse manure, all I'd be thinking about was how long until I could come back and experience it all again.

They were like heroin, nights like this. Winning 1-0, dominating the game and creating chance after chance, but never being able to relax – always nervous when the opposition came forward, the victory never secure – success always in the balance.

It might have only been the third tier of English football, but it was a joy to watch at times. Mark Stein, always alive to possibilities in and around the box, had diverted Lee Sandford's header into the net to score what would prove to be the winner – a mere flick of the neck muscles the difference between the ball being saved or ending up just out of the goalkeeper's reach.

The little man jinked through again and again after that, almost putting the game to bed but never quite managing to kill things off. But despite the pressure we had, West Brom almost equalised at the death, Gary Bannister dragging his shot wide when it seemed easier to score. Relief. Relief then an explosion of joy at the final whistle and the knowledge that we were top of the league.

'It was just like the old days,' said Lou Macari after the game. 'People will remember this ground when it used to be packed with big crowds, and it felt like those days were here again for this match.'

There were other big matches to follow. The fixture list kept throwing them up, one after the other. Brentford were another team gunning for promotion, and two weeks after our win over West Brom we beat them 2-1, Stein again scoring the clincher. Things were getting tense for everyone, and that tension spilled over into something rather unsavoury during our next game at Birmingham – another side challenging at the top of the table.

This one carried added spice due to the Macari factor; Birmingham were still bitter that our manager had walked out on them and they were determined to get revenge. I didn't attend but I remember a lot about the events that were relayed to us via the radio. The game was another tight affair with both teams getting chances.

It looked for all the world like we were going to come home from St Andrew's with a 1-0 defeat and our spot at the top of the table relinquished. In the final minute though, Wayne Biggins put in what could best be described as a rather physical challenge on Birmingham's goalkeeper as the ball bounced between them. It wasn't exactly the stuff of Nat Lofthouse, but it was the kind of thing that a referee would usually deem to be a foul, even accounting for the fact that goalkeepers weren't the protected species that they seem to have become in recent years.

Referee Ray Wiseman (bless him) wasn't interested though and the ball squirmed loose to our substitute Paul Barnes, who stroked it into the empty net to set off scenes of wild celebration.

It was misreported almost everywhere that our leveller was the catalyst for a riot, but that wasn't strictly true. What happened was that no more than 30 seconds after we'd equalised, the home team went straight up the other end and forged the sort of chance that would see the net bulge nine times out of ten. Somehow though, Paul Tait managed to place his shot, from all of eight yards out, straight at our goalkeeper Ronnie Sinclair.

The ball, however, still managed to bobble its way towards the line and the Blues fans began to celebrate, assuming that it was going to trickle in. Only it didn't because flying in from nowhere was Ian Cranson, who hooked the ball off the line and away from danger. Maybe some of the home fans hadn't realised this and were on the pitch celebrating what they thought was a winner, maybe some had realised what had happened and were enraged that the referee hadn't given a goal (even though the ball hadn't crossed the line) and maybe some were just so pissed off that they hadn't beaten us, despite spending all week getting wound up about Macari, that they just couldn't take it. And so it was that hundreds of Birmingham fans invaded the pitch and menacingly made their way to the end of the ground holding the Stoke fans.

Mark Chester, the author of *Naughty,* and a prominent figure among Stoke's hooligan element in the 1980s, recounted the moment that the away end came under attack, 'Birmingham got on the fence where many Stoke were already waiting to meet them, and the two mobs traded punches across the top. One lad later described how he'd been on the fence and seen a small black dot coming across the pitch and getting bigger and bigger until it eventually punched him. Another 20 of Stoke's top lads managed to get on to the pitch from the seats, dropping down from the roof of the executive boxes. They fought toe-to-toe with huge mobs of Birmingham.'

The scenes on the news would be described in the press as 'appalling', 'disgusting' and all the other disapproving adjectives that tend to get wheeled out when football violence rears its head again. Because, let's be honest, things might have improved since the dark days of the '70s and '80s, but the potential for trouble was still never that far away in the '90s.

To a 14-year-old sat in the safety of his own living room and watching on television, the initial reaction wasn't one of disgust or being appalled, rather that it all seemed terribly exciting. The talk on the playground at school the following Monday wasn't about the dramatic equaliser or the precious point we'd gained, it was the footage of a bloke wearing a grey coat who had stood on the fence at the front of the terrace and beaten the shit out of about six Birmingham fans, one after the other, as they'd tried to climb over. There were plenty of others too who'd stood up when it counted and basically done the police's jobs for them – using whatever means necessary to stop the home fans getting on to the terrace and attacking innocent Stoke fans.

Bizarrely, once the ground had been cleared, the players came back out on to the pitch to finish the game off. Wayne Biggins recalls the surreal situation of playing out injury time in a completely empty stadium:

'We were all in the dressing room starting to get changed and the referee came in and told us we needed to finish the game. Some of us went out there with no socks on! Both sets of players spoke to each other and we said, "You take the kick-off and we'll all just stand still." So we did – the referee blew the whistle and nobody moved for two minutes!'

I've never been someone who's enjoyed getting involved in physical violence. I'm a bit of a wimp to tell you the truth, and I'd always leg it given the chance rather than start trading punches with someone.

Watching it kick off is a different matter though. While I never wanted it to happen, when it did, I couldn't help but get the popcorn out and enjoy the spectacle. A voyeur of violence. We're all the same deep down, even those who write about how appalling it is. If there are punches being thrown and we're a safe distance away, we all watch it don't we?

Some of the other lads at school were a bit more physically robust than me and needed no excuse to arrange mass brawls with other schools or knock seven bells out of each other on the playground just for something to do. They were so excited by what had happened at Birmingham that they decided to form their own 'firm', which the rest of us were very impressed by, although in hindsight I don't think a bunch of 14-year-olds from Wolstanton would have had the Chelsea Headhunters quaking in their boots!

There were some serious consequences for one Stoke fan though. A young man by the name of Mark Beech had been making his way out of the ground, along with fellow Potters supporters, when a coin hurled by a Birmingham fan hit him in the face, which resulted in him losing the sight in his right eye. This was the cold reality of football violence. Because beneath all the bravado, the posturing and the glamour that impressionable teenage boys associate with hooligans and gangs, there were innocent bystanders like Mark Beech who had their lives ruined by the brainless actions of others. I knew that, and could weigh up the odds of getting hurt – particularly for someone like me who was rubbish at fighting, and so steered clear of the rush to enlist members to this new, very junior branch of Stoke's hooligan wing.

Although Stoke fans were guilty only of protecting themselves in the incident at Birmingham, we did seem to be involved in more than our fair share of confrontations, and the name of our genuinely notorious hooligan firm, the Naughty Forty, was often dropped into playground discussion by those looking to create a reputation for themselves as the lads not to be messed with. Some of the lads claimed to know members of this supposedly terrifying group of brawlers, and others claimed – without much credibility – to have fought alongside them at away games, but whatever the truth of these claims, football hooliganism suddenly seemed like it had entered the list of career options for a significant number of our school year group.

The Late Collapse

With 12 games left to play, Stoke sat atop the division, looking for all the world like they'd continue the form that had earned them that coveted spot and end up as champions. It was tight at the top though, and while West Brom's challenge was fading week by week, Birmingham and Brentford stubbornly kept pace with the Potters. Lurking in the play-off positions were other dangers – Huddersfield, free-scoring Peterborough and the 1990s version of the Crazy Gang, Danny Bergara's uncompromising Stockport County side.

To this day I don't know what happened to Stoke, but it was as though the side suddenly realised the position they were in and simply crumbled under the pressure. Two consecutive home games against a pair of relegation strugglers, Hull City and Bury, should have been the catalyst to open up an insurmountable gap, but it wasn't to be. In both games we played terribly, losing the first (on the Saturday) 3-2 and then following up in the second (on the Wednesday) by going down 2-1. Within five days Stoke had gone from league leaders and champions-elect to just another of the promotion hopefuls, scrapping for every last, desperate point.

'Those two games were so disappointing,' recalls Ian Cranson. 'I think it was the case of a long, hard season catching up on us. We worked just as hard in March and April as we did in pre-season and with a small squad, we'd all be playing 50 games a year.'

Football is never predictable though and the two home horror shows were forgotten after the Potters visited Huddersfield Town and came away with a 2-1 win before thumping Exeter 5-2 at home in the next game. Back on track? The title back in the bag? Not a chance, because we followed these results up with a 1-0 loss at Torquay, who were one of the worst sides I've ever seen us play. It was clear that Stoke would somehow always find a way of snatching defeat from the jaws of victory.

And so it was that after lurching from unexpected win to appalling defeat, Stoke entered the final two games of the 1991/92 campaign with their fate still in their own hands. It was tight and it was tense, but six points would have done it. All we had to do was dispatch Chester at home (oh God, them again) and then get something at Bolton, a task that looked trickier no doubt, but certainly not beyond a side that had made a habit of really showing up for the big games all season.

Typically, it was the Bolton game that people were talking about. The optimistic were already planning the parties, others were debating whether we could get something there against a side who'd long since dropped out of the promotion chase, but did at least sound like a proper football team. Nobody expected us to lose at home to Chester City though. Not again, surely to God?

We did though. We turned in a performance that was straight from the arse-end of Alan Ball's era, an abject 1-0 defeat in which we had plenty of chances but still somehow never looked like scoring. When Chester took the lead just before the hour, everyone resigned themselves to what was to follow. Stoke had three shots cleared off the line, Chester never got out of their own half again all game, but no one thought we'd score. It was painful stuff.

Birmingham and Brentford didn't err, they were both winning their respective games and by 5pm had both overtaken us with one game left. We visited Bolton the following Saturday needing snookers, and all we could do was pot the white. We lost 3-1 but it didn't really matter – the top two both won their games so we were condemned to the play-offs, where we'd face Stockport County.

It seems strange now that Stockport, a side who were always a byword for lower league also-rans, and have since slipped out of the Football League altogether, were, for a brief time, considered to be Stoke's fiercest rivals. Being situated only seven miles outside of Manchester, Stockport were always a small club who nobody really felt anything for, apart from perhaps a sense of sympathy that their catchment area was swallowed up by the enormous pull of the two Manchester clubs. The very fact that they continued to exist in the shadow of Manchester United was enough to elicit a sense of respect from any genuine football fan. What little respect that Stoke fans may have had for Stockport though, vanished the moment we experienced the displeasure of playing them.

Some would say they were uncompromising, others might describe them as rugged. I'd probably choose to describe them as the dirtiest, most cynical bunch of bastards I've ever seen on a football pitch. They were ugly to watch, utilising a game plan that involved nothing but launching high balls towards human giraffe Kevin Francis, a 6ft 7in beanpole of a striker who was a nightmare to play against. In midfield they had Jim Gannon, a hatchet man who, if you were being kind, you could describe as someone who did the unpleasant side of the game very effectively. Most of all though, they were organised and almost impossible to break down. Of all the sides we could have faced in a two-legged play-off match, Stockport were the last team you would have chosen.

'We didn't like them and they didn't like us,' recalls Carl Beeston. 'Everybody knew it. There was one game where there'd been a fracas on the pitch and it carried on in the players' lounge afterwards. Fists flying and everything.'

The first leg at the tiny Edgeley Park was another bloodbath. Stoke weren't exactly shrinking violets at the time either, and tackles from both sides went flying in. Unfortunately, Beeston went one step too far in flattening one of the Stockport players, earning himself a red card.

'It was Jim Gannon, I think,' he recalls. 'I didn't like him at all. Lou had made me captain and I was fired up, but Gannon was on at me, in my ear all game, and he was really pissing me off. I just lost it. I turned around, had a little look where the ref was, couldn't see him so yeah, I nutted him – that was it!'

Unfortunately the referee was only yards away and Stoke were down to ten men.

The home side took advantage and secured a 1-0 lead to bring to Stoke for the return. The game was still alive with that scoreline, we knew that, but when Stockport scored within 60 seconds of the second leg starting, that familiar feeling of inevitability began to descend. We'd been here only two weeks previous: Stoke were going to spend the whole game camped in the visitors' half, but the ball would go everywhere but into the opposition net.

As it happened, we did manage an equaliser on the night through Mark Stein, but with only ten minutes left it would prove to be too little, too late. The pill was a bitter one to swallow, but the despair would only be short-lived, because there was the small matter of a Wembley final only two weeks later in the football calendar. Our opponents for this historic occasion – Stockport County of course. All the talk around the city was now about revenge.

A Day Out at Wembley

At the risk of sounding arrogant, I couldn't tell you who won last year's Johnstone's Paint Trophy, Leyland DAF Cup, Zenith Data Systems Trophy, Captain Birdseye Twelve-Pack of Fishfingers Trophy or whatever bizarre sponsorship this tournament is being played under these days. The truth is that nobody outside of the two clubs who make it to the Wembley final has ever given two shits about it.

However, to the fans of those clubs who do grace the pitch of the national stadium for one afternoon in late spring, the day is just as memorable as any FA Cup final. In the 1990s, this competition exclusively for sides in the third and fourth tiers of English football (well, it *was then*) went by the name of the Autoglass Trophy. It was a cup sponsored by a firm that repaired broken windscreens, which probably tells you all you need to know about the level of glamour and stardust we're talking about.

Stoke had made steady progress throughout the early rounds, winning games against poor opposition in front of low, fairly disinterested crowds. It wasn't until after the Southern Area semi-final against Leyton Orient, which provided a 1-0 away win, that people began to really notice what was going on.

At this point, once we'd got over the shock of Stoke being in the southern half of the draw (we're proud northerners in Stoke and even calling us Midlanders will get you a dirty look) the realisation sank in that we only had to win one more match before the experience of a rare day out at Wembley would present itself. Stoke hadn't played under the twin towers since our 1972 League Cup Final victory, in fact that was the only time we'd ever played there, so even if this was the Bassett's Jelly Babies Trophy or the Anusol Piles Cream Cup, we didn't care. The city was suddenly in the grip of cup fever, and only Peterborough United stood in the way of us and the chance to play for silverware.

Peterborough were no pushover though. They had a 'crazy' goalkeeper called Fred Barber, who often ran out for games, for no apparent reason, wearing a Halloween mask. I can't even begin to guess what all that was about, but more worrying for us was that their star forward Ken Charlery was another of the league's extremely dangerous strikers. We'd seen first-hand the strike power that Peterborough possessed during a 3-3 draw on Boxing Day, and no one was taking a victory for granted. With a home leg to play first, we knew the importance of securing a decent first-leg lead against a side that were no slouches when it came to scoring.

Unfortunately, protecting our net was the hapless form of Kevin Pressman. Due to circumstances behind the scenes, it seemed that Lou Macari would rather play our overweight kit man, Neil Baldwin, in goals than give another start to veteran goalkeeper Peter Fox, so with regular stopper Ronnie Sinclair cup-tied, Macari turned to the loan market to secure an alternative.

Unfortunately, for all his transfer nous, Macari's track record in spotting goalkeepers was sketchy in the extreme. Pressman, despite possessing what looked like a decent CV, was another who played like a complete duffer. The Sheffield Wednesday man was responsible for at least two of the Peterborough goals as, unbelievably, another 3-3 scoreline was played out by two sides trading shots and goals blow for blow. It was entertaining stuff, but left Stoke in the uncomfortable position of needing to win at London Road or face a heartbreaking elimination at the final hurdle.

The second leg was unique in that, to my knowledge, it was the first time that a Stoke away match was broadcast on the nascent Sky Sports channel, then going under the name of BSkyB following Sky's merger with British Satellite Broadcasting.

Watching Stoke play on the small screen was a real novelty, but back in those days, hardly anybody subscribed to satellite television. Fortunately, one of our mates, Andy Bowler (known as Bowie), did. When the news got around that Bowie was the owner of one of these funny dishes that had started to spring up on the sides of houses, everybody was his new best friend. Come match night, the few lucky souls from school who'd bagged an invite round to Bowie's house to watch the game had to fight for a seat with the pals of Mr Bowler senior, whose popularity at British Telecom, where he worked, had no doubt also risen in the previous days.

I can't remember exactly how many of us were there that night, but it seemed like a lot. In fact the whole scene was a bit like stories you heard of life in the 1950s, when perhaps only one family per street owned a television at all and entire neighbourhoods would pile into one sitting room to gawp at the strange box in the corner emitting moving pictures and sound. I half-expected to turn around at 7.45pm and see a horde of faces pressed up against Bowie's front room window, all desperate for a glimpse of Autoglass Trophy action, but no, it was just the people in the room, squashed on to sofas, sat cross-legged on the floor and perched on armchairs who were witness to a night destined to go down as one of the most memorable from that era.

The game itself was nothing like the open, end-to-end first leg. It was cagey and tense, and neither side could really get a grip on proceedings. When Stoke won a free kick on the edge of the Peterborough box, what happened next surprised us all. Stepping up to the ball was midfielder Paul Ware – a utility player who'd come through the youth system but never really nailed a place down under any of the last three managers. Ware was committed and dependable, but never someone you would imagine stepping up to take a free kick even in a training session, let alone such an important game.

Was this some sort of ingenious master plan from Macari? 'No,' recalls the former boss when I put the question to him. 'Because I was in the dugout saying, "What the fuck's he doing taking that!?" There's no point me kidding anyone we'd worked on it for days because we hadn't!'

However, Ware did step up and the boy from Congleton absolutely smashed the ball through the narrowest of gaps and into the corner of the net. The Stoke fans in the ground went mental; *we* went mental. Stoke had done it – we were going to Wembley!

Nowadays, it doesn't seem like such an event, playing at the national stadium. There are semi-finals there, play-off finals, Tottenham even used it as their home ground for the 2017/18 season – it no longer feels all that special.

Back then though, it truly did. None of us knew whether we'd ever get the chance to see Stoke play there again; it had, after all, been two decades since the last occasion, so tickets – even at the prices that were being charged – were very much in demand. We purchased four, and it was the first and only time that our whole family – me, Mum, Dad and my sister, Clare – all attended a match together.

We took the train from Stoke station – a football special straight to Wembley – and I still remember the journey now. When you're in a cup final, even one as insignificant as the Autoglass Trophy, expectation pulses through the hours beforehand. In every expression, in every line spoken, you can sense it. There was excitement in the voices of every man, woman and child, from those who'd never been to Wembley before, to those who'd been there in '72. The older fans were given the opportunity to reminisce all over again about that glorious occasion and the open-top bus tour that followed our first, and still only, major trophy and they revelled in telling tales of that day to any younger fan who'd listen.

The sheer scale of the ground itself was also an experience for someone unused to such surroundings. Seeing it for the first time in all its 82,000 capacity glory reminded me of walking into the Victoria Ground for the first time as an eight-year-old and being taken aback at the size of everything: the pitch, the stands, the floodlights. To a child, everything seemed so enormous that first time – even the crowd appeared ten times larger than the actual attendance was.

Of course I'd become used to home games over the years, but this was something else. Stoke had sold out all of their 35,000 allocation and we were surrounded by an ocean of red and white flags and painted faces bathed in sunshine, a long way from those familiar Third Division fixtures played on rainy Saturdays.

I'm sure supporters of some clubs take days like these for granted. Those teams who reach finals every year – to them, Wembley must be a home from home, another routine to add to the many routines we have around football. The magic must wear off eventually, but that first time for me, at 14 years old, was probably the happiest I've ever been at a football match.

Macari had prepared his troops for the occasion, and suspected that his team's superior fitness and sense of unity would provide them with an advantage on Wembley's vast playing surface, 'Before the game I took the team away for three or four days, not to train them – because at that stage of the season they're as fit as they're ever going to be – it was just about resting them and preparing them to play at Wembley, which in itself was more demanding than any league fixture you can have because of the build-up to the game.

'The press coverage was three or four days before rather than just a day, so all that's different. Then you've got time to think about it, dream about it, dream about scoring the winning goal or trooping off as a loser. The main thing to get over to them was that every ounce of energy you've got, you'll need it at Wembley. It was a more demanding pitch than any other in the country. You'd see players lying down after 60 minutes with cramp because of how heavy the pitch was when it rained. It was about trying to convince the lads that they'd got a head start on the opponent because of how fit they were, which to be fair, they had.'

The final itself wasn't a classic. Stockport could spoil a game even at Wembley, but having played the Hatters, the Cobras or the Cheating Bastards (as we preferred to call them) four times already that season, we were becoming a little more adept at dealing with the unique threat they presented. Vince Overson and Ian Cranson at the heart of our defence made things as difficult as possible for the half-footballer-half-lamppost Kevin Francis, while their other danger man, Andy Preece, was also watched closely wherever he popped up on the pitch. But we had weapons too. Wayne Biggins was putting on a classy showcase of his talents on the pristine surface, while Mark Stein prowled with menace at all times, always hovering on the shoulder of the last man, always waiting for a sign of weakness in the opponent's backline.

It was the second half before he got his chance, but as he burst clear of the Stockport defence and bore down on goalkeeper Neil Edwards, there was never any doubt what was coming next. Stein lashed the ball in, the net rippled and Stoke players sprinted to the touchline in an orgy of celebration. The stands erupted. The look on Dad's face as he held both fists aloft is something that will always stay with me. Never demonstrative, always calm, sometimes appearing to be slightly distant from events on the pitch, that was the first time I think I'd seen him displaying unbridled joy at a football match. It was the love of the game returning – the sudden remembering of a forgotten happiness. It might not have been '72, it wasn't Chelsea in opposition, but it was still a day to treasure.

I have the match programme in front of me as I write this. The cover price of £3 seemed extortionate back then, 25 years ago. In truth there's little of substance in those musty-smelling pages – some action shots of the two teams, pen-portraits of the players involved, a rather twee advert for a model Wembley on a plinth, plus several pages dedicated to broken windscreens and what to do about them.

Just holding it brings the memories flooding back though. I'd like to think the players involved look back on the day as fondly as we do. Vince Overson, leading the team up the steps to receive the trophy from Bobby Moore, a proud grin on his face; Peter Fox, recalled for the final and doing a sterling job in keeping County at bay; Mark Stein, scorer of so many goals, but perhaps none as special as a Wembley winner and finally, Paul Ware, not in the squad that day due to an injury, but always remembered as the man who got us to the final.

I could just about remember the details of Ware's semi-final goal, but I searched for it on YouTube anyway to refresh the memory before writing this section. The strike was even more impressive than I thought it was, a little further out than I recall, and after watching the ball hit the net a few times on repeat, I looked down at who had uploaded it. It was Ware's daughters, and the tagline was 'Dad's goal, 20 years ago that took Stoke to Wembley.'

Paul Ware is the only member of that team no longer with us. Tragically he passed away in 2013, aged just 42. His daughters, Laura and Amy, are rightly proud of their father, for what he achieved in the game, but more so for his role in their lives as a loving father and a man who bravely battled a terminal illness for so long. Not long after Paul passed away, they published a highly acclaimed book detailing their father's life, football career and battle against the brain tumour which ultimately ended his life.

To all Stoke fans who remember him, Paul Ware was a modestly talented, wholehearted lower-league player who eked out every bit of natural ability he had through hard work and dedication to his profession.

We can't ever know the family man who his daughters describe as 'the best father any child could wish for: kind, caring and always there'. We won't remember the details of the cancer that Paul fought or the dreadful effect it had on him during his last days.

What we will remember though is 15 April 1992 and a ball being hit with the force of an Exocet missile. A young man running with joy etched across his face at scoring the winner for his team. And thanks to modern technology, people who were not even born then will see the footage and know who Paul Ware was. They too will see him as we remember him: frozen in time, forever 22, charging to the away end to celebrate, leaping into the air and pumping his fist in celebration. That goal was *his moment* and without it, none of us would have had our special day at Wembley.

Thanks for the memories, Paul. Rest in peace.

Season 1992/93
The Real Invincibles

A T the end of my days, if I could re-live one football season again, then no question it would be 1992/93. In everyday life, the social anxiety, low self-esteem and general uncertainty that accompanies being 14 or 15 years old isn't something I'd want to experience again, but being that age while supporting a football team who, for nine months at least, swept all before them is something I'd be more than happy to indulge myself with.

Like most teenagers, I didn't really know who I was at 14. I was uncomfortable in my own skin, awkward and unattractive, a powder keg of confused emotions that could blow up at any time. The only time I felt certain about anything was when I was watching Stoke, which always seemed wonderfully uncomplicated. Wear your shirt with pride, stand on the terrace and sing your heart out, worship Mark Stein for 90 minutes and watch us win again, then get home and bask in the glow of being miles clear at the top of the league. In a time of uncertainty and confusion, Stoke City was the one constant I could rely on.

The wider football world was changing though. Adverts started to appear on the television for Sky's coverage of something called the Premier League. Soundtracked by the Simple Minds song 'Alive and Kicking', a bizarrely homoerotic montage of early 1990s footballers working out in the gym and showering together was supposed to persuade us all to part with a monthly fee to have a dish stuck on the side of our houses so that we could watch

Wimbledon and Oldham Athletic kick each other to bits on a Sunday afternoon.

What was all that about? I'm no marketing guru, but I suspect that if you want to advertise a product as being desirable, showing a man like Colin Hendry topless isn't the best way to go about it!

'The Premier League: It's a whole new ball game' claimed the advert, which it really wasn't, because for all the talk of Super Leagues and breakaways that dominated the back pages, this appeared, on the surface at least, to be exactly the same as the old First Division had been the previous year. It was still 22 clubs full of ugly-looking British blokes with names like Barry and Geoff playing bad football on bad pitches. Sky's choice of window dressing is laughable now, but it signalled that something was about to change and a new audience was coming to football. The post-Gascoigne fans needed the packaging, needed someone to reassure them that what they were watching was a desirable form of entertainment and that's what Sky were trying to do.

Sticking The Shamen on the pitch at half-time to mime along to 'Ebeneezer Goode' and blasting all manner of pyrotechnics into the night sky to welcome Notts County out of the dressing room might raise a smirk now, but it was a way for Sky to say to the audience, 'This is different to what's gone before. This is football mark 2.0. Welcome aboard.'

The rest of us, those who'd been there through the years when entertainment at football meant Vinnie Jones stamping on people and watching fights break out in the crowd, just shrugged our shoulders and waited for things to go back to normal. It didn't take long, and within a few months Sky had ditched a lot of the superfluous razzmatazz and decided to let the football do the talking.

Well, they still employed Andy Gray to push some Subbuteo men around a pitch in the name of sophisticated analysis, the forerunner to Gary Neville and his magic pen perhaps, but they had to fill airtime somehow I suppose. As boring as it was to watch, it was still a step in the right direction away from the insipid 'sick as a parrot/over the moon' post-match analysis that the BBC and ITV had been getting away with for years.

However, despite a few higher-than-normal transfer fees flying around (the 'shock' of Alan Shearer moving to Blackburn for £3.2m – it seems quaint now), the £305m bonanza brought into the game by Sky's television deal, the re-branding to the 'Premier League' and the adverts trying to make battle-hardened, ageing footballers look glamorous, absolutely nothing changed further down the pyramid.

True, we were now playing in the Second Division rather than the Third, but it was still the same league full of the same crap teams who we'd really rather not have been playing at all, thank you very much. The prescient pundits all stated that the new money being ploughed into football's top tier would only create a schism between the rich clubs and the rest and kill the competitiveness that, even with the ugliness that surrounded it, still made the English league an interesting competition in the sense of fairness and unpredictability. The message was clear: the gravy train is leaving the station, and if you want a piece of the action, you'd better not waste any time getting aboard.

Down in the Second Division though, Stoke weren't even on the platform, we were outside the station, not even queueing for a ticket. At the start of the 1992/93 campaign, Stoke City had been out of the top flight for seven years and if we didn't want to be left behind forever, we needed to get our act together quickly. The club needed promotion like never before.

A Slow Start for the Unbeatables

With the disappointment of the previous season's play-off defeat offset by the glorious day under the Wembley sunshine, optimism was very much in evidence when Stoke fans discussed their team's prospects for the 1992/93 campaign. The feeling was that Lou Macari's men would learn from the experience of the previous year and be a better team as a result. Stoke were the bookmakers' favourites for promotion and looking at the squad we possessed, it was evident to see why.

The team's strength was built on defence, where Vince Overson and Ian Cranson continued their partnership in the centre. The two complemented each other in the same way that older fans remember Alan Bloor and Denis Smith combining moments of cultured play (the Cranson/Bloor half) with physicality and leadership (the Overson/Smith half). If it wasn't for a slight lack of pace, both would have been playing at a higher level.

Either side of the centre-backs were full-backs Lee Sandford, thriving at left-back but with the physical stature of a centre-half, and John Butler, always dependable and blessed with the ability to surge forward on occasion in the style of a modern wing-back. In reserve was a new arrival, Graham Harbey, who'd joined from West Brom for a modest fee of £60,000 and a young centre-back, Ian Wright, who would occasionally be thrown into action to cover for injuries.

Overson recalls fondly the mentality that made Stoke's backline seem impenetrable at times.

'We shared the same mentality. It was, "If you lot want to get past me, it's over my dead body." We worked as a group in training religiously – after most of the others had gone. Pej [coach Mike Pejic] drilled us into such a tight unit. We would be overloaded in many sessions – seven attackers against us four trying to score. It would start 0-0 and often finish that way. We had big hearts, big heads and we put a lot of work into it! Lou would always say you start with a clean sheet so your job is to keep hold of it. We were all winners.'

Another partnership that would have thrived at a higher level was that of Wayne Biggins and Mark Stein up front. The strikers complemented each other perfectly and as the previous season had drawn on, the accepted wisdom of Stein being a foil to Biggins, the goalscorer, seemed to be gradually reversed. The latter now regularly turned provider while Stein – the man who had taken several games to find his first goal – scored at a spectacular rate.

The dark cloud on the horizon, and there's always one when it comes to Stoke, was that Biggins still hadn't signed a new contract. A stream of contradictory rumours regarding his status flowed through the city – some saying he was set to sign, others linking him with various clubs. Unable to count on Biggins staying, Macari wisely brought in a back-up striker in the form of Graham Shaw, who returned to Stoke following a spell with Preston. That we were able to offload Tony Ellis in exchange for Shaw was a welcome piece of business. Shaw's arrival did, however, signal the departure of Paul Barnes, which many felt to be a mistake considering the young striker's goalscoring exploits with the reserve team.

If the team did have a weak spot it was arguably in midfield, particularly the wide spots. The arrival of bald-headed winger Kevin 'Rooster' Russell, so named due to a spiky haircut that had long-since deserted him, promised to address this, but the only other winger on the books was the tried-and-failed option of Tony Kelly. Macari would often play one of his central midfielders (either Carl Beeston, Paul Ware, Dave Kevan or Steve Foley) out wide to avoid picking Kelly, but many thought that a pair of flying wingers would have made an excellent side an unbeatable one.

Despite the optimism of 4,000 Stoke fans descending on Hull for the opening fixture of the season, the campaign opened with a disappointing defeat as Stoke laid siege to the Hull goal, only to lose 1-0 to a home side that literally had one shot on target all match. The abiding memory from this game is the footage of Russell dribbling around the goalkeeper and rolling a shot towards the unguarded net. One Stoke fan, convinced that Russell had opened the scoring, charged on to the pitch and began to celebrate, oblivious to the fact that the ball had hit the post and bounced out! If anything summed up our luck that day, it was that moment.

A hard-fought victory over Wigan followed, but this was another game when Stoke missed chance after chance and ended up hanging on for a narrow 2-1 win in a game they should have put to bed by half-time. Profligacy in front of goal was certainly the theme in these opening weeks of the season, as the Potters failed to dispatch team after team, drawing five of the next six games and losing the other 3-1 at Bradford. By mid-September, Stoke went into a crucial game against runaway leaders West Brom in 17th place, winning only one of their first seven games and looking anything but promotion favourites.

There was more pre-match pessimism after Ronnie Sinclair was injured in training, and rather than turn to Peter Fox, Macari brought in a new goalkeeper – Tony Parks on loan from Spurs.

Unfortunately, Parks was straight out of the same drawer as Kevin Pressman, and within 20 minutes had managed to fluff a clearance straight to the feet of the predatory Bob Taylor. As the striker advanced on goal, Parks compounded his error by charging out of his penalty area like a headless chicken, cleaned out one of his own defenders in the process and left Taylor the simple task of tapping into an empty net. If circus music had started playing at that moment, it really wouldn't have been out of place.

However, in typical Macari fashion, the team realised that for all the hype around the visitors' supposed 'total football', West Brom were doing nothing other than tip-tapping the ball around in their own half. While other teams might have stood back, admired this and congratulated Ossie Ardiles on 'playing football the right way', Macari's boys instead got stuck into their showboating opponents. After 20 minutes of being harried, hustled and kicked, West Brom's soft underbelly was exposed and Stoke stormed into a 2-1 lead through Steve Foley and Kevin Russell. For the first time, Stoke began to look like the side we thought they'd be.

Unfortunately, Parks had other ideas. The goalkeeper was blameless as Taylor stooped in to head the Baggies level on 70 minutes, but Lord knows what he was thinking four minutes later as his positioning allowed Simon Garner the whole goal to aim at from out wide. The winger duly obliged by slamming the ball into the net.

Once again, in a match they'd dominated, Stoke looked like they were going to throw the game away. The tables turned again though three minutes later as a rampant Russell streaked clear of the defence and planted an equaliser into the bottom corner. With seven minutes left Russell then turned provider, delivering a peach of a corner for Ian Cranson to crash home a thumping header and put Stoke into the lead again.

It was breathtaking stuff. The final whistle blew on an exhilarating afternoon's football when 23,000 people got to see what this Macari team was all about. Even with the handicap of an atrocious goalkeeper, even with the disappointment of twice going behind, the team dug in and kept going for 90 minutes.

Another crucial goal had arrived from a set piece, and I ask Cranson if the team did a lot of work on set plays under Macari. 'No, nothing major,' he informs me. 'It was a case of sending the big lads up, putting ourselves in areas we were capable of scoring from and trusting the delivery. Back then we were a big side – in today's game we'd probably be two or three inches shorter than what you'd expect, but we had a few players who were good headers of a ball and lads like Mark Stein and Wayne Biggins who'd be able to poach the knock-downs.'

Finally, Stoke had some momentum and following the West Brom game, promptly visited Mansfield and thumped them 4-0. Biggins ran up to the away following and kissed his Stoke badge, leaving many to assume that he must have been about to sign a new contract. It looked for all the world like the team was about to surge up the table. Of course, things are never that simple in Stoke-land.

The Biggins saga that had been dragging on since the start of the campaign finally reached its depressing conclusion, not with a new contract, but with the striker joining Barnsley for a fee of £200,000. The move, on all levels, seemed baffling. While Barnsley were in a higher division than Stoke, they were perennial relegation strugglers, doing little more than staving off the drop every year. Leaving a progressive outfit like Stoke to join them seemed to make no sense whatsoever, and all sorts of rumours began to surface, offering various fanciful reasons as to why Biggins needed to leave Stoke.

Macari had a simple explanation for the move. 'Wayne was a big player for us, but if anyone did move on back then, you didn't really begrudge them because nobody earned any money to speak of. If you did get a move you got five to ten per cent of the transfer fee. I remember moving from Celtic for £200,000 and having £20,000 in my pocket and thinking, "I'm rich!" At all levels that was the case, so when Wayne moved to Barnsley he'd have probably got five per cent of that fee. It would have been a lot of money at the time.'

That was backed up by Biggins himself, who admits today with a refreshing honesty that his departure was simply down to finances: 'My contract was up at the end of the season, we were having our first child and having scored 28 goals the season before, I felt I deserved a bit more than I was being paid. That's all there was to it. Barnsley was just down the road from where we lived and they offered me more money. I didn't have a clue I was going anywhere when I kissed the Stoke badge at Mansfield because I honestly had no idea I was leaving at that point – the Barnsley offer came out of the blue.'

To be fair to him, Biggins continued to do the business in the division above, scoring 18 goals to keep Barnsley clear of relegation trouble.

Despite the excellent season that Stoke had without him, it's impossible not to ponder just how much better things would have been had Biggins stayed. The partnership he had with Stein was almost telepathic at times, and you do wonder whether we'd have not only been promoted that season with the two playing a whole campaign in tandem, but would have broken all known records in the process!

Macari didn't dwell on the matter and immediately brought in a replacement – striker Dave Regis, cousin of the more famous Cyrille and a very different kind of striker to Biggins. Regis was big, pacy and powerful, but a little ungainly with the ball at his feet. Playing the sort of direct football that he preferred, Macari realised his team needed more physicality up front than the 5ft 5in Stein or the slightly-built Shaw could offer, so although Regis lacked the skill of Biggins, he provided a different kind of foil for Stein.

'He [Regis] had strength and power,' Macari recalls. 'It was an athletic family so we knew he'd got it in him. I can't remember what we paid for him, not much I think, so when you're paying next to nothing you're not going to get Pele are you? But we knew what we'd got to work with and he was another good lad, a good character, happy to learn, happy to work and on a matchday it would all tend to work out.'

The team shrugged off Biggins's departure and continued their good form, the next home game against Leyton Orient providing another memorable match.

Trailing 1-0 to a Ricky Otto strike and with only a couple of minutes left on the clock, it looked for all the world like Stoke were going to have to accept a frustrating defeat. Enter Mark Stein. As Stoke piled forward, Carl Beeston sent a shot crashing against the woodwork. Orient failed to clear their lines properly and when Ian Cranson sent the ball back into the danger zone, there was Stein to loop a header over the keeper for a dramatic equaliser. Most of us would have taken that after the 90 minutes of frustration we'd endured, but Stein wasn't finished there. Two minutes later and deep into injury time, Graham Shaw sent a low cross into the area. Sure enough, there was our goal-getter extraordinaire, positioned perfectly again to side-foot the ball home and send three-quarters of the ground into ecstasy.

While the dramatic conclusion to the match will live long in the memory, I'll also never forget the comedy of that night's match report in the *Green 'Un*. Working to such a tight deadline, the *Evening Sentinel*'s writers would be forced to write their report as the game progressed, which didn't exactly make for the best prose, and most weeks the report would consist of dry, factual 'this happened, then that happened' recounts.

In this particular game, the reporter had taken more of a risk and had spiced up his account with a bit more flavouring, telling the story of a frustrating afternoon for Stoke – an impressive piece of writing on the hoof that captured well the feeling of bombarding an opponent's goal for 90 minutes, only to lose the game. Although I'm paraphrasing massively here, the end of the report read something like this:

'There was more frustration for City as yet another chance went begging on 80 minutes, leaving Stoke with the feeling that this was simply one of those afternoons when nothing was going to drop for them. Then Stein equalised with two minutes to go then scored a winner in injury time. Stoke won 2-1!'

I could just imagine the poor chap's shoulders sinking as three minutes of action rendered everything he'd written irrelevant, 30 seconds before he was due to phone his report in!

The Playground Derby

One of the main sub-plots to the memorable 1992/93 season was the renewed rivalry with Port Vale, who'd felt the inevitable pull of relegation gravity following their stint in a higher division.

This mercifully ended a period of them lording it over Stoke fans, making all sorts of outrageous claims that decades of dominance would follow and that the natural order of things would be reversed forever. To say it gave us great pleasure to see them relegated would be an understatement. We were absolutely cock-a-hoop to see them back where they belonged and to have the chance of showing them who really were the top dogs in the Potteries.

The rivalry was intense, no more so than on our school playground, where the Stoke/Vale split fuelled a series of vicious breaktime football games. With only 15 minutes to let off some steam between lessons, as well as the need to shove barrel loads of crisps into our faces, we soon worked out that the traditional method of picking sides wasted valuable minutes and usually ended in an argument anyway. Instead, we played Stoke v Vale as numbers were fairly even on either side and there were always one or two neutrals we could shove on to either side to make the numbers up.

Playground football really is something else. At least at high school, the Vale and Stoke split afforded us a sense of order and the knowledge as to which way you were supposed to be kicking. At junior school there was never any such organisation and games would spark naturally into life as soon as someone produced a ball. Football was played during every breaktime, usually with a 'tenniser', as the risk to the windows was obviously too great to allow proper footballs on to the yard.

You'd think that using such a small ball would be a useful exercise in developing close control, but there was no chance of that as the ball would often disappear under a scrum of bodies with 30 kids all charging after it like some sort of violent 18th-century village game. God help you if you fell over, because if the ball was anywhere near you at the time, it would have been like diving head-first into a herd of stampeding cattle.

Nobody ever wanted to go in goals during these matches, so I worked out that one way to curry favour and avoid the ignominy of being picked last would be to volunteer myself as a regular goalkeeper. It wasn't that I possessed any more ability in this position than I did outfield, but I did possess a secret weapon –

namely, an enormous duffel coat. Whereas the other lads would throw their coats down at the start of the game to create the posts, I would keep mine on for tactical reasons. Whenever I had to face a shot I would stretch the coat out with my arms – in the style of a flasher – which meant I hardly ever conceded a goal, as the ball would usually bounce off the taut material.

I was also something of a natural clown, and throwing myself around like Bruce Grobbelaar would get a few laughs as I foolishly, and repeatedly, hurled my body across the concrete yard. There weren't so many titters from Mum though, who could never understand how I was getting through so many pairs of school trousers.

During my final year at junior school, mini-footballs hit the shops – tiny replicas of the Mitre balls used in the professional game – and I made sure that I had one for Christmas, instantly gaining a bit more playground-cred. There was a harsh lesson to be learned though, as when we all went up to high school, the bigger kids wouldn't come up to me and say, 'Hey, kid with the Mitre ball, can we join in your game?' Instead they would say things like, 'Give us that ball you little cunt,' and then steal it.

Other first-years who were naïve enough to bring any half-decent football suffered the same fate, or even the horror of seeing their beloved ball spitefully booted on to the school roof by a passing fifth-year. Therefore, we quickly learned that any football we took into school should be of sufficiently low quality to avoid the unwanted attentions of these older lads.

It does make me laugh when I think back to these days, as whenever I pass high school kids in the street now, they look so young with their wrinkle-free faces and pathetic bumfluff facial hair. Back then though, they were so much bigger and hairier than us that my memory still pictures them as all looking like 30-year-old men. It was the law of the jungle on that playground and if you did have your ball, your football stickers, or even items of clothing nicked, it was better to just keep your head down and stay quiet about it rather than go blarting to a teacher or your mum. That was pretty much the only way to survive.

The other danger was the ball being kicked into 'Gob Alley', which pretty much doomed all but the absolute hardest kids in the fifth year to a fate worse than death. The layout of our playground was that the yard itself was about 12 feet higher than the footings of the adjacent sports barn, and an alleyway, about three feet wide, separated the two. There was a gate at one end of the alley which was supposed to prevent access, the lock to which had long since been removed. At the top a badly-designed metal grille prevented children on the yard from attempting to bungee jump, abseil or throw themselves down into the alleyway in suicidal despair, but what it didn't do was stop footballs disappearing through the gaps in the metal.

As you can guess, the rule was that if you were responsible for the ball disappearing down Gob Alley, you were responsible for getting it out, and with that gate unlocked there was nothing preventing you from doing so. Well, other than the fear of what would happen next.

The name 'Gob Alley' gives a clue as to what that grim eventuality was, because as soon as a ball bounced tantalisingly close to that metal grille, time would stand still and hundreds of expectant eyes would be drawn to it. Sometimes it would bounce off and back into play, and a disappointed 'ooooooh' would be heard, akin to the noise a crowd makes when a shot goes narrowly over the bar.

However, on other occasions a massive cheer would resonate around the yard, which indicated the ball had gone down into the dark depths below. Pity the poor kid who had to retrieve it because as the clank of the gate sounded upon them entering that dark, dingy alleyway at the foot of the sports barn, that poor child would be met with the sight of a hundred faces peering down at them through the grille, and shouts of 'Gob Alley! Gob Alley!' would attract more and more malevolent participants to this rather unsanitary ritual.

The child would have barely taken their first step into the alleyway before the first projectile of phlegm would be launched, and within seconds, spit would rain down on them as they sprinted into the dreaded Gob Alley to retrieve the ball.

If they were lucky, the ball would roll somewhere near the gate and they might even get in and out unscathed. On other occasions it would cruelly bounce to the far end, forcing the unfortunate victim to make a 50-yard dash under a firing squad of phlegm. I remember this happening to one kid in the year below. Foolishly he went for it rather than face the beating that would have ensued had he not accepted his fate. He put up his hood and sprinted. He got the ball okay, and he got out alive, but only with his new Naf Naf coat looking like it had starred in a Japanese bukkake film. Disgusting isn't the word for it.

You might wonder what the teachers were doing while all this was going on. Well, I can honestly say that I never saw one during break or lunchtimes. Once the bell had gone it was every man for himself, and you just had to find a way to survive. To be frank, some of the teachers we had would have probably sprinted over and joined in with Gob Alley had they been around, so the moral of the story was always not to kick the ball in that direction!

Anyway, apologies for the digression and back to the Potteries derby, which carried a threat of violence that made a trip into Gob Alley seem like a walk in the park. All the talk in the weeks before the game at the Victoria Ground was where fights would be happening, our own wannabe hooligan firm strutting around making all kinds of unlikely claims as to where they would be meeting and what they were going to do to any Vale fans they came across on the day.

Fortunately, pre-match seemed to pass off fairly peacefully other than whispered mutterings of odd fights that had happened in town, but back in the days before social media and camera phones, nobody ever really knew how true these stories were. Aside from avoiding a beating, all I really cared about was whether Stoke would be able to continue an unbeaten run that now stood at eight games, particularly against an opponent who we simply couldn't afford to lose to – the piss-taking would have been endless.

As much as we hated them, even the most blinkered Stoke fan had to admit that Vale were a decent side at that level, and under the canny management of John Rudge, had a team of cheaply-assembled players, many of whom were capable of playing at a higher level. In Neil Aspin and Dean Glover they boasted a centre-back pairing very much in the mould of our own, and in the cultured Ray Walker and sought-after Ian Taylor, you could even argue that Vale had the upper hand in midfield. Man for man, there was very little to choose between the two sides and our rivals were clearly going to have a big say in the promotion picture come the end of the season.

Macari didn't enjoy the games, realising the pressure they brought on the players. 'Rudgey had done well at Port Vale and performed miracles, getting them where they were,' he recalls. 'He knew what he was doing, Rudgey. I used to see him at the same games as me, watching the same players.'

The Stoke manager recognised that midfield was an area that he needed to strengthen though, and handed a debut to former Birmingham playmaker Nigel Gleghorn, another of the manager's ex-players who he'd obviously identified as having the ability to improve his side.

It was a huge game to make a debut, and Gleghorn remembers Vale as being tough opponents. 'The games were very close against Port Vale,' he recalls, 'but we tended to have that little bit more resilience than they did – a bit of extra fighting spirit which gave us the edge.'

As is so often the case in these games, the occasion seemed to overshadow the match, particularly in the opening half, and 45 rather grim minutes ticked by as neither side dared to take the necessary risk. If a goal was to come, it would have to be something special, and unfortunately it was Port Vale's midfielder Paul Kerr who launched a speculative 30-yard strike at goal which found its way into Ronnie Sinclair's top-left corner.

The away end exploded into that depressing sight of Port Vale fans celebrating a goal against us with delirium. I felt sick, just as I had done in 1989/90. Where was Leigh Palin when you needed him? Thankfully, the nausea didn't last long as Ian Cranson, making a habit of scoring vital goals in vital games, got his granite-like head on to a Kevin Russell free kick, setting off scenes of equal jubilation on the other three sides of the ground. The game was in the balance again.

What happened with four minutes left is still talked about to this day as Mark Stein wriggled free in the box, only to see the Vale goalkeeper Paul Musselwhite bearing down on him. His feet like quicksilver and his centre of gravity low, Stein was able to push the ball away from Musselwhite's dive, perhaps poking it a little too far away from goal, but just far enough away from the keeper's outstretched arm. As Musselwhite groped in vain for the ball, his arm caught Stein's trailing leg. The little man was down in the box and the referee, a Mr J. Watson (God bless you, sir) pointed to the spot.

Stein dusted himself down, positioned the ball and calmly dispatched it into the corner, just out of Musselwhite's reach. The game was over – we were the kings of the Potteries! A surge of relief spread through the terraces and stands, people were dancing on the pitch. One poor bloke took his celebrations a bit too far, goading the Vale fans with a double fist pump celebration, only to end up with a police dog biting his testicles!

We were all deliriously happy with the result, but I'm not sure thrusting my plums into the face of a salivating police dog would be quite the move I'd choose to make. Still, we were able to go to school with our heads held high on Monday, ready to face the inevitable whining and moaning that Stein was a cheat, a diver, a charlatan and many other things that I'd best be advised not to commit to print.

It didn't matter though. All that counted was the final score of Stoke City 2 Port Vale 1 and the months of goading that we'd be able to enjoy before the return fixture. Only we couldn't even enjoy that, because with a sense of absolute mischief, fate had decreed that Stoke and Vale would meet each other not even a month later in the first round of the FA Cup. Bollocks. We had to do it all over again.

Predictably, Sky chose to pay us a visit with their dancing girls and fireworks for a cup tie which was unworthy of such razzmatazz. The game was the sliding doors scenario of the first game – what would have happened had Paul Kerr's shot not flown in – inevitably two sides grinding their way to a nervy 0-0 draw. Why have one Potteries derby when you can have three? It was off to Vale Park a week later for the replay and Vale's chance of gaining a quick revenge.

Things started well for Stoke on the night as Lee Sandford headed us into the lead. In a mirror image of the league game though, the home side equalised within a minute thanks to

Martin Foyle (a regular thorn in our side in these games) and as the rain lashed down on to the already worsening surface, Andy Porter put Vale into a 2-1 lead just before half-time.

Stoke knew they were in a game here and responded by going on the offensive in the second half. An equaliser looked on the cards, but with questions being asked whether the game would even be completed as the pitch became a mud bath, another iconic moment in Potteries football came to pass.

With Musselwhite going AWOL, substitute Dave Regis was presented with the chance to stroke the ball into an unguarded net from about 20 yards. While the shot was from a reasonable distance out, the striker was unchallenged and on any normal day you'd have put your house on him scoring.

This wasn't a normal day though, it was football being played in Biblical conditions. Regis took a while to sort his feet out, the connection between his brain and his size tens never being the quickest. Eventually he managed it though and sent the ball towards the net, not making the best contact, but surely enough for it to get there and spark wild celebrations on the away end.

The ball rolled across the turf.

We waited.

It was still rolling, but a bit slower now.

Still we waited.

The ball never got there. It sat in a pool of water about two yards from the line, taunting us. Regis looked horrified; Vale defender Peter Swan looked delighted, a huge grin across his face as he ran, nay *waded*, through the six-yard box and smashed the ball to safety. That's Dave Regis's moment right there. No nutmegging Bruce Grobbelaar at Anfield for you Dave, not even a winning free kick in an Autoglass Trophy game – a ball sticking in a muddy puddle on a wet night in Burslem. That's your career in a nutshell, mate, off you go now.

When that sort of thing happens, you know it's not going to be your night and Vale put us out of our misery in injury time, conditions again helping Martin Foyle to beat Ronnie Sinclair to the ball and give the home side a 3-1 win.

Regis reveals that he still frequently gets reminded about his infamous moment. 'It was going in I think but I didn't make a good connection – there wasn't enough pace on it and I slashed at it,' he recalls. 'Port Vale played well that night and they were a good side. I get reminded all the time about it – most weeks actually. The builders currently working on my house are Vale fans and they enjoy mentioning it every time I see them!'

We could blame the conditions all we liked, but it was the same for both sides and Vale, on the night, handled it better than we did. Macari was philosophical in defeat, maintaining that he still wouldn't swap his squad for John Rudge's, and despite the Vale fans turning the tables on us and claiming a 4-3 aggregate victory, the Stoke half of the playground insisted that we would be the ones laughing come the end of the year.

Things got even tastier on the yard though as challenges flew in with the same sort of reckless abandon as Steve Foley adopted with his lunge on Neil Aspin (another moment that's still talked about to this day). Yes, even a trip down Gob Alley was safer than one of our Stoke v Port Vale breaktime matches!

Teenage Away Days

While watching Stoke at home was fun, I longed to be part of the travelling army that descended on the unsuspecting grounds of the Second Division. Buoyed by the swashbuckling football that their team was playing, the Stoke fans travelled en masse everywhere the team was scheduled to play. Eventually, mum relented. I was 14 now, nearly 15, and all right, I could go to an away game without adult supervision on the proviso that I took the official coach and didn't do anything stupid. West Brom away on 23 January was the chosen day, a vital clash at the top of the table. My friend Thompo and I bought our coach tickets, excited by the prospect of a trip down the motorway without a grown-up in tow.

Unbelievably, Stoke hadn't lost in the league since that early defeat at Bradford; a record unbeaten run that stretched for an amazing 20 games and included plenty more iconic moments. The week after beating Port Vale we went to Burnley and completely outplayed the home side, winning the game 2-0 and treating the second half like an exhibition game. Then there was the 3-1 win at Blackpool in the pouring rain, no puddles of mud getting in our way this time, just Kevin Russell embarking on a mazy run across the sodden Bloomfield Park pitch.

'Blackpool away was good,' Russell remembers. 'I scored another brace and again missed the chance for a hat-trick – I was gutted. I've seen the video of that day – Steiny was class. His goals were ridiculous that season and I always felt we linked up well together. We always found each other and made the right run for the pass. It's not until you look back you realise the full contribution you made. I set up lots of goals that season. Many of those assists were really important.'

Stoke went to the top of the table that day. Then there was Paul Ware coming off the bench as an emergency striker against Huddersfield, scoring twice before Ian Cranson finished off the day with a 20-yard thunderbolt. All produced legendary 'mentals', but nothing to compare to Steve Foley's last-minute equaliser at Brighton on 9 January. That result, a 2-2 draw, ensured Stoke had set a new record of 19 games unbeaten.

It was simply impossible to see where or how Macari's team could drop points, so dominant were they in most games, and how resilient they were in games when things didn't go to plan. The team never, ever gave up, never knew when they were beaten, and to a man looked like they would happily run through a brick wall for the manager who had transformed them from a disorganised rabble into an efficient and ruthless football machine.

After a 4-0 cakewalk over a poor Mansfield side, we travelled to West Brom knowing that victory would take us ten points clear of our nearest challengers and would surely give us an unassailable lead at the summit. Thompo and I didn't do anything 'stupid' exactly, well not in the sense that Mum had used the word at least, but we did do something rather dozy.

Excited to be part of a vociferous away following, we failed to take any notice whatsoever of where our coach had parked – a grave error in a following of 8,000 fans! The game itself was a typical Stoke performance under Macari. Stoke took an early lead through Gleghorn only to be pegged back by that persistent menace, Bob Taylor.

The home side had their tails up and tip-tapped their way around with a little more purpose than they had at the Victoria

Ground, but there was never any real concern that Stoke would succumb to the threat.

Finally, with 69 minutes on the watch, Mark Stein did what everybody knew was coming and put Stoke into the lead – a position we weren't going to relinquish. At that point, West Brom accepted they were not going to beat us in this game and were never going to catch us in the league either. The belief drained out of them and their form began to slump. Stoke, however, just marched on with the look of champions – relentless and merciless, delivering result after result to maintain a vice-like grip on top spot.

'I didn't even realise the run we were on at the time,' admits Nigel Gleghorn. 'We just kept turning up and winning games. Even then, Lou would still send us on a training run on Monday morning – around the incinerator 30 times, around the Victoria Ground 20 times ...'

At the end of the West Brom match, the away end was in full voice, exiting the stadium to an array of songs celebrating what looked like a sure-fire promotion season, as well as the usual 'Oh I do like to be beside the seaside' song that always gets an airing every time we play West Brom. I can't say I've ever walked on a promenade and heard a brass band launch into a song called 'Fuck Off West Brom' but I live in hope that one day it might happen.

As we celebrated the three points and felt very grown-up after watching our first 'proper' away game, it dawned on Thompo and me that we hadn't got a clue which one of the coaches was ours. We remembered the number (we weren't that stupid) but there were hundreds of the things, all parked in random order. There followed a rather frantic search before we eventually found ours, ascending the steps rather red-faced and out of breath.

'You're just in time, lads, I was just about to leave,' quipped the driver, and we looked at each other in relief, not realising he was taking the piss as our coach was still boxed in on every side by Bostocks' finest!

Despite the unfounded fear that I was destined to spend a night in a car park in West Bromwich, the day had given me a real taste for life as an away fan, and for the next few months I attended every away game I could, even foregoing my inclination to be as lazy as possible by starting a paper round to fund such trips. While getting up at 6am and trudging round in the rain proved to be a pain in the arse at the best of times, it did have one perk. The afternoon rounds would afford paperboys first glimpse at the *Evening Sentinel* copies as they arrived at the newsagent's shop.

Information was thin on the ground in the pre-internet days, so the local paper provided an absolutely vital source of news for Stoke fans. That made paperboys a font of all knowledge for a few minutes every day, and I'd delight in completing my round, turning up for football on Wolstanton Marsh and telling all my mates the 'hot off the press' news.

Most days it was the usual space-filling waffle of players issuing rallying cries, injury news or soundbites about forthcoming fixtures, but just occasionally we'd get a transfer story. Sometimes it was speculation, which was exciting enough, but other times there'd be a new player's grinning mug on the back page, arms aloft with a Stoke scarf in his hands and the accompanying headline 'City Swoop for Birmingham Ace' or whichever team we'd bought the new bloke from. The appeal of alliteration always proved hard for the *Sentinel* journalists to ignore as City would always 'swoop' in these scenarios.

Nowadays, every part of a football transfer is played out on social media, from details of scouts appearing at games to agents deliberately leaking details of negotiations. From a player's name first being linked with a new club, it can take months before we get to see an identified target sign on the dotted line.

There are hold-ups, snags and problems with every deal, and whereas before we would have been completely oblivious to these behind-the-scenes shenanigans, in the modern world, someone's always feeding the white noise of the internet. We're aware of everything and nothing – fed a constant stream of truths, half-truths and bullshit as people-in-the-know, people who know people-in-the-know and people who know nothing but wish they did, fill Twitter, message boards and Facebook with endless posts about transfers and which teams are tracking which players.

Some people get addicted to it, reading into every half-clue posted by all manner of random nobodies and spend days tracking down the identities of possible signings on foreign websites. Even if we are aware that interest in a player is genuine, the protracted nature of negotiations causes constant stress to those who follow it closely, and the mood on a message board can swing from elation to suicidal depending on the vagaries of the complex transfer process.

One minute a player is signing and we're going to win the Champions League, the next he's not and we're going to get relegated. The whole thing is ridiculous and I tend to avoid it. Until a player is confirmed as signed, has the shirt on his back and is trotting out the usual crap about how, even as a child in Belgium, he dreamt about playing for Stoke, I'm not interested. Life was so much simpler in the days when the first we'd hear about a player joining was when he appeared on the back page of the paper wearing a Stoke kit.

Unfortunately, my next paper round-funded away trip coincided with the end of our unbeaten run. It had seemed like it might go on forever, but after 25 games we slipped to a 1-0 defeat at Leyton Orient. It still didn't stop me saving up for the mammoth trip to Bournemouth a few weeks later though.

A Marvellous Man

A few years ago, I worked for Social Services, assessing the housing needs of individuals with disabilities. During a rather ambitious project to re-assess every single person on our database, one of my colleagues returned from a home visit and sat down next to me. 'I've just met the funniest man,' she said. 'He reckons that he's a former circus clown, he's friends with Kevin Keegan, knows the Archbishop of Canterbury and has played football for Stoke City.'

'Was it Neil Baldwin?' I asked, knowing full well what the answer was.

'Yes,' she replied, a shocked look on her face. 'How did you know that?'

'Because every one of those stories he told you is true,' I said.

I first became aware of Neil Baldwin when a man dressed as a giant chicken appeared on our substitutes' bench at Bournemouth. Nobody knew what the hell was going on, but there he was as large as life – a man in a chicken suit, who spent the whole match sat next to Lou Macari. It was, of course, Baldwin, Stoke's kit manager – a man with possibly one of the most remarkable life stories I've ever heard.

More people are aware of Neil now thanks to the film *Marvellous*, a work that truly lives up to its title. Written by Peter Bowker and starring Toby Jones, the made-for-TV production, which aired in 2014, tells the story of how Neil overcame so-called learning difficulties to earn a job at Stoke City and become friends with all manner of famous and influential people along the way. From turning up at the Houses of Parliament and finding himself having tea with Tony Benn to setting up his own football team at Keele University (with Kevin Keegan as its president), Neil has packed enough stories into his 70 years to fill several lifetimes.

Describing Neil as 'the best signing I ever made', Lou Macari first noticed Baldwin as a slightly odd figure who hung around outside the Victoria Ground. Intrigued as to who this person was, Macari got talking to him and was instantly bowled over by Neil's infectious personality and amazing life story. He describes their first interaction with the warmth that has characterised their friendship.

'I think the film [*Marvellous*] is close to how everything did happen. I met him outside the ground – and people like Neil are outside every football ground, aren't they? There's one at every football club, so it was no surprise to see him there with his bag and things with stamps on them, looking for autographs! I chatted to him for a bit and the first thing that made me laugh was when I asked him what he did for a living and he said, "Well, I used to be a circus clown but I got the sack."

'So I said to him, "Fucking hell, you're the first circus clown I've ever heard of who's got the sack!" and I had the conversation with him, but as I walked away I thought hang on … circus clown … comedian … makes people laugh … I could use him, so I turned back and said, "How do you fancy a job?" I didn't even have a job for him!

'He said, "Doing what?"

'I said, "Never mind doing what," because I didn't know. "See you Monday!"

'He went his way, and I went mine and I thought I know, I'll make him kit man. He came in on Monday and I said, "How do you fancy meeting the players today?" And then, remembering his time as a circus clown I said, "And how do you fancy being introduced to them in some gear?" So I took him to the costume shop and bought a chicken outfit. I said, "Will you wear this?" And I thought, of course he will – he's an entertainer! And all the while I was thinking, I wonder how this is going to go down with the players?

'So I said to the lads, "We've got a new kit man, and I'd like to introduce him to you." Sure enough, in came Neil with the suit on, a big beak sticking out and everything. Straight away they all started laughing. I thought, it's worked!

'As a manager I could get quite annoyed, quite aggressive and players can only hear enough of it then it stops working, so it was something very different – and that was it. Neil built up the relationships with the players by himself – some he got on with, others he would annoy and there were some of the players *he* didn't like. He did all the jobs a kit man would do – getting the kit packed into boxes, on the bus and all those things. We had some great moments on those away trips.'

The stories of Baldwin's time at Stoke are both funny and heart-warming. They highlight not only the camaraderie that existed within that squad of players, but also the warmth in Macari, who didn't invite Baldwin into the club as an act of charity, but because he recognised the spirit and determination of the man to see no boundaries.

To this day, Lou Macari and Neil Baldwin remain good friends, and our ex-manager continues to speak glowingly about his former kit man. 'Neil's Neil,' he told the audience at a recent question-and-answer session in Stoke. 'Wherever he goes and whoever he meets he's still Neil from the circus. He doesn't change.'

Stoke v Port Vale Parts IV & V

After already facing our rivals three times in the first half of the season, there was a sense of disbelief when Stoke drew Port Vale in the Southern Area semi-final of the Autoglass Trophy. While retaining this trophy might not have been top of the agenda for Stoke in 1992/93, the prospect of facing Exeter City in the area final in what looked like a free passage to Wembley was too good to miss. All we had to do was see off Port Vale first and we'd have another trip to the twin towers to add the cherry on top of what was already an iced cake of a football season.

The problem was that Port Vale arrived at the Victoria Ground with the holy blessing of the football gods truly shining on them. I don't think I can remember a more one-sided Potteries derby than this game, but whatever we did on the night, the ball refused to go into the net. Mark Stein endured a personal nightmare, missing chance after chance before the inevitable happened. With literally their only shot on target all evening, Vale scored when midfielder Robin van der Laan diverted a header past Ronnie Sinclair.

Stoke continued to pour forward but it didn't matter – nothing was going to go right. To be honest, the match could still be going on now, 25 years later, and we still wouldn't have equalised. We lost 0-1, the Vale half of the playground could, briefly, claim superiority, and we had to watch our rivals go all the way to Wembley and lift the trophy. Mind you, by the time the final came around we weren't that sorry to see them do it, for their opponents in the final were none other than Stockport County – possibly the only team in the world that we hated more than Port Vale!

As pleasant as another day out at Wembley would have been, no Stoke fan would have swapped another Autoglass Trophy for promotion from the Second Division, so when we faced Port Vale in the depths of Burslem on a rainy Tuesday night in March, all we really cared about were the three precious points we needed to go ten points clear at the top of the table.

Our opening goal is still branded on to my brain all these years later – John Butler jinking down the right wing like Stanley Matthews, crossing the ball into the box, and then Mark Stein lashing the ball home with his first chance of the night. So many chances he'd missed in that previous derby match, but not this one. The ball flew into the net, sending the away end into delirium.

In the second half the lead was doubled when Nigel Gleghorn headed home from a corner, and that was the moment when we knew nobody was going to catch us. We were going up, the title would be ours, and for the first time in decades, we had a team to believe in.

'It was such a brilliant time,' remembers Carl Beeston. 'The group of lads we had loved Stoke just as much as I did. They wanted to do it for the club and for the fans, and there was a real sense of togetherness – we were there for each other. The fans were insane as well – 6,000 going up and down the country wherever we went. We worked hard and trained hard but we liked having a laugh as well. You wouldn't get that in a dressing room nowadays.

'It made it better with Lou being like he was – we'd always be trying to get up to stuff without him knowing. Honestly, ask any of the lads, we all respected Lou – what he'd done and who he was, and even though he was running us to death, you wanted to do the best for him.'

Every victory seemed to really mean something to those players, and it was wonderful to see the passion they displayed on nights like this. It's something that's becoming ever rarer in today's game, but there was never any questioning the commitment of those players who represented us in 1992/93. They truly understood what it meant to be a fan and to love your team.

We are the Champions!

Following the win at Vale Park, promotion seemed like a formality, but we still found time for the occasional wobble. The ghosts of 1991/92 came back to haunt us with two horrible home defeats to Blackpool and Hartlepool, 1-0 losses where both the opposing goalkeepers performed heroics for 90 minutes. These results pushed back the title being sealed to the night of 28 April.

Macari had moved to bolster his side with the loan signings of Liverpool legend Bruce Grobbelaar, who was unfortunately recalled after only four games, and right-back Dave Hockaday from Hull. The latter remembers coming into a dressing room that was high on confidence. 'I'd been with Lou for five years at Swindon,' Hockaday told the audience at a recent reunion dinner for Stoke's title winners. 'I knew exactly what the dressing room would be like – full of good honest pros who knew how to win a game. I had no doubt we'd be winning the championship.'

With three games left to play, Stoke needed three more points to be sure of clinching the crown, and Plymouth were the team standing between us and a well-deserved promotion.

These sort of nights are never the glorious procession that you crave them to be. They're scrappy, nervy, and neutrals in the crowd would be hard-pushed to tell who the promotion chasers were. Plymouth had nothing to play for other than spoiling the party, and with the way they went at us, it looked for all the world like they were going to do that.

Nigel Gleghorn had other ideas though. Somewhat against the run of play he put us into the lead, and from there on in we pretty much held on to what we had. Goalkeeper Peter Fox had been recalled for the run-in, and he single-handedly kept the visitors at bay with a string of stunning saves.

'I made a double save from Warren Joyce, which people do still talk about today,' Fox stated. 'I stopped his first shot from inside the area and then got up quickly to smother his follow-up from point-blank range. If I say so myself, I think that was a world class save.'

The swashbuckling attacking play of earlier in the season had gone – weighed down by the same nerves and anxiety that had cost us so badly the season before. But Fox held firm, helped out by the rugged backline that he marshalled so well that night, and as the minutes ticked by, we could sense that this was it. This was the night.

'It's hard to describe the emotion you felt,' recalls goalscorer Gleghorn. 'Was it elation or relief? In the end we kept the fans on the edge of seats for 80 minutes, but we got the job done in the end.'

An explosion of joy, and yes, relief, met the final whistle. An army of people surged on to the pitch, a joyous cavalry charge towards the players who bolted for the safety of the dressing room. Strangers hugged and danced on the Victoria Ground turf, lost in the elation of a rare triumph for the team who'd come back from the dead – resurrected by the miracle worker that was Lou Macari.

I'd never been part of a pitch invasion before – it was the kind of thing you saw on *Match of the Day*, the sort of thing that happened to other teams. Hereford fans charging around in parkas celebrating with Ronnie Radford – that's the one that always comes to mind. Even my dad ran on, bless him.

'It was a great feeling when the whistle went and all the fans began jumping around on the pitch,' remembered Mark Stein. 'There must have been 20,000 on going crazy. It was madness. I don't think we left the ground until about 12 o'clock and even then there were supporters milling around outside.'

Oh, wasn't school just joyous the next day. Forget those insignificant, tiny battles with Port Vale – the skirmishes for three points here or an Autoglass Trophy there – the war was over and we were the true victors. A small, silver trophy to add to the bare shelves of the cabinet, but really so much more than that. We'd won back our pride, our dignity, and our place as the Potteries' number one club.

We had Geography as our first lesson. Mr Lamb, a regular in the Boothen Paddock, told us we were going to watch a video on rock formations. We didn't though. He wheeled the old TV and Betamax combo into the room, pressed play and treated us to the full highlights of the previous night's game as a lesson starter. What a guy.

Just to top things off nicely, Port Vale missed out on automatic promotion when Stoke, already assured of the title, lost 1-0 at third-placed Bolton, allowing them to leapfrog Vale into second. How we laughed. Denied the automatic promotion they probably deserved, Vale faced West Bromwich Albion in the play-off final at Wembley. Peter Swan got sent off, they lost 3-0 and unlike Delilah, we laughed even more.

Season 1993/94
This Is What Loss Feels Like

I T'S hard to know where to pitch your expectations after a
promotion campaign. Stoke had been so much better than the
rest of the Second Division the previous year, the optimists
among the support (we do have some, believe it or not) were
talking of a second successive promotion and a glorious march
to the Premier League. With Mark Stein leading the line and Lou
Macari weaving his magic in the transfer market, it did seem like
we might only be another 12 months away from seeing Curiosity
Killed The Cat mime on our pitch at half-time in front of some
giant sumo wrestlers on a wet Monday night. What an incentive
to get promoted!

On the other side of the coin, there were the doom-mongers
who focused on the bigger names in the First Division – teams like
Nottingham Forest and Middlesbrough, who'd be a lot tougher to
beat than the likes of Mansfield and Bury had been, and forecast
a season of struggle ahead.

Most fans though were in between these two extremes and
had consolidation pencilled in as the most realistic aim – a
season of finding our feet at a higher level after the relative stroll
of 1992/93.

Looking back, we'd been promoted with a tiny squad. By the
time we clinched the title, Macari only had 16 bona-fide first-team
players at his disposal, so spent the summer of 1993 on a kind

of football trolley dash, charging through the aisles of the First Division, rummaging in the bargain bins and taking any out-of-date, unwanted or damaged goods footballers he could find. As ever, there was little money to spend, so to assemble the number of players he did by the following September was no mean feat – Macari practically had an entire team of new faces he could field if he'd so wished.

In goal there was Mark Prudhoe – a £120,000 signing from Darlington and a dead ringer for comedian Russ Abbott. Unfortunately, Prudhoe's goalkeeping was even more comical than his double's TV sketch show was, and the former Darlo man treated us to a season of wildly inconsistent displays. Having Ronnie Sinclair confined to the treatment room though meant back-up was needed, so Carl Muggleton also joined, initially on loan from Leicester City.

Macari was such a frequent visitor to Birmingham for transfers that one can only presume they were offering him a discount. Right-back Ian Clarkson was signed for £50,000 to provide cover and competition for John Butler, while Simon Sturridge, who cost a similar amount, was clearly an understudy to Mark Stein and another diminutive striker.

Further arrivals in the forward line were Nottingham Forest duo Gary Bannister and Toddy Orlygsson, the former a chronically slow forward who we pretty much knew had last seen his legs in the 1980s, while the latter was an Icelandic winger we knew little about.

Another old head who we *were* familiar with was Micky Gynn – a 5ft 5in Super Mario lookalike who'd given Coventry a decade's service and who'd scored the winning goal against us to end a rare FA Cup run back in 1987. However, at 33 he was another whose best days were surely behind him.

Gynn was joined by Kenny Lowe, who pretty much nobody had heard of, and at 32 and on a free transfer from Barnet, seemed a rather strange signing for a club in Stoke's position to make. It did seem at times that Macari must have been so desperate for new faces that he was sticking pins into his *Rothman's Football Annual* and signing whoever they landed on (providing they were free of course!)

The big signing though, the one we were all excited about, was Martin Carruthers. Carruthers was only 21 and had torn up the Pontin's Reserve League with Aston Villa (be afraid, be very afraid!), so we were clearly signing potential here rather than another short-term fix.

Several of the new faces lined up alongside the heroes of 1992/93 as Millwall came to town for the season opener. Almost 19,000 packed in to the Victoria Ground on a typically sun-drenched August Saturday and even got to enjoy the somewhat comical spectacle of Millwall fans stumbling over rows of seats as they attempted to storm the Butler Street stand. They were pushed back before anybody could get seriously hurt (more likely from banging their shins on the backs of the seats than from any punches being thrown) but on the pitch, the visitors looked determined to dish out a lesson to the division's new boys.

Despite a bizarre own goal from Mick McCarthy gifting us our first goal since promotion, Stoke had looked very much second best throughout the afternoon and finished the game comfortably beaten 2-1. The air began to escape from the balloon and those who'd predicted a continuation of our Second Division dominance quickly began to moderate their forecast. The First Division wasn't going to be easy.

Moving Up in the World

Things never stay the same for long, in football or in life. For the long-term football fan there are transitions to be made, mirroring the transitions that we all make as we get older. They creep up on us, and without thinking, we make small changes to our routines and in the process alter the world around us forever. I was approaching my 16th birthday in 1993/94 and following on from my independent expeditions to the away ends of the Second Division, I started to attend home games with that same group of mates who'd accompanied me on those exotic trips to places like Huddersfield and Leyton Orient.

It was a natural progression really, and one that's no longer fully applicable in the modern world of all-seater stadia and a game that's been sanitised almost beyond recognition, but most boys who began their supporting lives walking to matches clutching their dad's hand would have been doing so either heading for the main stand or maybe the paddocks. Dad and I had moved from stand to paddock a couple of years before, the move away from the thermos flasks and clean language of the Boothen Stand being something I'd no doubt been keener on than Dad had been, but he went along with it anyway, probably aware of where it would naturally lead to before long.

The paddock was undoubtedly a saltier experience than the stand, but it still wasn't the Boothen End. That's where I really wanted to be: in the belly of the beast, surging forward and back, listening to the foulest language imaginable and joining in with chants so offensive they would make your toes curl. The paddock was standing without the unsavoury extras – it got a bit more interesting if you were stood at the far end right next to the away fans, but where we were situated, the people weren't that much different to the folk who inhabited the stand behind us. How bad could it get really? Even Mr Lamb, my Geography teacher, stood next to us some weeks, while behind us was an elderly chap in a trilby, who surely shouldn't have still been standing up at his age, and who continually encouraged Vince Overson with a cry of, 'Come on Vincent!' in the plummiest accent you could imagine.

It was a novelty at first, being unrestrained by rows of seats when Stoke scored, being free, if you so desired, to celebrate by clambering on to a stranger's back or by charging along the gangways. However, this physical freedom was something of a double-edged sword. On one occasion, I almost broke my hand punching the wall in frustration, unable to find any other way of expressing my dismay at some event or other that had conspired against Stoke. Eventually though, I longed for something more from the matchday experience – an afternoon removed from parental judgement and restrictions. An afternoon where I was free to shout expletives as much as I liked without a disapproving look being cast in my direction.

It's all part of growing up I suppose, and the delicate balance of a father–son relationship as the boy pushes to become a man, and thus acts how he thinks men should act, while his dad rolls his eyes, having no doubt done the whole 'rebellious thing' himself years ago, realised the ridiculousness of it and falsely assumed that acting like a dickhead for a few years was some kind of optional choice that young men could be steered away from. Eventually, dad succumbs to the inevitability of it all, and off the boy goes to drink as much alcohol as possible, get into daft situations, smoke dubious substances and break a few minor laws, all the while thinking that he's the first person since James Dean to do it.

So that's what happened. I moved to the Boothen End to stand with Thompo, Bowie and Big Dave, leaving my dad back in the paddock, stood by himself. He no doubt did the same thing to his dad back in the 1960s, and my kids will inevitably do the same thing to me in a few years' time. So, for the best part of 20 years afterwards, I stood, and then sat, on the Boothen End with a group of mates. The constitution of the group evolved and changed over the years as people drifted in and out of the area and interest waxed and waned, even the stadium changed, but whoever was there at any given time, it was always great – blokes having a laugh together, a simple pleasure.

It was a good time to move to the Boothen End though in 1993/94. The feel-good factor was very much present and attendances post-promotion were at their highest for years. The games weren't sell-outs, and you could still just about pick your spot on the terrace, but there were still the mad surges after a goal had been scored, where you could end up about 20 feet away from where'd you'd started, winded, shaken and bruised, but grinning from ear to ear as you clambered out of the scrum of bodies.

Stoke picked up a bit too after that opening-day defeat, and soon began to hold their own in the First Division. The first dozen games brought a mixed bag of results. There were victories and some disappointing days, like the home defeats to Southend and Tranmere, when Ian Cranson became the unfortunate victim of one of the worst back-pass decisions I've ever seen.

The back-pass law was new for that season, and clearly some referees still hadn't got the hang of it. In this game, Cranson sliced a clearance so high into the air it practically rebounded off the moon before entering Earth's atmosphere again directly over his own six-yard-box. Mark Prudhoe could do nothing else but catch the ball as gravity deposited it into his grateful arms.

Quite how Mr P. Jones of wherever he was from – Lala Land I think – interpreted that as a deliberate back-pass I have no idea, but he couldn't wait to blow for a free kick and show the FA how he was top banana when it came to understanding new rules. Honestly, if Cranson tried to kick that ball again with the same trajectory and land it into his own goalkeeper's arms from that exact position in the penalty area, it would take him over a million attempts to do it.

It might seem like a minor incident in the grand scheme of things, but I've been waiting 25 years to get that off my chest, and if holding a quarter-of-a-century-long grudge over a refereeing decision in a mid-table nothing match classes me as mentally ill, then so be it. That's what football reduces you to.

Of course, Stoke enjoyed good days too – no more so than when we visited recently relegated Nottingham Forest in front of the Central TV cameras, resplendent in our classy new purple away kit. Everybody thought we'd lose, but Stoke turned up at the City Ground and put on a show and a half. We were 3-0 up by the 49th minute and Mark Stein was rampant.

Of course, we had to let Forest back in it just to give the watching public a bit of excitement, but visiting the pre-season promotion favourites and returning home with a 3-2 win was a sign that on our day, we could live with the best that the new division had to offer.

Dave Regis smiles as he recalls the game, 'I remember that one clearly. A Sunday televised game, the sun shining, big crowd with a huge Stoke following. I scored at the Trent End with a scuffed shot. I should have bagged a hat-trick that day, but it was one of those days where we all felt good and the win was a big statement. Stuart Pearce pulled a couple back but it was still a great win at a big club.'

This is What Loss Feels Like

'This man's magic. He scores goals that others can only dream about.' To any Stoke fan, that piece of commentary is every bit as famous as Kenneth Wolstenholme's 'Some people are on the pitch' line. Mark Stein was, of course, the magician in question, and Manchester United were the team on the receiving end of his latest conjuring trick – two goals from nowhere, sending Alex Ferguson's troops back up the M6 with a 2-1 defeat thanks to the merciless finishing ability of the man we rescued from Oxford's reserves. The man who had now become the hottest property outside the Premier League.

His first goal was lashed in from the right-hand side of the penalty area, crashing in and hitting the stanchion inside Peter Schmeichel's net. His second was even better – a thunderbolt into the Boothen End goal to win the game after Dion Dublin had equalised. 'I didn't have a goal celebration,' Stein stated when looking back on his favourite Stoke game in *Match of my Life,* 'I just used to love watching the Boothen go absolutely crazy. That night the place was rocking.'

It was a memorable night for any Stoke fan, and was also the setting for one of Lou Macari's favourite Neil Baldwin anecdotes.

'Waiting on the team sheets to come in, I'm hoping that Manchester United have left out a couple of players, which nobody did at the time,' Macari tells me, already chuckling to himself. 'I'm just hoping Alex has rested one or two to make it an achievable, winnable game for us. I get the team sheet, they're all playing. Schmeichel, Pallister, McClair, Mark Hughes, and I thought, fucking hell, they've got their best team out. I jokingly said to Neil, "Nello, you might as well take the team talk tonight. We're never going to beat this lot."

'Before I knew it, Nello's in the middle of the floor going, "Right lads, listen to me now," and he goes through this team talk of slagging off everyone who played for Manchester United, slagging Alex off and all sorts!

'So we go out, two great goals from Steiny, and we're clinging on from about the 85th minute, and I'm looking at the clock, looking at the referee, and looking at Nello in the back of the dugout. I'm mindful that come the final whistle he'll be jumping out on to the touchline and, knowing that Neil likes a celebrity, he'll be all over Alex.

'Bearing in mind that we were winning, I thought, that'll be the last thing Alex will want. Anyway, we get into added time, the whistle goes and we're all jumping up, hugging one another and I'd forgotten about Neil. Sure enough, I glance behind me to the dugout and he's gone -- I look down the track and he's up to Sir Alex and he's shaking his hand. Of course, Alex has just lost and doesn't like losing.

'Anyway, Alex comes up to my office after for a cup of tea and a sandwich. He says, "Who was the fucking big man on the track?"

'I say, "That's my kit man, boss." I always used to call him [Ferguson] boss. "He's an ex-circus clown."

'He says, "What are you talking about, circus clown?"

'I said, "Yeah, we signed him out of the circus."

'"Fuck off, you're kidding me," he says.

'I said, "No, I'm not, and I've got more bad news for you: he gave the team talk that beat you!"'

A memorable night for everyone, and the last great game we'd have with Stein in the side and Macari at the helm.

It was inevitable that Stein would end up leaving us. Newcastle had already had a bid rejected, so had Tottenham, and even though he kept delivering the goods for us like the true professional he was, Stein knew that at 28, this was probably his last chance to prove himself as a top-level striker and earn the sort of money his talent deserved. His toppling of the mighty Manchester United sealed his move. Chelsea were in with a £1.5m offer and the best Stoke striker of his generation was off to seek his fortune in the bright lights of London.

Losing Stein was a bitter blow, but with money to spend, and such an unbelievable record in the transfer market, Macari would surely be able to bring in a replacement.

Oh, wait, Macari's just gone to manage Celtic, his boyhood team, on the exact same day that Stein has left for Chelsea.

'I remember watching the television in the boardroom after the second leg of the Manchester United game,' recalls Peter Coates. 'We lost the game 2-0 and I saw on the screen that Celtic had sacked their manager, who was Liam Brady. It's funny how you react to things, and I thought, I bet they come for Lou Macari. Sure enough, the next morning I got a call – could they speak to him?

'When you're in football you have to tell your manager these things because, to be honest, they already know. I knew that Lou would have already been approached, and in fairness to Lou, he'd told me that he would only leave Stoke for two clubs – Manchester United or Celtic.

'All of a sudden – there it was.'

I can't begin to put into words the level of despondency that hit the Potteries on that particular day. It was like finding out that your mum and dad were divorcing, Santa wasn't real and your dog had just been run over all at once. Like many, I was numb with grief. I was in on my own when I heard the news, and I went outside and sat on our garden wall hoping that someone would come past who I could share the misery with.

Mrs Miller, our 90-year-old neighbour, wasn't interested – she just gave me a funny look when I told her that Steino and Lou were gone, but eventually the lad who lived opposite wandered past, and even though I barely spoke to him in everyday life, we shared a few minutes discussing how the whole bastard world had just ended. What the hell were we supposed to do now?

Chic Bates, Macari's faithful assistant, stepped into the breach, but he made it clear he'd soon be joining Lou at Celtic, so we couldn't even console ourselves by retaining one half of what had proven to be a great managerial partnership. We had to just wait and hope that one of our other strikers could step up and take on Stein's role as the team's focal point. The problem was that they were all a bit, well, crap.

That's probably a bit harsh on Dave Regis – as Stein's regular partner, he'd played his part in the opening quarter of the campaign, but none of the other options we had on the books seemed very promising. Simon Sturridge hadn't been given much of a chance yet (he would go on to prove an excellent buy), but had done very little in the few brief cameos he'd had, while Gary Bannister was even worse than we'd imagined he'd be.

The big let-down though was Martin Carruthers. Aside from a thunderbolt into the top corner in an early appearance against Mansfield in the League Cup, Carruthers was the sort of striker who would leave fans banging their heads against crush barriers, watching through their fingers when he went through on goal, or thumping walls in temper at his panicky finishing (I can't remember for sure, but it was probably him I blame for that injury).

He was fast and could certainly sniff out a chance, but something seemed to happen in Carruthers's mind as soon as he saw the goalkeeper come off his line. It was almost as if he envisaged a target appearing somewhere around the goalkeeper's knees and simply took aim at it. Either that or he closed his eyes and took a wild swing as soon as he got into the penalty area. Whatever it was, I've never seen anyone miss so many one-on-one chances as he did. It got to the point where you didn't even bother craning your neck, standing on tip-toes or getting out of your seat when he ran past the last defender – there was only the sad inevitability about what would come next.

But even Carruthers had his shooting boots on as Stoke faced Barnsley in the first game post-Macari, post-Stein. It was a strange experience on the terraces that day. Like seeing your favourite band make a comeback, minus the lead singer and lead guitarist, going through the motions on stage when everyone in the audience knows they're watching a shadow of the real deal – a tribute act.

Stoke without Steino and Lou was like The Doors without Jim Morrison; like Echo and the Bunnymen without Ian McCulloch – a shambling husk of the real thing.

A funereal atmosphere hung over the ground pre-kick-off, as if 15,000 people had turned up at a wake. Nobody knew quite what to say, or how to behave, or what we should do exactly. The soul of the club had suddenly been removed, 50 per cent of the terrace chant repertoire gone with it, and so we all just shuffled around, dead-eyed and grieving.

What happened next was quite unbelievable. Barnsley took advantage of a shell-shocked Stoke, racing into an early 2-0 lead and looking likely to pile on the misery. Somehow we dragged ourselves back level thanks to two own goals, and one of the most bizarre games in living memory played out before us as goals flew in at both ends. Stoke ended as 5-4 winners.

The players had fought like lions in difficult circumstances, and if Bates had even briefly considered hanging around a bit longer than planned, this game was not going to do a potential job application any harm whatsoever. Neither were the comments of captain Vince Overson, who made it clear who the dressing room wanted in charge. 'Chic is the man we'd like to see appointed,' said Overson. 'He has the respect of the players and we'd be 100 per cent behind him.'

Stoke went on to add another two victories under Bates's temporary stewardship. Firstly, a mazy run and shot from the increasingly influential Toddy Orlygsson illuminated a drab game against Sunderland to secure a 1-0 win, and this was followed by a confident performance on the road as Stoke came back from Watford's Vicarage Road with a 3-1 result, the side pushing themselves into play-off contention as a result.

As quickly as it had seemed to drain out of us, the belief had started to return. Eventually, Stoke announced that the man to step into Macari's shoes would be former Bristol City and Hearts boss Joe Jordan, another Scotsman who had ironically been working as Liam Brady's assistant at Celtic, prior to the pair's dismissal that prompted the Bhoys' move for Macari.

Jordan received one of the most emphatically positive welcomes ever afforded to a new Stoke manager, the Boothen End bouncing for almost the entirety of the next home game against Leicester, serenading their new manager with a chant of 'Joe Jordan's red and white army' for 90 minutes.

Stoke won 1-0, Mark Prudhoe making a world-class save in injury time, and as a result, moved into the play-off spots for the first time that season. Jordan, however, somewhat misjudging the mood, declared that this was 'another three points against relegation', thus demonstrating the dour, ambitionless pragmatism that would blight his tenure at the football club. Nobody really paid attention to the portentousness of Jordan's words though – we were just delighted to get another victory, and after all the wailing and gnashing of teeth that had followed Macari and Stein's exits, we were prepared to give Jordan our total support.

The Calamity Man

The honeymoon didn't last long, however, for Jordan lacked the charisma of Macari and people found it difficult to warm to him. His football, just like his personality, was dull and lifeless; his post-match interviews, win or lose, always sounded like five minutes of miserable growling. You couldn't imagine a Jordan team talk inspiring a player to do anything other than maybe close his eyes and slip into a coma.

In contrast, Lou Macari, for all his reputation as a disciplinarian teetotaller, was able to light up any room through his effulgent personality – a magnetic figure able to hold an audience in the palm of his hand whenever he spoke. Macari always had a twinkle in his eye and a sense of mischief – the sort of man who would appoint ex-circus clowns as kit men and play practical jokes on his players minutes before vital games in order to get a response out of them.

I wouldn't go as far as to say that the players 'liked' Macari given the physical torture he put them through in training, but come Saturday afternoon, to a man, they'd run through brick walls for him. Something about their manager inspired those players to be the best versions of themselves that they could be. That's how Macari was able to transform a bunch of Birmingham City cast-offs and jumble sale footballers into a disciplined unit of footballing commandos: a team of super-fit, hard-running, hard-tackling men willing to put their bodies on the line for the cause.

It didn't matter what formation Jordan played, or who he signed in the transfer market, he simply hadn't got *it* – whatever the mysterious, metaphysical properties of *it* might be. When Jordan stood and addressed a dressing room, or a room of reporters, or 20,000 Stoke fans via television and radio, these magical ingredients were always lacking.

Ultimately, if Macari told us that everything would be all right after a defeat, we believed him, because it was Macari saying it. Even during bad runs of form, we always felt reassured that it would turn around. That reassurance was impossible to feel with Jordan though. His voice carried the qualities of cold rain lashing against the grey, concrete tenements of Glasgow. There was no warmth to it, no feeling and no spark to anything he said or did. He was dourness personified and if we felt it, the players no doubt felt it too.

Carl Beeston was one player who struggled to make the transition from Macari to Jordan. 'Under Jordan, we didn't do too badly in terms of league position but everything was regimented and we all felt restricted,' he remembers. 'The atmosphere among the lads had turned flat; the away form was poor as well, with pretty negative tactics. He had a thing about the halfway line – mainly, don't go over it!'

It didn't help Jordan that his first signing was a disaster. While there could be no arguing that a more consistent goalkeeper than Mark Prudhoe was required if we were to continue challenging for the play-offs, it was Jordan's choice of replacement that quickly saw the goodwill and support of the Leicester game draining away at the same rate that our hope was.

Gordon Marshall, who Jordan would have been familiar with from his time at Celtic, remains, by some distance, the worst goalkeeper I've ever seen play for Stoke City. He was so bad that even the mention of his name, 25 years later, can reduce a man either to a catatonic state of post-traumatic stress or hysterical laughter.

For 12 games over the winter of 1993/94, Marshall conducted a one-man reign of terror on the nerves of all Stoke fans. During that unforgettable period, no ball was beyond punching into his own goal, no shot too soft to dive over or back-pass too tame to scuff. It was as if Marshall had set himself the personal target of having his own dedicated section in a comedy goalkeeping gaffes video, or was actually a random member of the public trying to pass himself off as a professional goalkeeper in an elaborate *Beadle's About* prank.

Searching for others' memories of Marshall is at least, an amusing experience. Threads about him on *The Oatcake*'s online message board quickly degenerate into pure comedy as fans share the trauma of having watched this man flap and flop around so haplessly all those years ago.

A quarter of a century later, Marshall has become a byword for bad goalkeepers, the daddy of them all, and no one who was there at the time will ever forget it. I believe the best thing I can do at this point is to simply stop writing and present you with a selection of comments from other fans who were witness to the phenomenon that was Gordon Marshall:

'I seem to recall one of the goals bouncing before him and simply going over his head and into the net, ala Lads & Dads when you'd have a little kid as goalie in full-size goals.'
'I remember his debut, Luton away, where we lost 6-2, I think it was. They used to have the goal klaxon on Radio Stoke then and it was going off every couple of minutes as the goals rained in.'

'The Millwall game was a stunning performance by Marshall. It was the last match before Christmas, and we'd battled for a point. Late in the second half the ball was hoofed into the Stoke penalty area. Marshall called and Ian Cranson ducked out of the way. The ball bounced. Marshall had come too far and it bounced over his head. A Millwall player just ran up and tapped it into the open goal.

A couple of minutes later the ball was played back to Marshall by Lee Sandford. A Millwall striker closed Marshall down. Marshall tried to be clever and knocked it around him, but only knocked it straight into the feet of another player who was advancing on goal. He just tapped it into the open net. The worst five minutes of keeping I have ever seen.'

'Charlton away was another one. A terrible performance capped by Marshall coming out for a cross only to miss the ball by about four feet & an easy header into the open goal for whichever lucky Addick was there.'

'After he conceded a comedy goal at home to Oxford, my dad stood up and booed him. Never known him do that to a Stoke player in 22 years of going to matches with him. That's how bad Gordon was.'

The worrying thing is that this is only a small selection of the mistakes that Marshall made during this spell. His final gaffe was against Oxford, when he dived to his left to save a low shot, palming the ball into the air.

Instinctively, he flicked his right arm up, even though there were no Oxford players following in, somehow managing to punch the ball into his own net as a result. The crowd erupted in anger, their patience long since having broken with this fool who was costing us points every single week, and also with the manager who continued to pick him.

For some reason, I wasn't stood on the Boothen End that game, I was in the paddock again. I remember being stood right next to the players' tunnel, perhaps having charged there in anger after the whistle, and I've never seen a more broken expression on the face of a footballer as Marshall trudged from the pitch.

I, along with many others, couldn't contain the anger we felt, and Marshall was subjected to a volley of verbal abuse as he despondently ambled off the field. I'm not proud of doing this, but in my own defence, I was 16 years old and didn't really know any better. I wouldn't have even thought about the emotions that Marshall would have been going through at that moment – the effect of the abuse on his self-esteem at a time when his confidence was clearly at an all-time low. I just let rip.

I still remember what I said, too. It was horrible and unnecessary. 'Fuck off and die, Marshall, you useless twat.'

On one hand I suppose footballers get used to that sort of thing; developing the mental fortitude to ignore disparaging comments and angry 'heat of the moment' rants being a necessary part of what is, after all, a well-paid profession. But there must still be the odd one that gets through the armour – words infused with toxicity that skewer through the skin and into the soul of the person they're directed at, burrowing around inside them and ringing out in their brain at 3am when the defences are down and even the most mentally resilient characters are at their most vulnerable.

In contrast to the frenzied melee around the tunnel, there was an older chap stood by the wall as Marshall ran, or perhaps dejectedly trudged, the gauntlet that day – someone in his late 40s or early 50s who tended to stand in the same spot every week. I didn't know his name or what he did, but I'll always remember his actions as our beleaguered goalkeeper passed him. As everyone else screamed abuse, red faces and throbbing veins, profanities and spittle flying in from either side like a volley of arrows, this chap stood, leaning against the wall, sanguine and impassive.

As Marshall passed him, he said nothing, he just leaned over the wall and patted him on the shoulder – a small gesture of humanity that's stayed with me ever since.

There are some footballers who probably don't help themselves when it comes to avoiding abuse from the crowd. Those who turn up, don't bother trying and still pick up their enormous salaries are those who I do find it difficult to defend. If you're picking up £50,000 a week and deliberately giving very little back in return then sympathy is going to be thin on the ground when people start directing verbal abuse your way.

However, there are other players to whom that doesn't apply – the Gordon Marshalls, the Tony Kellys, in recent years perhaps the Darren Fletchers or Salif Diaos. Guys who tried their best, but, for one reason or another, were just simply not good enough. Looking back as a more phlegmatic man of early middle-age, rather than a hot-headed teenager, I do feel a bit of remorse about some of the personal abuse I shouted at the players, particularly Marshall on that day against Oxford. He'd have heard it all right, the paddock was close quarters to the tunnel, and it's all I can do to redress the balance a bit, all these years later.

As awful as he was for us, and by God he was awful, Marshall can't have possibly been as bad a goalkeeper over his whole career as he was during that one brief spell in 1993/94. He was capped by his country, only once perhaps, but played a total of 101 times for Celtic, 171 times for Falkirk, 159 times for Kilmarnock and 67 times for Motherwell in the Scottish Premier League. It's easy to make jokes about Scottish goalkeepers and to laugh at the quality of the Scottish top flight, but assuming that Celtic apart, the rest of the division is about the same quality as the bottom end of the Championship in England, that's still a standard way higher than Marshall's performances for Stoke would suggest he was capable of performing at.

There was only one thing for it. To restore the reputation of Gordon Marshall, I'd have to ask the people who watched him for these clubs and find out whether he truly was as bad as he seemed to be for Stoke. What follows is an account of my attempt to redress the balance.

Saving Gordon Marshall ... (Because he probably wouldn't be able to save himself!)

I start the search for Gordon Marshall by tracking down his current whereabouts – he's working as a goalkeeping coach at Aberdeen, and has worked at a number of top-flight Scottish clubs since retiring. It's clear to me from my initial research that Marshall's a highly respected coach, but it's not praise for his coaching skills that I'm intending to highlight – it's positives from his playing career.

My first internet search throws up a recent article from the *Daily Herald*. It was written as a preview for the 2017/18 Scottish League Cup Final between Celtic and Motherwell, and centres around Marshall not only playing for both clubs, but making howlers in two separate cup finals. The tone of the article is quite complimentary towards Marshall (it would be – he had agreed, after all, to provide the writer with a few quotes), but all things considered, this is not a good start.

Undeterred though in my mission to at least partly restore the reputation of the man, I head off to trawl Scottish football websites and forums – dark, grim corners of the internet that they are – for some positive opinions about Gordon Marshall. Fans don't need to be as diplomatic as journalists and I know I'll get a warts an' all view on any player, past or present, if I look in the right places.

As I wade through the various Celtic message boards looking for anything complimentary about Marshall, the true nature of this task became apparent to me.

'How he ever played for us is unbelievable.'

'A complete joke of a goalkeeper.'

'Absolutely diabolical.'

Worryingly, they were the only printable comments on the thread I found entitled 'Gordon Marshall'. The rest was a two-page assassination, albeit heavily based on his association with Rangers as a youngster as much as it was about his goalkeeping. All right, so Marshall – or 'The Hairdresser' as the Celtic fans call him, referencing his qualification as a barber (something I'd forgotten about until now) – was obviously never good enough for a fanbase as big and demanding as Celtic's, but perhaps he's thought of more fondly somewhere a little more forgiving, and less sectarian, like Kilmarnock?

In desperation for something positive to write about the man, if only to assuage my guilt, I tweet a request for comments about Marshall to a handful of Kilmarnock fans who at least look like they might be able to string a few sentences together. If they don't reply with something nice, I may have to resort to hoping that the big man's mum is still alive and getting something on record from her. He played 159 games for Kilmarnock: surely he can't have been as bad for them as he was for us, and, it appears, for Celtic as well?

Thankfully, someone soon comes to my rescue. A Kilmarnock fan tweeting under the name of 'The Murph' answers my prayers. Bearing in mind that up to this point, I've spent the whole of my Sunday morning trawling the entire worldwide web for something nice to write about our former goalkeeper, his tweet has me literally laughing out loud. Here it is folks, the most positive thing that anyone on the whole internet said to me about Marshall:

'We've certainly had worse goalies than him.'

Gordon Marshall, loathed by Celtic fans, derided by the Stoke faithful, but finally his reputation has been restored. Kilmarnock FC have apparently had *worse* goalkeepers than him.

Joysticks For Goalposts

With Joe Jordan in charge, the joy of attending matches was dissipating fast. Getting to the ground was a chore as well when you were 16 and nobody could drive. Some weeks we'd walk all the way from Newcastle, a four-mile hike that didn't seem as bad on the way down as it did on the way back up the almost vertical banks of Hartshill and Penkhull – inclines similar to those of Everest's summit. Other weeks, if Dad was feeling charitable, I'd get a lift own with him in the car. Some weeks, although it wasn't that often, we'd give the game a miss completely – something that would never have happened under Macari.

There was something else starting to distract us – football computer games. It seems ridiculous to admit that my mates and I sometimes missed the real thing in order to play a simulated version, but watching Jordan do things like play five men in defence at home to Bath City in the FA Cup was killing my buzz every Saturday. It made more sense to take a joystick round to someone's house and play *Kick Off 2* and *Sensible Soccer* rather than watch useless lumps like John Clarke (another awful Jordan signing) hoof the ball over the stand roof every time he attempted a clearance.

I've always loved football games. Even as a 40-year-old man I still play *FIFA* online, my reactions getting noticeably slower with each version that's released. Games weren't always that sophisticated though, and people of my age will no doubt have played games like *Pong Football*, *Footballer of the Year* and early management simulations like *Football Director*.

The other big names from the Amiga-dominated era of the early 1990s though were *Sensible Soccer* and *Kick Off 2*, probably the *Pro Evolution Soccer* and *FIFA* of their day, and entire school playgrounds were split by loyalty to one title over another.

Sensible Soccer's gameplay was beautifully simple, with a vertical scrolling pitch and a fairly limited number of ways that a goal could be scored. However, it was fast-paced, fun and addictive, and was also fully editable, featuring a list of surreal custom teams already edited into the game. This was where the fun lay, as teams of Mass Murderers took on a side of *Neighbours* characters among other highly unlikely match-ups. Regardless of any issues with graphics or realism, how could anyone fail to appreciate the sight of Harold Bishop slide-tackling Adolf Hitler?

To a 16-year-old with a highly developed sense of the absurd this was comedy heaven and I spent hours editing in all manner of daft teams. Rather than taking the usual option of controlling Stoke, most of the matches I played were with a side comprised of people who lived in our street, the star striker being Mrs Miller – remember her? Yep, the 90-year-old spinster who lived next door. In the unlikely event that you're reading this, Mrs Miller, that's why I sometimes couldn't help but smirk as I walked past you in the street. I wasn't cruelly laughing at your frail form, bent over and shuffling slowly along the road – I just couldn't stop thinking about you tossing your Zimmer frame aside to plant a diving header past Genghis Khan. I can only apologise for my youthful insolence.

Kick Off 2 was revolutionary at the time in the way that ball control had to be learnt and perfected, rather than passes automatically sticking to a player's feet, as had been the norm prior to this iconic title being released. As a result, the game was harder to master than *Sensible Soccer*, but a lot more rewarding once you were practised enough to embellish the basics with a few fancy dribbles and one-touch passing moves.

My mates and I were so obsessed with *Kick Off 2* that we formed a league, with home and away fixtures being played at each other's houses after school or at weekends. The home player was afforded the right to choose the game conditions – such as wind, weather and pitch type – which saw the lesser players in the league deliberately making the environment as awkward as possible to drag the better ones down to their level (a plastic pitch and high-wind combo being a particularly nasty one).

The Manchester City of the *Kick Off 2* league was a lad called Brooksy, who also used the devilish tactic of allowing his excitable boxer dog into the bedroom during games, and encouraged it to start sniffing around your bollocks as the match was going on. I think he finished the competition with a 100 per cent home record due to that bloody dog!

As PlayStations and Xboxes started to grow in popularity, these two games were replaced at the top of the gaming charts by *FIFA* and *Pro Evolution Soccer*, which have both improved year-on-year, seeing off a few other short-lived titles in the process to maintain something of a football game duopoly for the last decade.

I made the mistake a few years ago of downloading some old football games using one of the many emulators available on the internet, and soon realised that the magic lay solely in the memories that I had of them. At the time though, we were more than happy with these simple games and relied on a healthy dose of imagination to turn even the most primitive piece of programming into a capacity crowd at a Wembley cup final.

Writing this makes me sound and feel like an old man, but it saddens me to visit any message board dedicated to the modern football games and read all kinds of ungrateful, hysterical flouncing from spoilt, spotty brats, squealing displeasure because Lionel Messi has got the wrong colour boots on in the latest incarnation of whichever game they're playing. Well, guess what: back in the day of *Pong Football*, star players didn't wear boots, because they didn't even have any legs – or a head. They were just faceless bricks, moving up and down in a straight line ... a bit like watching Dave Bamber in real life.

Bertie's Return

As the season entered the home straight, Stoke had fallen out of the play-off picture and most of the crowd, those that weren't playing computer games at least, were dying with boredom every week.

Whoever the opposition were, Joe Jordan set his team up to not lose, which was an outcome he didn't often achieve. After a run of only seven goals scored in 14 matches between January and March, the crowd began to call for his head. Jordan responded by making three signings, which gave the side a much-needed boost and heralded the best football of his reign – not that the standard was ever particularly high.

First through the door was former favourite Wayne Biggins, who'd ended up following Lou Macari to Celtic after his controversial Barnsley move. Unbelievably, considering how good he'd been for us, Biggins was considered to be a waste of space by Celtic fans. His name still crops up in 'Worst Ever XIs' on their fans' forums, and he was, by all accounts, so desperate to get away from Celtic and return to Stoke that he reportedly sang 'Delilah' all the way down from Glasgow when the Scottish giants accepted our £100,000 bid!

'It was a bad move for me,' admits Biggins. 'There was upheaval at the club, the chairman was getting stick off the supporters, the players weren't behind the club – I thought it'd be a brilliant move for me at 33, but it didn't turn out that way. Looking back it was a mistake, but thankfully I got the chance to come back to Stoke under Joe Jordan.'

There was another Stoke legend who was having a difficult time north of the border as well. Rumours were rife that Lou Macari would soon be losing his job at Parkhead following Fergus McCann's takeover and the apparent failure of Macari and his team to improve the Bhoys' fortunes. I'm sure I wasn't alone in selfishly hoping that Celtic lost every single game they played to hasten Macari's departure and convenient return to Stoke at a time when our own manager was walking on ever-thinning ice.

For now though, Jordan was doing everything he could to curry favour – and, to be fair, there were few fans who weren't excited when Liverpool winger Mark Walters arrived on loan. Walters was 30 and probably just past his best when he came to Stoke, but this was still an incredible signing for us to make, even on a temporary basis. The final member of the trio was Micky Adams, who went under the radar a bit considering the status of the other two, but even at 33 he brought some energy and experience to a side that looked devoid of belief.

The upturn in Stoke's fortunes was immediate, and Stoke went on to win four of the next six, with all three of the new arrivals making an impact. Biggins had lost a bit of pace but still demonstrated that same class he'd displayed in his first spell, while Mark Walters possessed the sort of trickery we'd not seen since the days of Peter Beagrie. Unfortunately, Stoke had lost too much ground in that awful spell in January and February, and the play-offs were just too far out of reach for an unlikely end-of-season assault on promotion to materialise. Three draws ended the season and Stoke finished in tenth spot, only four points away from the final play-off position.

It was a position we'd have probably all taken back in August, meeting as it did, the club's objective to consolidate and build foundations for the future. There wasn't a Stoke fan alive though who didn't ponder the obvious 'if' scenarios. If Mark Stein hadn't left, If Lou Macari hadn't left, If we'd signed Walters and Biggins a month sooner.

Four points was nothing. We all knew that in the alternative universe where our two heroes had stayed, Stoke would have found themselves competing for a place at the very top of the English game. It wasn't to be though, but when news came through that Celtic had decided to sack Macari at the end of the season, we all breathed a sigh of joyous relief and waited for the inevitable to happen.

Only, it didn't.

What the hell were the board playing at? Macari was available again and other teams would soon snap him up; all we had to do was fire the dismal Jordan and we could go again. It'd be like Lou had never even left! What were we waiting for?

Whether it was a misplaced sense of loyalty, decency, call it what you will, or whether Peter Coates genuinely believed that the improved end-of-season form was Jordan turning the corner, I don't know. Whatever the chairman's reasons, Jordan would continue in his role as Stoke manager while we all looked longingly and pleadingly in the direction of the man we considered to be our true messiah.

The Messiah Returns

NOTHING can stir a football fan's emotions like change. Sometimes it's the desire for change: baying mobs banging on the stadium doors demanding the head of the manager, the chairman, the tea lady or anyone else we deem culpable for poor performance on the pitch. Even when a successful manager is departing, the concern is still tempered by the excitement of what a new man could bring to the team. The unknown seduces us with its exotic promises.

It's the same in the boardroom – fans love takeovers, always assuming that the incoming party will be an improvement on the last lot – benevolent fairy godmothers who'll throw cash over the first team squad like pixie dust, transforming them into world-beaters within weeks. Unless you're Manchester City, it rarely works out that way.

However, give us talk of new stadiums, new shirt colours or new badges and change can go and take a running jump. Even when the evidence is irrefutably pointing at change being vital for progression or, in some cases, survival, we cling stubbornly to the past – chuntering into our scarves about 'tradition'. This is the paradox of football support – we want to move forwards and backwards at the same time, discovering new horizons while remaining firmly rooted in the habits of the past.

The dawn of the 1994/95 campaign was dominated by the prospect of change. An acrimonious boardroom battle had ignited towards the end of the previous season when director Bob Kenyon began a campaign to oust incumbent chairman Peter Coates. Most fans instantly rallied around Kenyon's cause, drawn in by promises of investment in the team, seduced by the familiar fantasy of a new face in charge.

'Bob came in and seemed to want to take control of the club,' states Coates. 'He never made any offer, but he was very good at playing the media. He was the new kid on the block promising to make it all different.'

Meanwhile, the ugly reality of the Victoria Ground's dilapidated state meant that change one way or another was needed in order for Stoke to comply with the Taylor Report. Discussions about a new stadium on the Trentham Lakes site began to appear in the local press. It was only talk at first, then artists' impressions, then chief executive Jez Moxey and council leader Ted Smith talking about flagship developments and funding streams.

Some were excited by the prospect of a new start in a stadium fit for the new millennium, but many others weren't. Instead, the traditionalists clung to the architects' plans for a rebuilt Butler Street Stand and the prospect of seats hastily screwed into the existing concrete of the Boothen End. That was as much change as we could handle, thank you very much – the Victoria Ground is where we play and where we'll stay. Oh, and that modernised club crest you'll foist upon us in another five years' time? You can stick that up your arses as well.

On the other hand, most supporters knew that only a move made any sense. The Boothen End, the oldest part of the ground, was an eyesore, while the Boothen Stand was looking almost as tired. Neither of these stands could be expanded due to the residential areas that surrounded them, while that was also the case for the Stoke End, which had at least already been redeveloped in the early 1980s. Only the Butler Street Stand had sufficient land behind on which to expand – an absolute necessity given the reduced capacity that seating installed on to existing terraces would have brought about – but the proximity of the River Trent meant that the club would have had to finance the redirecting of the river and also cope with the loss of numerous car parking spaces that any expanded stand would have swallowed up.

Southern Supporters Club chairperson Monica Hartland summarised the situation when writing in *The Oatcake*, 'It [the Victoria Ground] is the ground which holds the record as being the oldest one in the league to have hosted professional football – and it is increasingly giving that impression.'

Hartland went on to detail not only the shocking state of the stadium exterior but also the turnstiles that were in need of replacement, the 'wholly unprofessional' offices, foyer and interiors, the 'appalling' toilets and the 'hideous, space-taking, incongruous floodlights'. All in all, it didn't make pretty reading, and anybody who took a long hard look at their surroundings couldn't have argued.

Around the country, new stadiums were being built in places like Middlesbrough, Sunderland and Derby. Remaining in a decaying ground for no reason other than nostalgia and convenience would have been a mistake, and deep down, everybody knew it. While some argued that a new ground would be a soulless structure of breeze blocks and plastic, and that supporters would be inconvenienced by the extra travel that would be necessary, it seemed a small price to pay for the potential that a new stadium would bring. This was a once-in-a-lifetime chance that Stoke couldn't afford to pass up.

Oatcake editor Martin Smith pointed out, 'What would future generations of Stoke supporters think of us if they learned that the reason they didn't get a new ground in 1997 was because it was too far to walk from the pub?!'

In many ways, the argument for a new modern stadium was clearer-cut than the argument for a change of ownership. Peter Coates in 1995 was by no means the multi-millionaire Peter Coates of the 21st century. His investment in the club was modest at best, transfer kitties were limited and the wage bill always prudent. Stoke's financial profile was undeniably that of a club treading water. The fans, as fans do, demanded more. Was Bob Kenyon the right man to realise their ambition? It was hard to know. Kenyon talked a good game, as you'd have expected him to, and made promises of substantial investment in the team – but did he have the financial power and clarity of vision to make a difference in the long run?

As a lifelong Stoke fan, there was no doubt that Coates wanted the best for the club. However, there were some who thought his passion for Stoke was outweighed by a desire to use the club as a convenient vessel to further his own business interests – namely Stadia Catering and Provincial Racing. The argument was that Coates was using his position as a football club chairman to build his network and business portfolio, eke out more influence and power for himself with the Football Association, while neglecting to invest in the team.

The calls for change became louder and louder the more that Kenyon spoke to the press. Eventually Kenyon challenged Coates to 'match my million' – a statement that sounded like the premise for an awful game show, possibly hosted by the late Keith Chegwin, but was actually a challenge for the incumbent chairman to put his money where his mouth was and prove that he, too, had the desire to move Stoke forward.

In many ways, Kenyon was in an easier position than Coates was. As the party seeking power, he could fire off promises like party poppers, give us the sexiest election manifesto possible, and then grin like a Cheshire cat as the supporters inevitably rallied behind his cause. I certainly did – making a crude 'Coates Out' banner with an old bedsheet and some of Dad's Ronseal. There was a reason those fence panels went rotten, Dad, but blame Peter Coates, not me.

Perhaps seeing my sad-looking homemade protest being passed around the Boothen End during the opening game against Tranmere prompted the chairman into action? So eager had I been to hold aloft my creation in the garage that the paint had run on several letters, lending the words the look of a badly designed horror movie video sleeve. 'Crikey, they're writing "Coates Out" in dripping blood,' the chairman might have said. 'I'd better do something!'

More likely was that he was beginning to find Kenyon an irritant, so by September, both Kenyon and fellow director Paul Wright had been voted off the board – vengefully booted into touch like rebel backbenchers by a spiteful prime minister. With the only interested party in boardroom Siberia, the protests against Coates began to lose urgency and vigour. What was the point exactly? If we were successful in forcing Coates to sell, who would want to take the club on?

Some fans had formed a pressure group, others had not renewed season tickets and there were various protests and boycotts being mooted on an almost constant basis. Nothing ever really crystallised though. There was widespread frustration with the board, but frustration rarely removes people from power. The raw anger that would explode from the stands and force the chairman to step down was still two years away.

If the dream was a Kenyon-led Stoke City, managed by the returning Lou Macari and playing in a redeveloped Victoria Ground, the reality seemed to be moving us in the opposite direction on all fronts. The board were showing no signs of getting rid of Joe Jordan, and the PR exercise to persuade the fanbase that a move would be for the best gathered pace with every passing week.

Putting aside sentimentality and the residual fear of the future that forms the character of Stoke-on-Trent, logically the move to Trentham Lakes did make sense. By moving, the club would be eligible for a grant from the Football Trust, would receive money from the sale of the Victoria Ground, and if embarking on the venture in partnership with the city council, would also be able to count on the local authority to stump up 50 per cent of the shortfall.

Then there were the logistical problems of a football stadium being situated in the middle of a town centre: even in the 1990s, parking was a nightmare, and the labyrinth of dark, terraced streets that surrounded the stadium was nirvana for those intent on causing trouble. As much as we loved her, the Victoria Ground *was* a tired old stadium that had been left behind in the '70s. Where once there was a modern ground to be proud of, now stood only an archaic monument to the past, ravaged by age and years of neglect. Initially, moving was presented merely as an option. In reality, it was the *only* viable option.

Macari's Return

The prospect of funding a new stadium had the Stoke board bringing in their own age of austerity years before George Osborne even dreamt of sealing up the government's piggy bank. Talk about operating with a smaller squad of higher quality players was not matched by the actions of Joe Jordan, who brought in a number of players on free transfers.

John Dreyer, an experienced centre-half, arrived from relegated Luton; midfielders Keith Downing and Jason Beckford joined from Birmingham, having only made a handful of appearances for the Blues the previous year; and finally Ray Wallace, the least famous of the Wallace brothers and an unexciting utility player, came from Leeds. As a collective, this didn't look like a small squad of high quality – it looked like a ragtag bunch of cast-offs who'd been found abandoned in a sack by the side of the motorway.

Of course, the board tried to redeem themselves by making a marquee signing to point to if anyone accused them of lacking ambition. Canadian striker Paul Peschisolido was the man to serve as the veneer that would cover a rotten transfer policy and a creaking squad.

A well-known figure due to his relationship with tabloid favourite and Birmingham board member Karen Brady, not to mention his impressive goalscoring record and photogenic boyband looks, Pesch was the sort of transfer to get fans excited. His reputation probably outweighed his ability, in truth, but on the surface this at least looked like a belated attempt to replace the much missed Mark Stein. The board claimed this to be a record signing, although that depended very much on their valuation of striker Dave Regis, who went the other way in the deal. Stoke's cash outlay on Peschisolido was no more than £280,000 and we'd also lost our best striker in the process. Whether that epitomised ambition was questionable.

Predictably, the season didn't start well. A fortuitous opening day victory over Tranmere and hard-fought draw at Burnley at least put some points on the board, but after a trio of defeats – including consecutive 4-0 losses at Reading and Bolton – there was a sense of inevitability about the fate that awaited Jordan.

It was an easy and obvious move by the board to quell the growing unrest, and probably one that should have been made before the start of the season: Jordan was sacrificed. The writing had been on the wall even longer than that 'Mills Out' graffiti, and Jordan had been reading it for months, describing Macari in his autobiography *Behind the Dream* as being a constant shadowy companion throughout his ten months as manager. Jordan knew exactly what had gone before him and who he was constantly being judged against – the only man the fans wanted to manage their team.

'God: supreme being, creator and ruler of universe; superhuman being worshipped as possessing divine power; idol; adored person' read the front cover of the next issue of *The Oatcake*. The dictionary definition, next to the personification of the Lord himself: Lou Macari.

Macari returned with Stoke having shaken off the pallor of Jordan's regime, the team briefly bursting with the old vibrancy again for a run of three straight wins. Stoke were in the top half of the table and the crisis seemed to be over, affording Macari the time to settle back into the hot seat and find his groove again with the pressure off.

The Central TV cameras were in town to capture the glorious occasion as West Brom provided an obliging supporting act on a wet Sunday afternoon at the Victoria Ground. The terrible weather didn't matter though – all that counted was that Stoke were going to give Lou a victorious homecoming, and inspired by a rare clinical performance in front of goal by Martin Carruthers (who notched twice), Stoke ran out 4-1 winners on a rain-soaked pitch.

'The players did everything I asked of them, which was to go out, work hard and get around the pitch,' said a beaming Macari following the final whistle. 'The fans will appreciate what they saw. They like to see players go out and earn their wages and that's what they saw this afternoon.'

It was like he'd never been away. And maybe, somewhere deep down, he knew he wouldn't be away for that long. With stunning prescience, Macari had actually told the *Evening Sentinel* on the day of his departure, 'If things do not go right for me at Celtic, and things do not go right at Stoke, and I had the chance to come back, I would not hesitate.' Clairvoyance was obviously another talent the little Scot had at his disposal alongside excellent motivational skills and an eye for a player.

Fortunately, for all of the poor signings that Jordan had made, the bedrock of the team that Macari had originally built was still present. The rearguard of Butler, Sandford, Overson and Cranson was intact, albeit two years older, while the midfield still benefitted from the ageless guile of Nigel Gleghorn and would also soon welcome back the classy Carl Beeston after 18 months on the sidelines. The rest of the side though had deteriorated since the title-winning season of two years previous. With his trusty lieutenants of 1992/93 all getting older and a lot of dead wood on the books, the difficulty of the situation that Macari had inherited would soon become apparent.

John Dreyer was my Pen Pal

Evening Sentinel Letters Page
Sentinel House
Bethesda Street
Stoke-on-Trent, ST1 3GN
July 1994

Dear Sir,
I have to say that I'm appalled by Stoke claiming that they are an ambitious club. Evidence to the contrary can be found simply by looking at the signings that have been made over the summer. For example, how can someone like John Dreyer improve a side that's supposed to be challenging for promotion? I admit that I've never seen Dreyer play before, but 30-year-olds on free transfers from clubs in lower divisions don't tend to be great players.
Yours sincerely,
N. James

They say the pen is mightier than the blanket daubed in creosote, and my contribution to the summer of discontent was not only limited to badly painted 'Coates Out' banners, but angry letters to the local paper. There's something rather quaint about angry letters in newspapers in 2018. Even though the rest of the world has found more instantly gratifying ways of unleashing their anger for no purpose other than to faintly amuse others, there does still remain a section of society who shun social media, preferring instead to enclose their vitriol in an A5 envelope, purchase a stamp, walk to a post box in the rain, then wait a week for their bitterness to appear in print.

Sometimes, and this is a real treat when it happens, particularly angry letters will elicit equally irate responses from other readers, all of whom will go through the same painstaking process of scribing their enraged feelings on to paper and trudging to a nearby post office to 'fire' off their riposte. These sort of miserable exchanges can go back and forth for weeks on end, like two men locked in a depressing war of attrition, throwing one rock a month at each other until one of them gives up or dies of boredom.

Nobody was disagreeing with my letter though. I'd like to think that when it appeared in all its snarky glory, a collective nodding of heads ensued among the *Sentinel*'s readership, which would have been far larger in 1994 than it is now, given that 25 years ago there were very few outlets in which to read the disgruntlement of our fellow citizens. Well, I say nobody – there was one man who read it and clearly didn't appreciate the thrust of my main argument. That was John Dreyer.

'I read a letter from a Stoke fan in the paper,' Dreyer stated indignantly in an interview some months later, 'saying that he'd never seen me play before. Well, the reason for that is that I've spent most of my career in the top division.'

Ooooh. Get you, John Dreyer.

I was strangely proud of myself in a way. Dreyer had read my letter and it had pissed him off! The only problem was that I'd since been proven to be talking absolute horse shit, because within weeks of actually *seeing* him play, it soon became obvious that he was a bloody good defender. Why Luton had let him go I have no idea, but he was performing so well at the start of the 1994/95 season that he regularly kept one of the imperious duo of Ian Cranson and Vince Overson out of the team.

There was only one decent course of action to take. I felt an overwhelming need to apologise to Dreyer. It probably should have been a letter to the *Sentinel* and a public acknowledgement of my idiocy, but I opted for a personal letter addressed to him at the club instead, basically saying sorry for jumping to the incorrect conclusion that he was crap, and congratulating him on an excellent start to the season.

That was it. My conscience was clear – I felt better about myself and the world in general. A couple of weeks later, I received a handwritten reply from Dreyer saying he appreciated me taking the time to apologise and that he could understand the fans' frustration. I can't remember what else he wrote, but it was a well-worded and thoughtful letter which struck just the right tone. Even though I was 16 at the time and not as easily star-struck as I would have been at a younger age, I remember being chuffed to bits at receiving personal correspondence from a Stoke City footballer and showed it to a couple of mates, as well as my dad and my grandad.

I thought nothing more of it until Christmas, when I opened a present from my grandad. There, in a frame, was a picture of John Dreyer – not even in his football kit but dressed in his civvies, striking a pose straight out of a Littlewoods catalogue. What the fucking hell is this, I thought?

Originally I suspected Grandad was just taking the piss, but when I found out that Stoke were actually stocking framed photographs of players in bad catalogue model poses, an equally likely scenario would have been my nan visiting the club shop on the lookout for presents, recalling my story and incorrectly assuming that this meant I'd be receptive to having some kind of homoerotic tribute to John Dreyer on my bedroom wall. Sadly, I'll never know. The frame came in useful though – sorry, John!

Despite Dreyer's best efforts, it simply wasn't happening for Macari on his second coming, at least not straight away. After beating West Brom, Stoke went six games without a victory. The board did, however, provide some cash for the manager to bring in winger Kevin Keen (£300,000) from Wolves, who immediately looked a smart acquisition and scored on his home debut with a superb finish in a 1-1 draw against his former club.

When Saturday Comes (Almost)

There was also a clutch of (surprise, surprise) free transfers too. However, with the season underway, Lou Macari had to think outside the box when it came to recruiting new talent.

He told *Duck* in 2017, 'Money was still really tight but we worked hard at getting good lads in to the club. We bought two players out of the army for 500 quid that season! One was a chef, and I don't know what the other one did! Justin Whittle and Gary Holt. They came into a squad that was already fit and worked hard, but those two soldiers blew them away on the training ground.

'We signed Larus Sigurdsson from a team in Iceland for next to nothing and he was the same – a beast in training. After his first day, some of the coaches told me that he was shockingly bad but that Iceland win over England in the Euros was no shock to me – I found them to be polite, professional, honest and fit lads – their attitude was better, too.

'Anyway, I was in the office after Larus's first session and some of my coaches said that he didn't understand the game and that his positioning was poor. The next day I was out there watching and I asked them, "Do you not think there's something there already without your coaching? He's as strong as an ox, has electric pace and he will recover from his mistakes, no bother."'

Less successful was the cameo of local non-league player Shaun Wade, 22, who arrived at Stoke on a month's trial from Newcastle Town and came off the bench late on in a 1-1 draw against Sheffield United. This was the kind of story that simply wouldn't happen in today's game, but Macari was always a risk-taker. Wade was a prolific scorer in semi-professional football but admits he was shocked by the jump in standard.

'It was totally different. Everyone was a lot fitter than I was used to. I thought I was fit, but until you go and do that ... I was well out of my depth fitness-wise, probably football-wise at first too. It takes you a month to settle in anywhere doesn't it?' he said.

Wade didn't get that long though. With Stoke's striking options limited, and Macari having seen enough potential in Wade to throw him into the first-team squad, the striker was named as substitute. He came on to a deafening roar from the crowd, proceeded to run around hell-for-leather for ten minutes and capped his one and only professional football appearances not with a goal but by kicking the opposition goalkeeper up the arse!

'By the time I'd got on it was over, I was off again!' says Wade. 'It is what it is though and it's good that people still talk about it.'

In some ways, Wade's story resembles the film *When Saturday Comes* but without the Hollywood ending or Sean Bean involved anywhere. Bean's film was the tale of a non-league player being plucked from obscurity to wear the colours of his local side (ironically in the film, Sheffield United) and of course, there's the predictable ending with the protagonist scoring a hat-trick in a cup final and everyone living happily ever after. Unfortunately, it was Wade's trial with Stoke that ended his hopes of a professional career.

'I did my cruciate in a reserve game,' he remembers. 'It took them six months to find out what was going on. Back then, nobody seemed that interested – you find yourself slipping down the pecking order and with my age and everything, it was probably a case of wrong place, wrong time.

'I went back to Newcastle Town after, and at first I was knocking goals in left, right and centre, then my knee went again. I had my cartilage on my other knee done and then after that I was in and out – fit for a week then injured for two. I had to pack it in really; I'd got to go on to a building site during the week, and you have to look after your family don't you, so it was one or the other. I was never the most skilful player – I was no Chris Waddle – I was all blood and guts and snot – a bit of a ramming rod, so once my physical attributes had gone, that was it. By 27 I was done.'

I ask Wade how he feels now looking back on how close he came to becoming a professional footballer.

'It's still a bit raw to be honest, even now,' he says. 'I don't think I really fulfilled my potential. I could have done more, but these things happen, don't they? There were other clubs interested in me at the time – Preston for one – and things might have worked out differently had I gone there, but I had a young family and those sort of things to consider so that was that, really.'

A Cult Classic

Macari was doing his best on limited resources, but the wins were often hard-earned and entertainment was thin on the ground. While my mates and I still attended all the games, our attention would often wander and we'd end up talking more about what we'd watched on TV the night before, with one show in particular often being the centrepiece of our conversations.

While I'm acutely aware that the phrase 'essential post-pub viewing' has a reduced relevance in these modern times of streaming on demand, back in the 1990s there was one (fairly) late-night show that had young men the length and breadth of Britain staggering home from the boozer, or in our case as under-age drinkers, staggering home from the car park at Festival Park, to tune in and get their weekly fix.

No, I'm not talking about *The Word* – unless watching desperate students drink pints of old ladies' piss was your thing – and I'm not even talking about the surreal soft porn madness of *Eurotrash*, but the legendary *Fantasy Football League*, starring David Baddiel and Frank Skinner, ably assisted of course by former professional gambler Angus Loughran, aka 'Statto'.

Fantasy Football League initially started on Radio Five and was presented by Dominik Diamond. It was based around the emerging concept of fantasy sports. In the programme, minor celebrities bid for their 11 players at an auction, and the concept was then used as a framework around which to discuss the week's football. Transposed to television and shot on a set designed to replicate the flat that Skinner and Baddiel had once shared in real life, the show was at its peak between 1994 and 1996, with a series of live specials also filmed for the World Cup in 1998 and the European Championships in 2004.

It soon became apparent that it wasn't the fantasy football element of the format that made the show work, but the chemistry between the two hosts, the affectionate goading of Statto and the surreal sketches that would crop up throughout. Many of the segments were recurring, with 'Phoenix from the Flames' being a particular highlight. This would involve Skinner and Baddiel roping in a footballer from past or present and attempting to recreate a famous moment from their career.

One of my personal favourites was the re-enactment of Jimmy Greaves catching a dog on the pitch in the 1962 World Cup. *Saint and Greavsie* had been a running joke on the show for years, and Skinner and Baddiel played them with gleeful irreverence in countless sketches. The latter's drink problem was often referenced in the mirth, something that reads as more problematic than it actually was given that Skinner himself was also a recovering alcoholic.

In the sketch, Greavsie recalls how he got on to his hands and knees and enticed the interloping dog over, only for it to promptly urinate all over him as he made a grab for it. 'Hey Jimmy,' quipped Frank with a twinkle in his eye, 'I bet that wasn't the first time you crawled home covered in piss.'

It was a brutal jibe but also delivered with affection, and Greavsie was obviously happy to be the butt of the joke. Ian St John was somewhat less enamoured by the comedians' portrayal of him, and the concept of the show in general. 'We were on the show once. They didn't tell us anything pre-show,' St John told *The Guardian*. 'I said, "I know what they're going to try and do, they're going to try and take the mickey out of us," and we were not prepared to have that ... it was probably the worst show they ever had.'

Taking the mickey was what *Fantasy Football* did though, and for every Greavsie – playing along with the joke – there was a St John, unhappy at having the piss ripped out of him on a weekly basis. The most infamous example was Nottingham Forest's Jason Lee, a striker who, with all the goodwill in the world, was way out of his depth as a Premier League player, and whose goalscoring ineptitude and unusual haircut both became running jokes, shoehorned into as many segments of the show as possible. The lampooning quickly spread from television to terrace, causing the sensitive, misfiring striker to comment that *Fantasy Football League* had shattered his confidence and ruined his career.

The Lee saga was perhaps a rare example of when the show overstepped the mark, and I think Skinner and Baddiel had got so carried away with the success of the joke that they'd missed the possible racial element to some of the sketches depicting him and his haircut. Generally though, the piss-taking was affectionate rather than acerbic.

It could be argued that *Fantasy Football League* was the seminal point in the so-called 'lad culture' that grew around it, clearing the way for the growth of publications such as *Loaded* and *FHM*, which in turn led the way for degenerative magazines like *Zoo* and *Nuts*, misogynistic 'comedians' like Dapper Laughs appearing on television and the lamentable concept of 'banter', where pretty much anything goes in terms of what's said and to whom on the basis that it's all just one big laugh.

Whether you think that the role of mainstream media is to shape and influence the times in which we live or to reflect them is a wider debate, but no one can argue that *Fantasy Football League* looked, sounded and to all intents and purposes *was* just a few ordinary blokes talking naturally about football in the way that blokes do and probably always have done.

At the time it was a revelation to see that on television, as what had come before was the usual array of talking jackets, lined up in front of the cameras, speaking in clichés. *Fantasy Football League* ripped all that apart. Overnight, Saint and Greavsie were sat in their sterile TV studio looking sad and irrelevant. Now we had blokes on the screen who talked like we did. More articulate, funnier versions of us perhaps, but ordinary blokes like us all the same, on television and providing content that would not only be talked about in the nation's pubs and football grounds, but would go as far as actually shaping terrace humour.

Nothing that has been broadcast since has quite captured or shaped football humour quite like *Fantasy Football League* did in its heyday. Sky's *Soccer AM* was well thought of at first, in the days of Tim Lovejoy and Helen Chamberlain, but its broadcast time meant that it was impossible for it to replicate the biting edge of the show that was its main influence. Nevertheless, Frank Skinner doesn't feel that there's any place for *Fantasy Football League* in the modern world, and that it was a show very much of its time.

'I like that people [still] like *Fantasy Football*,' he told Digital Spy in 2014. 'But you don't need it anymore. *Match of the Day 2* is quite comic, and there's *Soccer AM* and *A League of Their Own*. Saint and Greavsie were the two pioneers of football comedy, but we continued the tradition. There's almost no serious stuff. Even on Sky they feel they have to do gags in the punditry bits. I think it's no longer required.'

It's probably a good thing that neither Skinner nor Baddiel feel inclined to bring the show back, and personally I don't feel that it would suit the modern age as well as it did the more relaxed football (and television) landscape of the 1990s. By its very nature the show had to walk a fine line at times, especially during the live broadcasts, and in an age where offence is quickly taken, and one mistake is enough to destroy a career, it's probably better to leave the show as a treasured memory of a time when such a format genuinely seemed like it was cutting-edge stuff.

One thing's for sure though, I've never seen Brigitte Nielsen on any other football show, drunkenly staggering around with her breasts half-hanging out. 'Sit down Brigitte, you're making a twat of yourself,' quipped Baddiel at the time. I don't care what Skinner says, *Match of the Day 2* has never been as entertaining as *that*!

The Legend of Keith Scott

By the turn of the year, Stoke looked very much set for another unexciting season in mid-table. Wins would usually be followed by losses, places gained in the table one week would be given up the next as Stoke bobbed around in the no-man's land between 10th and 14th. We needed something to excite us – even something like the memorable events of Selhurst Park on 25 January 1995.

It might seem odd to talk about this in what is essentially a book about Stoke City, but there have been few moments in football quite as iconic as the moment that Eric Cantona launched himself into the crowd at Crystal Palace, aiming a kung-fu kick at a supporter who'd been abusing him from the touchline. A true 'where were you?' moment for supporters of any club.

While commentators berated Cantona for his unprofessionalism and ill discipline, I absolutely loved him for what he did, the same as I loved Zinidene Zidane for his headbutt in the 2006 World Cup Final. Both were moments when the usual codes of socialised behaviour that we expect in such high-profile settings were transcended by the rawest primal human emotion – the urge to seek instant vengeance on someone who's wronged us. In that moment, something snapped within Cantona, prompting what, on one hand, seemed an absurd reaction, yet on the other – taken outside of the constructed confines of what we consider to be the appropriate responses of sportsmen – it made perfect sense.

Walk up to someone in the street and insult their race, religion or parentage and what would the expected reaction be? A kick in the throat would be the least you'd deserve. Walk up to someone in the pub and call his mother a whore? In Stoke you'd be on the floor before you'd uttered the last syllable.

I'm not a fan of Manchester United – I can't stand them in fact – but I'll always make an exception for Cantona, as who could fail to be entertained not only by his sublimely arrogant style of play, but also by his unwavering desire to follow only his own desired path? Even the humble shirt collar was utilised as a token of dissent to the mundane conformists. Permanently upturned, a message delivered with three inches of cotton – I am not like these other men.

That was what we needed at Stoke. Something mercurial, talismanic. We could live without karate-kicking the crowd or the stuff about the seagulls following the trawler, but the ability of someone, anyone, to get us off our seats again was what was missing. With perfect timing, Macari announced we were in for a new striker, and maybe this would be the man to provide a touch of Cantona-style unpredictable genius to the Victoria Ground. Step forward Mr Keith Scott.

'Lou Lands a Great Scott' wrote Ian Bayley in the *Sentinel* – possibly deserving an award for the most inaccurate headline in the history of journalism. However, it wasn't just local journalists under the impression that Scott would be the answer to Stoke's striking difficulties. Macari too seemed to be convinced that he'd found the right man. 'Everyone knows we've been looking for a strong front-runner for some time,' said the manager. 'We believe Keith fits the bill.'

I'm aware that in a previous chapter, I described Dave Bamber as the worst striker I'd ever seen don the red and white stripes. Believe me, Scott runs, or should I say jogs, him a close second. Scott was more Eric Morecambe than Eric Cantona. He wouldn't have ever moved fast enough to launch a karate kick at the crowd, and would have possibly ended up booting himself in the face if he'd tried it.

Having watched Scott make his debut against Middlesbrough, if I were Macari I'd have been tempted to try and get my money back under the Trade Descriptions Act. Scott looked as much like a professional striker as my gran did.

Of course, this is all the sort of grossly unfair stuff that overweight, armchair expert fans like me assume we have the right to say about professional footballers. Having said all that, I have no doubt that if Scott had wandered on to one of the Sunday league pitches I used to trundle around each week, he'd have absolutely taken the piss out of me and every other player on there. To put things further into perspective, Scott was a prolific lower-league goalscorer for Wycombe Wanderers, so much so that Swindon Town took a gamble on him and paid £375,000 to take him into the Premier League – where he scored for them at Anfield of all places.

Football is a game of fine margins at the top. The differences between a good player and an average player are minuscule, and all sorts of factors can influence whether a player is perceived as good, bad or the worst player of all time. Whatever the reasons for his woes at Stoke, Scott looked like a man who wanted to be somewhere else every time the whistle went at three o'clock on a Saturday afternoon. Some of the chances he missed were scandalously bad: shots from two yards out blazed wildly over the crossbar, headers from virtually on the line missed when it was easier to score. Before too long, it looked like he didn't even want the chances because everyone in the ground, including himself, knew he'd miss.

Fans all like to think that if we were blessed with the opportunity to wear the shirt of whichever team we support, we'd run ourselves into the ground and leave nothing on the pitch at the end of the game. That's what we tell ourselves, but anyone who's played football at even a semi-decent standard knows what it feels like to be drained of confidence on a pitch – to know deep down that sometimes you're out of your depth.

I often experienced this playing for a team that regularly finished near the bottom of the lowest division in one of the local six-a-side leagues. Most weeks we faced teams who were about as rotten as we were, but on the occasions that we faced league leaders or – God forbid – teams from higher divisions in the cup, many of whom used to feature a few semi-professional players, the difference in class was so noticeable that the game, from first minute to last, ceased to be enjoyable. I hated these sort of matches when I'd be up against someone bigger, quicker, stronger and more skilful than me. I didn't want the ball, because I knew that any mis-control would be pounced on and I'd be left looking and feeling stupid.

I'd hide in these matches, hoping that the ball stayed well away from me, and doing only the most basic things if it didn't – hacking it into touch like it was a bomb, usually. If there'd been more than one man and a dog watching in these kind of games, I'd have had the crowd on my back, no question.

If I imagine what that feeling of inadequacy would be like accompanied by 15,000 people yelling abuse at me, well, I can barely comprehend what it would be like. Forget all the badge-thumping bravado of fans, I'd have done exactly what Scott seemed to do out there once he realised he was out of his depth – plod dejectedly through the 90 minutes and hate every second of it.

Having invested £300,000 in his new striker though, Macari felt compelled to give him a fair chance, and consequently Stoke's results crashed through the floor while Scott was leading the line. Between January and early April Stoke only won three games out of 16, and what had looked like an uneventful season suddenly started to take on the appearance of a relegation battle.

Crowds started to drop as well. Only 9,700 watched a dismal 2-0 defeat to Portsmouth in February, complete with the usual missed sitter for Scott. A 1-0 loss to Reading a month later was even worse. Stoke were destined not to score, and it wasn't only the usual villain of the piece Scott passing up chance after chance – Martin Carruthers was also up to his old tricks again. After this game, Stoke plummeted to 20th place in the league and only managed to scramble away from the relegation zone thanks to a couple of hard-fought, grinding wins around Easter.

For the first time ever, the unthinkable started to happen. While no one would have ever called for his head, people began to grumble about Macari. Where was the verve and panache the team had shown during his first spell in charge? Why was he persisting with the beyond-awful figure of Scott? The manager hadn't helped himself when signing John Gayle for £70,000 – another target man who was about as mobile as a double garage.

This smacked of panic, and something drastic was needed to pull Stoke out of trouble.

The Anglo-Italian Cup

In a league where fixture congestion is still an oft-repeated complaint of managers, it seems nonsensical that the football authorities would foist possibly the most bizarre cup competition in the world on to clubs already playing a 46-game league season. However, that's exactly what they did in reviving the Anglo-Italian Cup: a long-forgotten tournament that ran for four seasons in the early 1970s.

Originally the cup was introduced as a close-season competition for clubs in England and Italy to generate players' wages over the summer, but was scrapped in 1973 due to a lack of interest. It was briefly revived a few years later as a semi-professional competition, but again didn't last long due to the obvious logistical problems in taking amateur sides all the way to Italy to play football matches in front of virtually no spectators. In 1992, the Football League decided to bring the competition back for a third time as a replacement for the Full Members' Cup – another pointless trophy that served little purpose other than to clog up the fixture list.

The format this time involved English clubs playing a preliminary round between themselves, with the qualifiers progressing to a group stage where they would play four games against Italian sides. The two English teams with the most points from the group stage would face off in a two-legged semi-final and then face their Italian equivalents in a one-off final game. To make things more complicated, the format was tweaked every year depending on the number of teams who bothered to enter. By 1994/95 many didn't.

Sensing that a day out at Wembley would generate some money, Stoke took the competition seriously – in theory anyway; on the pitch the players sometimes looked about as hurried as a man jogging to the shop for a newspaper. The previous season's tournament hadn't been a great success for the Potters and the team had lost both games in Italy (3-0 to Padova, 2-1 to Pescara) in front of small crowds. Even so, the first game managed to spark violence as a large group of Italians attacked Stoke fans in Padua.

One supporter, a Stoke fan from Liverpool known to many only as 'Scouse', was stabbed and left hospitalised.

'I travelled on the supporters' club coach,' recalls Scouse, 'the plan being to book into the hotel, look around the town, go to the game, overnight stay in Padua, drive to Bologna for the San Marino v England World Cup qualifier, then home after that game. Somewhere along the way, the venue of our game was changed – something to do with accommodating an Italian under-21 match – but we were assured there'd be a coach to take us to this new venue. When we got there it was like a non-league ground: one reasonably-sized stand opposite one covered terrace that 300 Stoke fans were housed in.'

On the pitch, Stoke put in a dreadful display and lost 3-0. However, even during the game there were signs that things could turn ugly.

'There was some trouble by the exit gates that suggested the Italians were trying to get at us, but there didn't seem to be that much concern among the Stoke fans at that point,' says Scouse. 'Anyway, the game ended and we headed back to Padua. On arrival back at the hotel, a few were warning to take care as the Italian Ultras were thought to be back in town. A quick change of clothes, and as some were dragging their feet about getting ready, three of us headed out towards the town square.

'Hindsight is a wonderful thing, but at the time what struck me was how quiet and deserted the streets were. The first small bar that took our fancy was in a passageway leading to the main square. We opened the door but it was full and less than inviting, so we closed the door again and moved on. Over the years, whenever Padova has come up, I always wonder whether we'd have been safer in there or if we'd already given ourselves away.

'We entered the square from the bottom right and there was a large group of about 20 Italians in the top left-hand corner blocking the exit from the square. We knew we were in trouble at that point. Then we saw movement in the shadows of the colonnades opposite – there were even greater numbers there.'

Scouse understandably requests that the finer details of the attack itself are left out of his account. He describes to me though how the Italians descended on the small group of Stoke fans, armed with metal bars and knives, about the terrible injuries he sustained, about staring into the mirror in the hospital afterwards and not recognising his own reflection, about the lack of consular help, about the fruitless search for a law firm to try and seek justice for what happened to him. However, he also talks about the kindness of the Italian nurses, the friends, fellow supporters and patients who supported him after the attack and, at the time, also saved him from greater harm.

'When you're massively outnumbered, it's a fine balance knowing when to bluff and when to take flight,' he reflects. 'Often in those circumstances you'll be given nothing more than a passing blow. But this time it wasn't to be. Perhaps I was slow off the mark, perhaps I froze, perhaps I didn't want to be the first to flee. All questions I've asked myself over the years.'

Eight years on, the bitterness from Heysel was still present in the Italian psyche. Clearly, travelling to Italy in small number, or any number, was fraught with danger and the potential for revenge attacks, especially considering the persistent knife culture of the Italian terrace, lent an air of tragic inevitability to the assaults that took place on Stoke fans that night. English teams had only just been allowed back into European competition in the early 1990s, so to set up a competition between clubs from the two nations involved in the tragedy leading to the expulsion was foolhardy in the extreme.

Neither Italian nor English fans were interested in the competition, and attendances in both countries were extremely low. The sides entering the tournament were all from the second tier of their respective nations, so half of the teams we played – Cremonese, Piacenza, and Cesena – sounded to us like products you'd find on the pasta aisle in Sainsbury's. We hadn't heard of them and they hadn't heard of us. What was the point?

The one memorable experience from the tournament was the visit of Fiorentina. The Florence side had been relegated from Serie A the previous year, but still boasted internationals such as Stefan Effenberg and Gabriel Batistuta in their ranks. At a time when facing European opposition meant a fixture against Wrexham, this was a one-off opportunity to see Stoke play a European giant, albeit one that had fallen on hard times.

Stroking the ball around with panache, resplendent in their iconic purple kit, for older fans the visitors would have brought back memories of those nights under the floodlights against Kaiserslautern and Ajax – the days when Stoke had genuinely earned the right to face the famous sides of Europe and did so on an equal footing. This was different, but while the circumstances that led to Stoke v Fiorentina was a single game in a meaningless joke of a competition, the night itself boasted enough glamour and allure to bring 8,000 fans to the Victoria Ground to witness an entertaining 0-0 draw.

Even the players themselves seemed to be taken aback a little at facing a side like Fiorentina. 'We were a bit lethargic in the first half,' admitted Ian Cranson following the match. 'It was a question of getting used to the different pace and style of the game. We took the game to them more in the second half though and almost got our rewards.'

Stoke upped their game in the 1994/95 competition. A 3-1 away win over Udinese looks like an incredible result now, even though the Italian side weren't the established Serie A outfit they are today, being more of a yo-yo club in the '90s – the Italian version of West Brom. Two other victories and a draw against Italian sides meant Stoke qualified for the semi-final and a fixture against Notts County for the right to play at Wembley.

Two absolutely dismal games ensued, a two-legged nightmare that ended scoreless after 210 minutes of football. I pity the poor sods who were there to witness it, but unless Italian giants were in town, I wasn't interested! I did listen to the penalty shoot-out on the radio, and would have inevitably jumped on the bandwagon had we got to Wembley, but it wasn't to be. We lost 3-2 on penalties and Notts County went to the final instead, where they beat Ascoli 2-1 in front of only 17,000 fans.

The following season was the last for the Anglo-Italian Cup and it was finally put out of its misery. On this occasion, Stoke failed to get out of the group stage after drawing all four games – not that anyone cared. Taking a place in the final though were Port Vale, who at least had the prestige of playing the mighty Genoa for the trophy. However, any jealousy we might have felt changed into mocking laughter as the classy Italians went 5-0 up inside an hour, eventually allowing Vale to sneak two late goals, probably through pity. I've tried to find the attendance figure for this game in order to take another cheap shot at our rivals, but none of the usual websites seem to have a record of it. Rather than do some proper research I can only assume this means there were no people present whatsoever – which probably isn't that far from the truth!

City Get Off Scott-Free

'Who's the best player in training?' *The Sun* asked Paul Peschisolido in a Q&A session.

'Nigel Gleghorn,' he replied. 'Runs all day and doesn't break sweat.'

'And the worst?'

'Keith Scott. Talks all day and does break sweat.'

Brilliant. And an accurate summary of where the problem lay. The phrase 'carrying a chip on one's shoulder' is said to derive from the old American bar room practice of placing a wood chip on the shoulder and daring others whom you want to fight to knock it off. There'd have been a queue five miles around the block to knock off what Scott was carrying on his shoulders – namely, his head. Eventually, even Macari had to face the truth that his almost perfect transfer record was now tarnished. There was no alternative but to remove Scott from the team and hope that one of the other options could step up and find some form from somewhere.

Peschisolido had done well overall but wasn't prolific – he'd go on to finish the season with 13 goals, but the question was who should partner him. Simon Sturridge was too similar in stature to Pesch and was injury-prone, Martin Carruthers had a case of the yips every time he got near the goal, while John Gayle was Keith Scott minus the attitude. It was time to gamble and so in came a Portuguese striker – Jose Andrade, or was it Zay Angola? This man had so many different names, he was either a spy or under a witness protection scheme. It didn't matter – he was with us on trial and Macari, showing the same sense of bravery he'd employed with other triallists, threw him into action and (you'd imagine) crossed his fingers, closed his eyes and hoped everything would turn out fine.

After 27 minutes of his debut, Jose Andrade had opened his account and notched a vital equaliser against fellow strugglers Bristol City, now managed by our old friend Joe Jordan. If there was one thing that Jordan wasn't going to do in an away game at 1-1 it was attack, and so Stoke continued on the front foot – the visitors pretty much hanging on to what they'd got. With only a minute left to play, Peschisolido popped up to strike a winner and all but condemn Jordan to relegation, which is exactly what he (and we) would have suffered had he still been in charge of Stoke. It hadn't been plain sailing since his return, but suddenly Macari's side looked like they believed again.

The victory was followed by a 1-0 win at another struggling side, Swindon. The downside was that our new hero, Andrade, broke his leg, leaving Macari with the same set of tried-and-tested failures that he had to choose from before the mysterious Portuguese triallist had arrived from nowhere. At least there was daylight between Stoke and the relegation trapdoor now.

Despite a typically dismal defeat to Port Vale in the Potteries derby – a habit that was becoming more than annoying – Stoke recorded a further two victories. The first was a 4-3 thriller over Millwall, and included another late winner, this time from Kevin Keen. The season – a forgettable one in truth – ended with a 3-2 win at Kenilworth Road over Luton, a late goal again clinching it. The scorer? Keith Scott!

From having his management questioned by the more critical elements of the support and those with exceptionally short memories, Macari finished the season by winning the April Manager of the Month award. Stoke finished 11th, a position that looked far more comfortable than it was, and we also managed to overtake Port Vale in the process.

All's well that ends well, maybe, but the signs were there that a squad overhaul was urgently needed. If Macari planned on approaching the board, cap in hand, and asking for some cash for transfers, he had another thing coming. Despite making an operating profit for the first time in years, every bit of revenue appeared to be heading into the pot marked 'New Stadium'. When it came to a transfer kitty, Stoke hadn't even got the money to buy the pot. It promised to be a difficult summer.

Season 1995/96
The Year of the S.A.S.

THE longest year in history is 1995. For some people in Stoke at least, it never seems to have ended. Dads who were there, man, 23 years ago still sport Liam Gallagher scowls and haircuts, and even their own kids are following suit – children born five years or more after the release of *Definitely Maybe* are all 'Mad fer it, our kid'.

That the remnants of 20-year-old fashions still remain visible in Stoke and cities like Stoke doesn't only evidence a cultural void in modern society, it also suggests that Stoke's a place that prefers its culture packaged up elsewhere and imported. What are the lads up to in Manchester? We'll have some of that.

In a modern world where culture beyond the most anodyne mainstream pap has to be sought out and sifted for, it's sad that many people don't seem to have the time, or maybe the inclination, to do just that. Most would rather stick with what they know until someone from the big city comes along and shuffles us all along towards the sign marked 'evolution'. Nobody's done that for two decades though. That's why Oasis tribute bands still do so well round here.

We might have only been bystanders at someone else's party, but the years between 1994 and 1996 were the last time when the average man in the street felt like something was happening in Stoke-on-Trent. People were listening to the same bands – to Oasis, Blur, Pulp, Supergrass; people were reading the same books – Irvine Welsh and Alex Garland novels flew around college and university campuses; people at least *knew* of Damien Hirst and Tracey Emin. Britpop might well have started as an idea in the columns of the London music press two years prior or, depending on whose opinion you're reading, may have had its origins in the summer of baggy and The Stone Roses in 1990, but wherever the place and whenever the time in which the movement's origins lay, by 1995 it seemed that music, literature, art and football were all part of the same common language.

That's how it *seemed*, at least. Or maybe blokes of my generation say and write crap like that because it's a way of justifying the laziness of choosing empty nostalgia over the effort required to keep pace with today's cultural conversation.

'I don't listen to new music. All crap innit?'

'I haven't read anything either. Books aren't as good as they used to be.'

'I hate modern football.'

'I don't watch any of these new films.'

'What's art?'

Many of us are guilty of that at times, myself included, and it's too easy to lose touch when there's so much noise to sift through and not enough time to do it. Some people give up entirely, others try but find that they're listening or reading in isolation – not enough people are discovering the same things at the same time for art of any kind to become the cultural and social currency that we once took for granted.

Twenty years on, there's a modern sneering that Britpop as a movement was little more than a regurgitated sliver of the 1960s, and I wouldn't exactly demand that anybody making such a claim put down their pint and step outside immediately. However, at least there was an array of shared reference points, even if the array was a series of slight variations of the familiar white-boys-playing-guitars theme and most of them sounded like The Kinks.

While many people indulged no further than buying a couple of Oasis or Blur tapes from the local petrol garage, the spotlight that hit this small handful of juggernaut acts was powerful enough to illuminate the odd and the obscure operating at the periphery – the likes of Super Furry Animals and Spiritualized for example, great bands who might have been ignored in any other era.

Regardless of Britpop's historical cultural relevance, for once it seemed like Stoke-on-Trent wasn't being left behind. We might not have been at the centre of the room, holding court and setting the agenda, but we were at least in the building and at the party. Venues like Trentham Gardens and Kings Hall opened their doors to music fans again.

Platinum-selling acts like Radiohead, Manic Street Preachers and Cast all played in Stoke during this period, and the smaller venues like The Stage and The Wheatsheaf were getting in on the act too, hosting the Second Division of British music: Mansun, The Longpigs, Shed Seven et al deeming Stoke to be worthy of a visit on their British tours.

It was a good time to be 17 or 18 years old and at college or university in the city. The local music scene was healthier than it had been for some time too. Local gigs were well attended, and The Stage's 'unsigned' nights seemed like events rather than bills consisting of the same bands going through the motions of selling tickets to small groups of friends and family members attending only through a sense of obligation.

The whole nation seemed to be moving forwards, culturally and politically, excitement and hope building at the imminent end of Tory rule as voters flocked to support Tony Blair and New Labour; Blair sensed the zeitgeist and allied himself with the names and faces of Britpop, talking with faux-laddishness of Newcastle United and Alan Shearer in interviews, positioning himself as a vote for culture, for sport, for the man on the terrace and the kids at the Oasis gig.

It'd be useful for narrative symmetry to say that following Stoke City carried the same sense of excitement and promise: that something was happening, that we were part of the wider conversation, that guys from all these bands, the new breed of alternative comedians and the cool, new actors off the telly were sat on Frank Skinner and David Baddiel's sofa on *Fantasy Football League* talking about players from our team. Or that maybe we'd be high-profile enough for someone to get into a football argument with the Gallagher brothers on our behalf via the pages of *Loaded* or *NME*, but, of course, we weren't. We were as crap and as hopeless and as irrelevant as ever.

Maybe that's a more suitable narrative though, because what's more Stoke City than managing to be the only blight in the life of the youth of Stoke-on-Trent? Remaining stubbornly useless as everything else suddenly seemed to become exciting is a very Stoke City thing to do. And that's certainly what we were doing. By the end of the season, Sky would bid £670m for the rights to televise Premier League games for another four years – over double the value of its previous deal. Many clubs were falling over themselves to get in on the action, spending money on new players to try and get a seat at the big table. Stoke didn't seem arsed at all about any of it.

There was absolutely nothing for Lou Macari to spend and the fans, even accounting for the issue of the potential new ground, wanted to know why.

The Squad

Jump forward to 2018 and I'm stood in a pub with Lee Hawthorne, assistant editor of *Duck*, *The Oatcake*'s baby brother in the fanzine world. Lee's roughly the same age as me and has been writing for fanzines for years – attempting to start, in his own words, a 'dreadful' one when he was just 15 that lasted a mere two issues. He's been contributing regularly to *The Oatcake* and *Duck* in the 25 years since and is also working on a book aimed at the football nostalgia market. His speciality is tracking down 1990s footballers and interviewing them, something I've been doing a fair bit of in recent months too.

A Champions League match plays on the pub's television screen, but neither of us are watching it properly. We're both submerged in the '90s zone, discussing the peculiar psychological effect that results from spending virtually all of your free time with your head in a decade that ended nearly 20 years ago.

The present somehow stops being present, life becomes a series of images that pass before your eyes, just like these footballers on the screen are doing as you spend more time than is healthy pondering where players like Justin Whittle and Dave

Kevan are, and acting like some kind of saddle-sniffing stalker to try and get a few good quotes from them.

Then there's the disorientating experience of having spent so long writing about a particular season that it almost becomes the present. If someone had asked me at the end of last week after a particularly heavy session of writing and research who the Stoke manager was, I'd have probably answered 'Lou Macari' and would be able to reel off the results from 1994/95 more easily than I could recall how our current side got on last Saturday.

'There's a line in the *Trainspotting* sequel that sums it up,' says Lee. '"You're a tourist in your own youth." That's exactly how I feel.' We talk about why we're doing what we're doing: picking at the psychological malaise that leads you to wallow in times past to escape an unsatisfactory present, but we also swap stories and possible leads to old footballers like a pair of anorak-wearing saddos swapping train numbers on a platform at Stoke station.

We get on to the defence. I don't need to explain who 'the defence' are, do I? It can only be four names: the lads who Macari put together in 1991. The guys who served the club for the next five years as the regular backline, the odd intrusion from interlopers like John Clark notwithstanding. Three of them were either into or just on the cusp of their thirties when Stoke won the title, but four years later they were still around and expected to provide the foundation for a Stoke team a division higher.

'I can't get hold of Ian Cranson at all,' I explain. 'I've tracked him down to working for the local authority and have his direct e-mail address, but I just keep getting his out of office. I don't even know if he's still working there to be honest.'

Lee has a contact who is a friend of a friend who might work with him. Might. This is what it's come to. Sending e-mails to strangers on the basis they *might* know someone. In 1995/96, Ian Cranson, a man who'd suffered injury throughout his career, was 32 and picking up more strains and tears with every game he played.

Vince Overson. Captain. Leader. Legend. 'Massive Fucking Unit' was even older at 34 and starting to add the weight that naturally creeps on to certain types of physique with the passing of time. Lee met him a couple of years ago when our man was employed at Carlisle. He's dropped off the radar since then though, which takes some doing when you're the size he is!

He was always my favourite though, Vince – I even had a mini-bust of his head sitting in my bedroom. Yes, really. This four-inch high horror show looked more like Frankenstein's monster than our club captain, but as Overson was such a legend in my eyes, and I obviously didn't realise how weird this gift was, his tiny eyeless head sat atop my bookcase for a good while, silently surveying his new kingdom of unwashed teenage underpants, empty Pot Noodles and a collection of suspiciously crusty gym socks stuffed under the bed. Christ, it's no wonder I couldn't get laid.

Moving on, Lee Sandford was the baby of the bunch. At 27, he was probably at his peak as the 1995/96 season approached. Lou Macari felt he would have played for England had he been more disciplined off the field, but Sandford was still good, even if, as rumour had it, he liked the odd lager in his down time.

Sandford is easy enough to track down – he has his own website and works as a financial adviser, offering advice on the stock market. I haven't tried to contact him. He doesn't fit the profile of ex-players who seem like they'd have time to talk about the good old days. That's just something you sense when you've been moving in the murky circles that we both have.

The one we're both intrigued by is right-back John Butler. He was the first one to leave Stoke – the first of the gang to die. Not literally thank goodness, but he joined Wigan Athletic on a free transfer, which is pretty much the same thing. 'A few people I've spoken to have told me things about John Butler,' explains Lee, 'that just don't match up with the image of him that you got from watching him play football. He was supposed to be an absolute pisser on team nights out – a bloke who would do absolutely anything once he'd had a few beers. Drunken fire-eating and all sorts, I was told. I don't know how true it is, but how do you go from being a seven out of ten every week full-back, who works as a van courier now, to drunken fire-eating? It doesn't make any sense.'

'Have you managed to track him down yet?' I ask.

'Not yet. All I know is that he lives in Wigan and drives a van.'

'Not much to go on is it?'

'No, but I do have a list of van couriers in Wigan.'

I think he's joking. Is he joking? I'm not sure. This is the level of obsession that you can reach once your brain sees finding a particular ex-footballer as a puzzle that needs completing.

Without Butler in the squad, there was no alternative for Macari but to promote understudy Ian Clarkson to first-choice right-back. He wasn't very good but there was no one else. It's a good job that Clarkson stayed fit all season (he ended up making 43 appearances that year) because he literally was the only right-back at the club. The same for Sandford at left-back, where there was no natural understudy and no money to buy one.

John Dreyer, another golden oldie at 33, suddenly seemed to be out of favour, despite showing excellent form whenever he was selected. Back in stalker mode, I track John down to non-league Ware FC. Appropriately named I guess, and the answer is it's in deepest Hertfordshire. The team play in the Bostik League. There are jokes to be made here, I know.

I fire off an e-mail to the club secretary, jokily making reference to my letter to John all those years ago and asking if their manager can give me a call. The secretary, a chap named Stephen King, although I assume it's a different one, responds and seems faintly amused by it. He assures me that John will drop me a line soon. He doesn't though – he's probably scared, I reckon. Perhaps I shouldn't have mentioned the picture frame as well?

Making up our defensive options were the two rookie centre-backs that Macari signed the previous season. Icelandic youngster Larus Sigurdsson and ex-army man Justin Whittle. We knew that with the creaking limbs of Overson and Cranson taking the first team spots, both understudies were likely to be getting plenty of action. Playing in front of either Mark Prudhoe or Carl Muggleton in goals, they'd need to get up to speed very, very quickly.

'What about Gleghorn?' I ask Lee. 'Have you managed to get hold of him?'

'Yeah, but he's not that quick to reply,' Lee answers. 'There's only so many times you can ask isn't there?'

Another mate of mine spotted Gleghorn recently, running an amateur side in Salford. I knew he'd done some work for Cheshire

County Council, so my own enquiries had stretched to contacting that particular local authority and asking whether they had an e-mail address for him.

'Unfortunately, Cheshire County Council are unable to give out the e-mail addresses of employees,' was the reply, which I'd kind of anticipated.

I replied back, asking directly if Nigel Gleghorn worked for them.

'Cheshire County Council are unable to disclose the names of its employees.'

Fucking hell, was this the county council or MI5? I wasn't going to be beaten though and so snooped around on the Cheshire County Council website until I found the name of a random employee – an HR person who job applicants could send their applications to – and used the exact format to send Nigel an e-mail, which probably would have got to him, had he actually worked for Cheshire County Council. As it happened, it bounced back, which at least gave me the answer to my second question.

Doing this kind of thing though makes you feel like you genuinely are mental. If you're reading this, Nigel, don't worry, I gave up. Even though you were one of my favourite players, you can save the restraining order.

And Gleghorn *was* bloody good. He was another of Macari's old brigade – at 33 he was strolling majestically through games like a visiting admiral, controlling the pace and tempo in the style of one of the old singers at Vegas, effortlessly crooning his way through the classics while keeping an audience in the palm of his hand. He didn't break sweat in training and he didn't need to in games.

He was the embodiment of the Macari philosophy that the manager had inherited from the great Jock Stein at Celtic: let the passers pass, the runners run and the tacklers tackle. Teams and systems were set up to play to their strengths. Gleghorn was expected to do nothing that his body wouldn't permit him to do.

Running was the job of Ray Wallace and so was tackling. Wallace couldn't pass his own piss, so as soon as he won the ball, which he was effective at doing, Gleghorn would be along to take it from him like a concerned parent who'd just noticed their child had picked up scissors. The two had a wonderful synchronicity when playing together. It would be telling that once Gleghorn did move on, Wallace instantly went from cult hero to liability.

'Who'd have thought Graham Potter would be where he is now?' says Lee, referencing our former left-winger's emergence as one of the most promising young managers in Europe. 'No chance of getting an interview with him at the moment.'

Absolutely none. Because as we were stood there in the pub watching Chelsea and Barcelona compare wage bills on the Stamford Bridge turf, Graham Potter was preparing the Swedish club Ostersunds FK to take on (and beat) Arsenal at the Emirates in the Europa League. Potter had taken his side from the Swedish Fourth Division and the obscurity of Scandinavian part-time football to European competition. He'd have a lot more important people than a couple of nostalgic dickheads in Stoke wanting to know his secrets.

'I did get Kevin Keen though,' Lee tells me. 'I interviewed him for three hours at a Premier Inn in Wycombe. Cost me a fortune in petrol.' Keen was stationed on the opposite flank to Potter. Neither of them were particularly quick, but both could deliver a reasonable cross. 'Passers pass, crossers cross' I can hear Macari's voice channelling Jock Stein as I write that. So that's what Keen and Potter did, and I don't think I saw either even attempt to beat a man all season.

And what of star man Toddy Orlygsson, the scowling Icelandic midfielder with a touch of magic? He was sold to Oldham for £180,000 after several months spent sulking about the terms of his contract. The midfield had two men as cover – Carl Beeston, still spending so often on the treatment table that the physio's room was renamed 'Beeston's Quarters' and Mark Devlin. Yes, him again! How he was still at the club I have no idea – he'd hardly played since breaking through into the team under Graham Paddon, but he was still knocking around the place. I had a theory that he'd perhaps taken to walking around the training ground with a clipboard and an envelope a few years ago to look busy, and people had forgotten that he was one of the players. However, he was here and he was a body to fill the bench some weeks.

Up front it was still a case of picking Paul Peschisolido and then pulling a name out of the hat to see which one of Keith Scott, John Gayle, Martin Carruthers or Simon Sturridge partnered him. All seemed equally useless, but there was no alternative but to keep experimenting and hope that something clicked with one of them. It was the George's Marvellous Medicine approach to strike partnerships – throw in different ingredients in different combinations every week and hope that one week, the alchemic potion would start fizzing and frothing. Predictably, it didn't. At least not for a while.

Neither Lee nor I knew where any of those guys were now, other than assuming that Paul might be at home doing the housework while Karen Brady hired and fired people on *The Apprentice*. I had a mental image of our former striker whipping on a false moustache and pinny then giving it 'I Want to Break Free' Freddie Mercury style the minute that his wife went through the front door. There was no chance of interviewing Pesch now – or ever sleeping properly again – not with that image stuck there.

Still chuckling, I made my way home and decided to make a final check on my e-mail inbox. In there was a message from Ian Cranson.

'Hi Neil. How can I help?'

A Poor Start

I'm going to start this section by talking about Muhammed Saeed al-Sahhaf. He might sound like a long-forgotten triallist from Egypt, but he's not (you know the ones – they used to get mentioned in the *Evening Sentinel*, play one reserve game then disappear into a Narnia-like void, never to be seen or heard of again).

Al-Sahhaf wasn't even a footballer, he was the Iraqi Minister for Information during the 2003 invasion of Iraq. That poor sod was the man who Saddam Hussein employed to reassure the public that the Iraqi army were defeating the invading Americans as Baghdad literally exploded behind him. Well, even that guy had an easier time of it than Jez Moxey, the chief executive tasked to oversee the project of Stoke moving (or maybe not moving) grounds, while simultaneously acting as a human shield to protect the board from the anger of fans.

Moxey was a master of spin, and his job was to try and keep the natives onside while the board decided which direction they were going in and sought the finances to fund it. Previously the general manager at Partick Thistle, Moxey had an impossible job acting as a buffer between fans demanding the board spend money on the team, and a board that either didn't have that money available or were refusing to acquiesce with the fans' wishes and buy some players.

Before the season even started, Moxey faced a hostile crowd at the Jubilee Hall at the end of July, but handled it in a typically unflustered and diplomatic fashion. Moxey was smooth – maybe a little too smooth – and fans soon christened him 'The Fat Controller' after the rotund character with the top hat and black suit in *Thomas the Tank Engine*. There were rumours that Lou Macari didn't see eye-to-eye with him either and the two of them were said to lock horns on a regular basis.

Macari certainly pulled no punches when writing about Moxey in his autobiography, complaining that Moxey went beyond his remit of overseeing the new stadium's development and began to try and have influence over the players that Stoke bought or sold. Macari's view, not unreasonably, was that a chief executive 'should keep his gob shut' on football matters, and it was clear that Moxey wasn't inclined to do that. There were also regular arguments over the issue of whether Stoke should move grounds.

'I favoured staying put,' Macari admits. 'The ground and the atmosphere – that was worth 20 points a season, teams having to walk down that little tunnel – the crowd were so close to the players that people could touch them. There was no escape in there, was there!?'

But the decision was out of Macari's hands and he accepted that he would have to work within certain constraints.

'I used to know exactly what was in the bank account at Stoke. Mike Potts, who was the secretary and a friend of mine, would say to me, "Hey, don't go out trying to sign someone for £30,000 this week – we've only got £27,250, and we've got the wages to pay!" I knew what I could achieve and what I couldn't achieve so

I never used to bother Peter on the phone asking for more money and he didn't used to bother me. He'd come in after the game and we'd have a laugh and a joke and that was the top and bottom of a good manager–chairman relationship. I knew when there was money and when there wasn't.'

There certainly wasn't in the summer of 1995, and Moxey's presence was rumoured to have put the first cracks in what had otherwise been a solid relationship between manager and chairman. The bad atmosphere in the dressing room was also down to a new initiative that Stoke introduced for players signing new contracts – namely, paying players their signing-on fees on a pay-as-you-play basis. Signing-on fees made a huge difference to players' incomes at a time when wages were still not totally out of sync with the kind of salary the general public would earn.

The players rightly pointed out that if they were to get injured then, through no fault of their own, they would be not only forfeiting the usual win bonuses that tended to top up the modest basic wage they were on, but also the signing-on fees that they would have previously been paid as a lump sum. The club risked losing any players who were out of contract, but also risked disaffecting the whole squad. The players would no doubt have responded with unity to a situation that would affect them all eventually. By trying to pinch pennies, the board risked invoking a mutiny.

Ian Cranson was one of a number of players who felt the system was wrong. 'It was unfairly weighted in favour of the club,' he recalls. 'I'd already been playing on reduced terms because when I signed a new contract in 1992, I'd been injured and so I was promised that if I proved my fitness, the club would put me back on to the wage I'd been on when I signed. Even though I played 60 games that season, that didn't happen. The concern was that the club could put something in the contract to say if you played so many games you'd get your bonus. If you were one short of that number, what would stop them not picking you so they didn't have to pay you? They said they wouldn't do that, but having seen what had happened with my contract situation before, I wasn't so sure.'

However, as unpopular as the system was, most players eventually ended up signing. 'Eventually everyone came round to it,' says Carl Beeston. 'It was a different game back then, you hadn't got agents there and so you had to do it yourself and see the manager, which is never an easy thing to do. Personally I hadn't got as much of a problem with it because with the state of my ankle I could understand where the club were coming from. I thought it was going to come in massively but after a season or two it went.'

As Macari found himself getting bogged down with players' contractual situations and an increasing number of administrative tasks, he decided to renegotiate his role to a director of football-style position, allowing him to oversee recruitment and leave more of the day-to-day training to his coaching team of Chic Bates, Peter Henderson and Mike Pejic – a former Stoke left-back and as old-school a disciplinarian as you're ever likely to come across.

Without the fresh blood that was needed to improve a squad that had only pulled away from trouble late on in the previous campaign, coupled with an unhappy dressing room, it seemed inevitable that Stoke would struggle. The team actually made a reasonable start, drawing 1-1 with Reading at home on the opening day then following up with a superb 3-2 win at Leicester's Filbert Street ground. It proved to be a false dawn though, and a 1-0 defeat at home to Port Vale prompted a poor run of form more in keeping with what people had expected.

Just like Lou Macari did, I absolutely loathed those mid-to-late 1990s games against Vale as they all followed the same pattern. The away game would be a dour struggle in which we would usually fall behind and then manage to scramble an equaliser from somewhere. A draw in a local derby was the kind of result you'd take all day long, but it was the home games that all seemed to be cloned from one miserable archetype.

In this Groundhog Day football match, it would piss it down with rain, Stoke would play appallingly and Port Vale, despite huffing and puffing and at least looking like they cared, would be almost as bad. For some reason, the Central TV cameras would always be in attendance to broadcast this filth to the whole of the Midlands, and any viewers stupid enough to tune in would, I imagine, either switch over to *Countryfile* on BBC2 instead or maybe start self-harming. If I hadn't been there in person for every painful re-telling of the same story, I'd have been convinced that ITV had kept last year's tape and just stuck it on again, hoping that no one would notice.

Whether it was the presence of the cameras or the sense of apathy that was creeping in, no one could fail to notice that only 14,000 fans were inside the Victoria Ground for a Potteries derby. What the hell had happened? This fixture had ignited the six towns and beyond for weeks in 1989 – or 'the Day of Leigh Palin' as only I referred to it. And only three years before, we'd witnessed those five epic struggles as both sides went toe-to-toe for promotion. Now the ground was barely half-full and Stoke's players never seemed to want to be there.

Even though I wasn't at school anymore, it was just as horrible walking into Stoke-on-Trent Sixth Form on Monday morning and getting the same kind of grief and piss-taking, only a slightly wittier, more articulate version from the handful of Vale fans who were just about clever enough to do A Levels. We hadn't even got the prospect of a 'Gob Alley' revenge either at sixth form, so I just had to take it on the chin.

The situation wasn't helped by my being a very visible Stoke fan, wearing as I did a Stoke managerial coat – the type that Joe Jordan used to wear in the dugout. Even Vale fans I didn't know, or to be honest people in general, used to mock me when they saw that coming.

Although it was a birthday present, and I had no money to buy a replacement, I still cringe when I think about that coat. How on earth did I think that this kind of thing was acceptable attire for a 17-year-old, especially when I was looking for a girlfriend?! I'd have been better off going in with no coat and getting hypothermia than wearing that thing. I can just imagine a group of girls sat in the canteen as I walked in wearing such a crime against fashion:

'Wow, look at him over there dressed like Joe Jordan. Sexy!'

'Yeah, I went back to his place last week. He's got a Vince Overson bust on his bookcase, and a picture of John Dreyer too.'

'God, stop it, you're making me horny.'

For years afterwards, I refused to wear any Stoke clothing – leisurewear, replica kits, anything at all because it brought back memories of having to wear that bloody coat. Maybe it wasn't such a great time to be at college after all!

A Rallying Cry and the Wrong Kind of Battle

Stoke followed up the appalling Port Vale defeat with a hat-trick of losses and a black cloud seemed to hang over the whole club as Stoke sank into the bottom three. The whole club appeared to be fracturing from within. Lou Macari's statements to the press smacked of pure frustration as a lack of cash scuppered his move for winger Rick Holden, and with results worsening he was ordered to resume his position in the dugout and get back into the thick of the battle.

There were rumours of players falling out with each other, falling out with the manager and falling out with fans. Well, I say 'players', but most of the time the trouble seemed to centre around striker Keith Scott, who it appeared was so unhappy at the club, he could suck all the joy out of summer. Eventually, enough was enough and after another dressing-room bust-up, Scott was told not to bother turning up for training again.

With one alleged source of negativity removed from the dressing room, Vince Overson issued a rallying call to the players – a battle cry for everyone to start pulling in the same direction. The change in performances was instant.

'Vince was the leader and he was bloody good at it,' recalls Carl Beeston. 'If Lou or whoever was having a go, we'd look to Vince to say something on our behalf. You always need those sensible lads who'll keep everyone else in check – your Vince Oversons, Ian Cransons, Nigel Gleghorns.'

In the first game following Overson's public appeal for unity, Stoke battled to a 0-0 draw with Tranmere, but suddenly looked more like the kind of side we'd become accustomed to watching. In the space of one week, the team had gone from pointing fingers and moaning at each other to fighting for every ball again and were unlucky not to get all three points that day.

More was needed though. A renewed sense of motivation and urgency could get Stoke so far but ability was still lacking in key areas, noticeably up front. Stoke did enough to claw themselves away from the bottom three (a 4-1 win at Wolves being an unexpected highlight) but there were many drawn games and points thrown away through poor finishing.

Respite was provided by a fantastic 1-0 aggregate win over a strong Chelsea side in the League Cup, but Stoke were on the receiving end of a thrashing in the next round as Kevin Keegan's Newcastle team came to town and strolled to a 4-0 win, with players like David Ginola showing true Premier League class.

This was a night that would be remembered more for what happened off the pitch.

I was lucky to have been offered a lift by someone who parked fairly close to the ground, and we were able to get away without really seeing anything happen other than the usual posturing that you tended to witness whenever there was a decent away following. However, other fans saw and were involved in trouble on a scale that hadn't been seen since the 1980s.

The media's portrayal of the 'Toon Army' as some kind of party-loving funsters couldn't have been further from the truth as they landed in Stoke with the mentality of an invading army – large groups of them roaming around the town, loudly announcing their presence and pretty much sticking a sign above their heads. 'We're here. What are you going to fucking do about it?'

I don't condone violence, but if you turn up in someone else's town, city or country and start strutting around like you own the place, then there's only going to be one outcome. Which may well have been the Newcastle fans' intention, the same as it's the intention of England fans who march through foreign cities yelling songs about the war, insulting the customs of whichever nation's hosting them and throwing a few pint glasses at the locals. 'We were only having a sing-song,' they plead into the news cameras, wide-eyed and indignant that the police took umbrage to this and tear-gassed them.

The real trouble, however, was ignited when a rumour spread like wildfire that some Geordies had glassed a young girl in a pub in Shelton – The Bell and Bear – the story even being reported in news bulletins on Signal Radio.

'Stoke town centre went up like a furnace as the story spread from pub to pub,' wrote Mark Chester in *Naughty*. 'There was still five hours until kick-off and suddenly any Geordie about to enter Stoke town was going to get burnt. All reasoning went out of the window. Late-comers were turning up in the pubs straight from work, seething about the awful story they'd heard on the car radio, not bothering to go home and get changed for the match. Everyone began hunting the Geordies.'

One of the Stoke fans who did see the town centre turn into something resembling a war zone was a chap known to many as 'Big Vern'. 'It was the most violent evening I've ever seen in Stoke,' he recalls. 'There was the rumour of the young girl getting glassed and after that anyone in a black and white shirt was fair game. One thing that stays in my mind is one Stoke fan walking alone by Stoke market opening a car door, booting the passenger in the face and walking off casually while four young lads were overturning a minibus a little further down the road.'

It sounds like one of the exaggerated stories that you read in hooligan books, but it was true. The minibus being overturned was also seen by Shents, one of the lads I sat next to on the Boothen End for years at the Britannia Stadium.

'It was totally lawless,' he tells me when I ask him for his memories of the evening. 'I came up on the train with a mate from London and all the way back to the station there were gangs of blokes attacking Newcastle fans. When we got near the station there was a fight going on right in front of us. One of the blokes, in a Stoke accent, stopped fighting and said, "Are you two Stoke?" Obviously I said "yes", so him and his mate stopped attacking this Newcastle fan, let us past, and then just carried on! It was ridiculous but terrifying at the same time.'

In some ways the night that Newcastle visited was a last hurrah for the old world of gangs assaulting strangers in dark streets, 'Got the time, mate?' and the sight of terrified people running for their lives down mazes of alleyways. It's never really happened since. Not on that sort of scale. We've had pockets of fighting in and around the new ground of course, but it's always isolated and apologetic – pathetic-looking scrums of five or six blokes clinching each other and swinging half-hearted haymakers as the rest of the crowd walk past them.

These sort of ungainly wrestling matches can go on for a good few minutes until the porky pugilists either get bored or someone takes pity on them and separates them. 'Leave it, Kev, it ain't worth it,' or whatever excuse one side or the other can find to rescue themselves from the hell of sustained physical exertion.

The ugliness of that night was that anyone seemed fair game to be targeted. Forget all the bullshit about the supposed moral code that hooligans live by, never hitting shirters and all that self-justifying bollocks, everyone who saw the violence that night tells the same story. The attacks on Newcastle supporters were random, merciless and not restricted to those who were 'game' and looking to fight back. There were stories of people young and old being repeatedly assaulted: people who were just there for the match and in the wrong place at the wrong time receiving barrages of punches and kicks, which didn't always stop when they hit the ground.

This was what we left behind. Of course there were things that went with it: The injustice of the working class all but losing the game that 'belonged' to them; the impromptu social groups that formed on terraces; the rite of passage where boys could stand with their fathers in an environment that Mum wouldn't really know or approve of; young men graduating to different parts of the ground as they grew and assimilated with the micro-cultures that existed on each part of the terrace.

There were a million life lessons to be learnt in those old grounds.

Football had a different social system back then, one that can't be replicated in all-seater arenas where moving from one place to another is impossible and the only place to aspire to moving to is a seat slightly nearer the exit so you can get off the car park quicker. And groups of teenage lads just don't go to games together any more like we did – they don't have the financial means to afford it.

That's the downside of the modern game. However, the upside is you don't see young boys, old people or women being punched by 15-stone blokes or panicking children crying because they let go of Dad's hand as he got caught up in the melee.

It's easy to be seduced by the romanticised nostalgia of terrace culture from a vantage point of 20 years down the line, but we can't mourn the passing of that experience without acknowledging the ugliness that came with it. Today, there's probably a middle ground to be sought that sits somewhere between the wild west of the old days and the gentrified game we've been left with – maybe affordable safe standing areas are a step towards that compromise – but that's another argument for another day. Back in 1995/96, the days of the old world may have been numbered, but there were still nights when the open sores were exposed and the ugliness was presented once more to the watching world.

Here Comes the SAS (Sheron and Sturridge)

All fans are frustrated managers, or at least frustrated scouts. We love to pass judgement on players like we're some kind of experts, arguing the merits of one player over another on forums, social media or over a pint in the pub. Opinions were less entrenched in the 1990s. You were free to slag a player off one week and praise him the next because nobody was sober enough to remember that you'd called this week's hat-trick hero 'a fucking donkey' last Saturday, and even if they did, you'd get a bit of piss-taking at your expense and that was the end of it.

In the world of online forums though, every word is immortalised in html code, searchable and quotable and able to be weaponised by people whose entire lives are lived online. For some, being proved wrong about something leads to a crisis of self so psychologically damaging that they will argue black is white and that day is night before they'll admit that yes, the other day, they were talking complete bollocks.

God only knows what you'd find if you could somehow Google the opinions of Stoke fans on Simon Sturridge before 4 November 1995. Sturridge had been at the club for two years and had done absolutely nothing up to this point. We'd decided he was going to be the next Mark Stein, based very lazily on the fact that he was black, played up front and was quite small. However, pretty soon, 'Studger' had been written off as a cheap gamble that hadn't paid off.

Opinion began to change on that Saturday as he scored twice after coming off the bench in a 5-0 win against Luton. All right, the visitors were awful that day, even John Gayle scored, so maybe it wasn't time to get too excited just yet. We'd let him have a start the following week at Southend and see how he ... fucking hell

... Studger's just banged in a hat-trick! Southend were put to the sword and Sturridge took the match ball home the following week with a smart side-foot finish and two absolute belters. Where did that come from? Whatever we'd said about him before was forgotten. Five goals in two games and he WAS the new Mark Stein now.

Can anyone remember anyone who said otherwise? Nah, we'd *all* seen *something* in him. Honest.

He was at it again at Portsmouth the following week, notching another in a 3-3 draw.

'Well, he's just on a lucky streak isn't he?'

'He's scored against some awful teams, let's see him do it against the top six.'

'He's still shit. Because I said he was some time in 1994, I'd rather die than admit I was wrong.'

If there had been football forums in 1996 then that's the kind of thing you'd probably have read after that game at Portsmouth (I'm sure someone will correct me in pointing out that there were some online football forums available in 1996, the difference being of course, that they weren't populated by the idiotic general population). In reality though, Sturridge had gone from zero to hero in a matter of three weeks.

This section isn't just about Simon Sturridge though, otherwise it would be entitled 'Here Comes the S' which I'm sure you'll agree sounds rubbish. Sturridge had a partner in crime, and that man was, of course, Mike Sheron.

Sheron was, in many ways, a typical Lou Macari signing. A player with pedigree who'd lost his way over recent years and was now available for a song.

The young Sheron started his career with Manchester City. He played 71 times for them in the top flight, 100 times in total, and also won 16 England under-21 caps in the process. How on earth had he ended up in the reserves at Norwich having scored only twice in 28 games?

Macari's scouting paid dividends yet again. 'I remembered Mike's time at Man City and when you watch games you make notes,' he recalls. 'I knew that Mike was an up-and-coming young player back then. We saw that he was at Norwich and hadn't done anything there so I went to watch him and there was nothing wrong with him. He had all the same attributes he had as a kid – always in the box, always looking for a goal, always doing the right things and I said to my chief scout, "I can't see much wrong with him. I wonder what the problem is?" so we made a few enquiries and it was put to us that, no disrespect to Norwich, but living there in the middle of nowhere, after living in Manchester, it's like chalk and cheese, so maybe it's something as simple as that.'

Another theory of Macari's is that Sheron might have just needed a different kind of managerial approach than he was getting at Norwich. 'Martin O'Neill was the manager there at the time, but Martin might not have been the right manager for Mike. Mike was quite a quiet, gentle character so he might not have responded to Martin's style, but I watched him a couple more times and thought he might be worth considering.'

This is not to say that Macari was incorrect in his assertion, but Sheron himself pinpointed a long-standing injury as the reason he began to struggle at Norwich. 'I never really got fit and I had this repetitive hamstring injury,' he recalls. 'As a goalscorer they can't wait to throw you back in the side, as if it's going to be cured by magic, but it doesn't really work like that. I was really in the doldrums at Norwich.'

Sheron credits the intensive fitness regime that Macari put him through as the catalyst for his old sharpness to return. 'He got me as fit as anything,' he remembers. 'I'd be doing laps around the pitch on a Friday afternoon after everyone else had gone home and with being on the bench at the start of my Stoke career, it was exactly what I needed.'

It didn't take long before Sheron was starting games and he soon developed a partnership with Simon Sturridge that's still talked about to this day as one of the best front pairings that Stoke have fielded in the modern era. Sheron himself wasn't blessed with blistering pace; he was similar to Wayne Biggins in the way he played, possessing an excellent first touch, good positional sense and the ability to shoot accurately in and around the box. Sturridge wasn't quite the Stein equivalent we'd cast him as, but he was still busy, tricky on the ball and provided a suitable foil to his strike partner.

What makes a strike partnership like that work? It's hard to put a finger on exactly why certain players catch fire while playing together yet others, even though they may be individually brilliant players, simply can't gel on the field. It's the football equivalent of a marriage. We call it 'chemistry' – a blanket term for what we feel yet can't define about the presence of another. It isn't always the best-looking woman in the room that makes your heart skip a beat, it's the person whose conversation runs to the same beat as your own – the person who knows what you're thinking because they're usually thinking it too.

On the football pitch, there's a game playing out in all of our heads – the players we gel with are the ones who actually do run into the spaces that our mind unconsciously pictures them in. Some players don't even need to look where their partner's running; they know where they'll be running, because it'll be the same place as they're at in the game going on in that player's mind. 'A telepathic understanding,' the commentator will call it as seemingly blind passes find their intended target. Sturridge and Sheron were in tune with each other, the same as Biggins and Stein, Greenhoff and Ritchie, and even Fuller and Sidibe were in later years.

'It was a bit mix-and-match at the start,' remembers Sheron. 'We had Carruthers and Gayle and Peschisolido, but it was me and Simon that hit it off – he was a great foil for me.'

I ask Sheron what he thinks makes a partnership click. 'It's about recognising the runs each other are making and the space we'd create for each other. In some ways we were quite similar – he was a little bit smaller than me, but he was nippy and fit. He was a joy to play with to be honest.'

It wasn't just the strikers who were doing the business though. The defence, marshalled superbly by the young Icelandic centre-back Larus Sigurdsson, specialised in clean sheets, enabling Stoke to win four consecutive games 1-0 in November and early December, the final one of which, over West Brom, put Stoke into the play-off positions. A remarkable achievement given the awful start to the season when relegation was predicted by many.

Another run of five clean sheets in February cemented Stoke's position as unlikely promotion chasers. A slight dip in form had people beginning to worry, but two games in April all but sealed Stoke's position in the top six come the end of the campaign.

Firstly, Luton away on 9 April has to be a contender for game of the season. I'd been listening to the game on the radio at a friend's house. Trailing 1-0 and assuming we were going to lose, I left with about ten minutes to go and walked home, unaware of the drama that was unfolding at Kenilworth Road as I trudged the familiar steps back to my parents' house, all the way cursing that we'd come away with nothing. I checked Ceefax when I got in and almost fainted. Luton 1 Stoke 2 (Sturridge 86, Sheron 90). Two goals in four minutes. I almost wept with joy and still had to try and find another source for the information, unable to accept that yes, we had actually come from behind to force a sudden and unexpected turnaround. This was the kind of shit that other teams pulled on us all the time – I couldn't believe that we were now the ones pulling off the heroics!

'I remember that one,' says Mike Sheron. 'I didn't play too well, but Nigel Gleghorn sent in a free kick and I got in between two defenders and headed it in with a minute to go. Chic Bates came into the dressing room afterwards and he laughed and said, "You were crap for 89 minutes, but you've just won us the game." He was right too, but when we kept the opposition down to nils and ones, it always gave us a chance to win any game. Quite often we did!'

Eight days later, following a dramatic last-minute win over Portsmouth, Stoke faced Charlton at the Victoria Ground with Sheron on the verge of making history. The striker had scored in six consecutive games – including the 90th-minute goal in that 2-1 win against Pompey – and needed just one more to break the club record. By the 29th minute he'd done it – a clinical finish from Simon Sturridge's chipped pass that zipped into the far corner of the net in front of an ecstatic Boothen End.

Sheron stood triumphantly, arms aloft in front of his adoring fans, drinking in the moment. He described the feeling of elation to Simon Lowe in the book *Match of my Life:* 'You know with the Boothen End all singing my name, I felt like the next thing I was going to do was win the World Cup for England. It was just utter ecstasy I suppose. I'll always remember that feeling. It didn't ever get bettered in my career, even previously at Manchester City.'

Stoke certainly was a golden period in Mike Sheron's career, which, truth be told, never really took off anywhere else after the initial promise he'd shown as a youngster. Heading towards the play-offs, even though we were acutely aware that the club's squad was small and short of quality in some areas, we knew that possessing a striker with a golden touch gave us a chance.

The very fact we were going to be in the play-offs was unbelievable given the chaotic conditions the season had started under – but as unexpected as the achievement was, it was also a chance that nobody dared to imagine us squandering. The foundations simply weren't in place for a sustained assault on promotion season after season, so this seemed like a once-in-a-lifetime shot: a stand-in fighter plucked from obscurity to challenge for the title at short notice. We had to win. We simply had to.

The Play-Off Heartbreak

Only Martin O'Neill's Leicester team stood between Stoke and a date with destiny at Wembley. In the first leg at Filbert Street, a game televised on Central TV, Stoke took the game to Leicester and should have won. It was a nervy contest but we had the better chances. Graham Potter's header, for example. Graham fucking Potter's header. How did it not go in? It didn't though and we came back with a 0-0 draw and a home leg to play. If we could repeat that level of performance the following Wednesday at home, and just nick a goal from somewhere, we'd be going to Wembley. There was no reason not to be confident about our chances.

A deafening rendition of 'Delilah' rung out from all four sides of the stadium before the return leg at the Victoria Ground – 20,000 people knowing that the fate of their club rested on the shoulders of only 11, but if the sound of their voices – that burgeoning swell of noise – could pump the adrenaline through the muscles and veins even one per cent quicker, they would sing until their hearts burst from their chests.

Looking back on the teams that started the night, Leicester's line-up would be recognisable to anyone old enough to have watched football during that era: Muzzy Izzet, Neil Lennon, Emile Heskey – all players who went on to play in the top flight and on the international stage. On the other hand, Stoke had Mark Devlin starting on the right wing and a bloke who'd been bought out of the army for £500 in central defence. Leicester might have only finished one place away from Stoke, but their team sheet, even then, looked worlds apart.

Stoke, however, had a 12th man. The crowd roared every touch by a home player – routine clearances by defenders, three-yard passes by midfielders, comfortable catches by goalkeeper Mark Prudhoe – all were treated like match-winning moments. Vociferous backing can only do so much though. Cheers and roars don't impact the legs like 46 long, hard games do. Leicester looked lively, Stoke looked leggy. If this was our unexpected title shot, we were hanging on to the ropes, throwing slow and tired punches, the footwork ambling and heavy. It seemed only a matter of time before the heartbreak would arrive.

Thirty seconds after half-time, midfielder Garry Parker arrived in the box to slam Heskey's cross into the top corner. Hope drained away even with a half left to play. If only we had someone to bring off the bench to change things – a game-changer like Paul Peschisolido, for example. We didn't though. We'd sold Peschisolido back to Birmingham for £400,000 a few weeks beforehand. With the team so close to glory and the squad so desperate for reinforcements, the board's response was to sell the only credible back-up we'd got to Simon Sturridge and Mark Sheron.

It seemed criminal at the time, but perhaps showed how utterly desperate the board were to raise funds for the new ground at whatever cost to the team. The project was going to cost £15m, and even with the city council's stake in the project, the grants from the Football Trust and various sponsorship deals, Stoke were still several million short. The financial situation at the club was desperate.

In the short term, the scenes on the pitch seemed more so. Stoke had nothing left to give and no one to turn to. The game petered out into a 1-0 loss. Leicester went on to win promotion and the Stoke faithful knew it was all over. This was the closest the club had come to returning to the top flight in 11 years of trying, and it would be unlikely to happen again any time soon. Frustration and anger spilled from the terraces on to the pitch – fans fighting with stewards and the police. There was no justification for some of the scenes that followed – I vividly remember the shock of seeing someone punching a police horse – but we all felt it.

I went out that night, this being a time when nightclubs would open pretty much every night of the week to accommodate student revellers, and I'm sorry to say that I behaved appallingly too. I tipped a pint over someone's head for no other reason than they were a Manchester United fan ('they deserved it!' I can hear you scream), and spent most of the night staggering around the dance floor acting like an obnoxious arsehole. I suppose that's being 18 though and having little to no sense of perspective.

Failed attempts at promotion, relegations and many other kinds of football misery have already been heaped upon you several times over by the time you reach 40; I've had 32 years of shit things happening to my team now and I expect there'll be many more to come. I wouldn't say I treated triumph and disaster the same exactly (sorry, Rudyard) but the latter gets a shrug of the shoulders rather than beer being thrown over people or horses getting whacked in the face. I'm getting old I guess.

It's Coming Home

If Britpop and the period now referred to as the years of 'Cool Britannia' had a pinnacle from which the only way would be down, it was Oasis at Knebworth in August 1996. For two consecutive nights, the Gallagher brothers played to a combined crowd of 250,000 people – the biggest gig in British music history and the moment that three years of optimism swelled into something so enormous and overblown, the whole movement began to eat away at itself from that moment on. Before the hangover though, came the party – and the European Championship in England was a huge part of that never-to-be-forgotten summer.

In the build-up to the tournament, Frank Skinner and David Baddiel recorded what seemed like an instant classic football anthem with Britpop act The Lightning Seeds – the ubiquitous 'Three Lions' and its 'Football's coming home' chorus – and fans of all clubs put domestic rivalries aside for a summer that seemed like one three-month-long festival of football and music. For the first time in many years, it seemed acceptable for British patriotism to be celebrated. Union Jacks and St George's crosses were everywhere, from Spice Girls' dresses to rock stars' guitars, and miniature flags flew from the windows of the nation's cars with pride. It truly seemed like the good times had returned.

Of course, the press did everything in their power to derail it, such is the way of the English tabloid, going to great lengths to report the misdemeanours of the England side when on a pre-tournament tour of the Far East. Players misbehaving in nightclubs became the running story of the summer, hooliganism for once having taken a back seat on the press agenda. Now there was a new stick to beat the national team with and the papers couldn't put it down. Players in various states of undress, tied to chairs with alcohol being poured down their throats, or causing damage to airline property on long-haul flights became the subject matter of daily headlines.

Most football fans weren't bothered by this though. These antics were just an amplified version to the sort of high jinks all young people were getting up to over that summer. I spent most weekends and a holiday in Ibiza with a group of lads from college, a mixed crowd of Vale and Stoke fans, and we tended to watch the England games together too, usually in the pub with beer flying everywhere and people climbing on tables to get a better view of the big screen.

We got up to some ridiculous antics on that holiday. I have a vague drunken memory of stealing a pallet truck from outside a small shop and riding down the street on it as if it were some kind of industrial-sized scooter; a couple of my mates swam 500 metres out to sea and climbed aboard someone's yacht at night; there were numerous misdemeanours in nightclubs and hotels fuelled by cheap alcohol. We were no different to other groups of lads letting off steam, and even though England footballers were a little older than we were back then, with money in their pockets and already drunk on the euphoria of fame, they wouldn't have been any wiser. Stick a group of young men together abroad, give them access to alcohol and the result is inevitable.

When the moral outrage had subsided, England started poorly, as is standard in tournaments, drawing 1-1 with Switzerland before a moment of Gazza magic sealed a 2-0 win over Scotland in a fiercely contested game. There was also the 4-1 win over a Holland side that featured future Stoke player Peter Hoekstra – a game that was, in truth, the only really great England display of the competition. The 0-0 against Spain that followed in the quarter-final was memorable for being the only competitive penalty shoot-out victory that England had registered in a major tournament, before beating Colombia in the 2018 World Cup.

However, the semi-final was a familiar heartbreak. A hard-fought, end-to-end battle with the Germans ending in a 1-1 draw and the usual, predictable, inevitable defeat on penalties. The camera lingered on the glum faces of Baddiel and Skinner as the crowd stoically sang 'Football's coming home', proud of their team but choking back the tears of yet another defeat at the penultimate hurdle.

Just like the years that followed Italia 90, football received another shot in the arm following Euro 96. Attendances rose further and the Premier League was now the most popular league to watch across Europe. Within a decade, music was dying on its arse again – a combination of TV talent shows and free streaming sites killing record sales – while Tony Blair's Labour Party, after sweeping to power as expected in 1997 ('Labour's coming home', Blair informed us) were getting hammered in the polls following the Iraq War and preparing to make way for a resurgent Conservative Party.

Gazza was a more immediate casualty and a long, painful decline followed as his addictions and mental health problems really began to take hold. First there was the admission from Gascoigne that he'd assaulted his wife, Sheryl, and his battle with alcohol became a constant source of news for the tabloid press. He was often portrayed as the personification of the irresponsible footballer on yet another late-night bender: gulping back spirits while strapped into 'the dentist's chair' in Singapore, which was of course the incident immortalised during the celebration of Gazza's stunning strike in the victory over Scotland.

It doesn't take a qualification in psychiatry to conclude that football itself was the ultimate anti-depressant for Gazza, and as his ability to perform at the top level began to wane, the psychological safety blanket that the sport provided began to slip away with it, exposing Gazza to his own demons. If the tail end of the 1990s was a comedown for everyone, nobody was hit harder than Gazza.

The popularity of football exploded though. The sport just got bigger and more bloated every single year, each new TV deal becoming more eye-watering than the last, wages and transfer fees spiralling more and more out of control. The last two decades have been a never-ending Knebworth for football, a concert that's just kept growing and growing in size. But growth can only ever last so long, then there will surely follow an almighty implosion and collapse. Where Stoke will be at that time I have no idea. The only certainty is that it will happen.

Season 1996/97

Things Never Stay the Same

OVERALL, the final few seasons at the Victoria Ground were a mixed period for Stoke fans. We witnessed the dazzling Macari years sandwiched by the mind-numbing but mercifully brief Joe Jordan era, followed by the unlikely tilt at the play-offs. The football wasn't always fantastic, but for a group of teenage lads discovering the fun of alcohol and clubbing, the terraces were just another setting for the carefree laughs and male bonding that these wonderful years afforded us.

Things changed though in the autumn of 1996 when most of my social circle departed the Potteries to attend various universities and I made the decision to further my education in Stoke-on-Trent. I'm not exaggerating when I say that career-wise, I paid the price for that decision for about 15 years afterwards. Without wishing to make excuses for my lack of ambition and foresight, there were several factors involved in me staying.

Firstly, I'd started my first serious relationship with a girl called Louise (she didn't spot my Joe Jordan coat from afar and go weak at the knees, I'd thankfully moved on from that and finally saved up enough to buy something a bit more stylish!). We fell in love like you do when you're 18 or 19 and don't know any better, thinking that your first relationship, the first time you feel the rush of those endorphins, must mean it's the one. The intensity of young love might be nothing more than a cruel biological trick, but it's potent enough to nullify whichever part of our brain's responsible for applying common sense. Our neural wiring tends to go haywire during those first few months of a new, teenage love and nobody should be held accountable for any decisions they make during it!

The second reason was that, like most students, I was absolutely broke. I'd just been made redundant from my part-time job at the glamorous supermarket that was Discount Giant (the biggest name in low prices, as anybody who ever heard the advert always felt compelled to sing at me) following a takeover from Morrisons so I had no income other than my student grant and loans. Mr Morrison obviously didn't fancy taking on the various reprobates that made up the Discount Giant workforce so we were all given a meagre redundancy package, forced to hand over our smiley-face green dungarees, empty our pockets of stolen pick 'n' mix and troop off into the sunset.

Finally, I'd be lying if I said that the prospect of not being able to watch Stoke every week wasn't a factor in me choosing to remain at home. It's no exaggeration to say that if I could travel back in time, I would gladly kick my 18-year-old self squarely in the bollocks for making such a ridiculously short-sighted decision. I had the A Level grades that would have given me the pick of pretty much anywhere in the country outside of Oxford and Cambridge, but instead I chose to remain at home so I could watch Ray Wallace run around in midfield like a headless chicken.

So stay in Stoke I did – to study Psychology at Staffordshire University. What the hell was I thinking? I chose that degree for no other reason than I quite liked watching *Cracker*, a TV drama starring Robbie Coltrane as a forensic psychologist.

Was it being in love that caused me to make such laughable life decisions, or was it just being young and having no sense whatsoever? I don't know, but in the summer of 1996 I decided to enrol on a degree course that every other indecisive drifter latched on to as well, probably for the same hare-brained reasons I did. That was how I came to make my own small contribution to the excess of unemployable Psychology graduates spat out of British universities in the late 20th century. None of the people I knew on the course, those I'm still in touch with anyway, have become psychologists or used the subject in any discernible way in any of their jobs since graduating. Many, like me, ended up bumming around in low-paid jobs for years afterwards as a result. I hope you're reading this, Robbie Coltrane, because it's all your damn fault!

Apologies, I'm ranting off-piste again. It does happen from time to time, but the point is that by the start of the 1996/97 season, most of my mates had left the building, leaving only me and Big Dave in Stoke. I love Big Dave, I've known the guy since we were both four years old and at infant school, but it's a different vibe when there's just two of you going to the match rather than a crowd. And there's a life lesson in itself, applicable to football and general existence. If something's good, it's not going to stay like that for long – so make the most of it while it's there. As a teenager though, you don't see the changes coming, they just creep up on you and wham ... suddenly people are missing from your life.

I remember thinking at the time, oh well, the lads will be back during the holidays and there'll be plenty of games that'll fall in those weeks at Easter and Christmas. People change though. Thompo moved to London and started talking with a strange faux-Cockney accent, obviously ashamed of where he came from. On the rare occasions when he did come home, he never told us, and we never saw him on the Boothen End again. I haven't seen him for 20 years now. He probably started supporting Arsenal for all I know.

Change really was on the horizon – literally, in the case of where we would soon be playing our home games. Earlier in 1996, the decision had been made that redeveloping the increasingly ramshackle Victoria Ground was not a feasible option. Instead, the club, in partnership with the city council, would definitely be going ahead with plans to build a new 28,000-seater stadium on the Trentham Lakes site – a location that sounds deceptively picturesque, but was actually situated adjacent to the busy A50/500 roundabout and the industrial chimneys of the incinerator belching out smoke across the Potteries skyline.

However, the club had done their research on the kind of ground they wanted to build. A fact-finding mission to Middlesbrough's brand new Riverside Stadium, which had been built 12 months previously, had been carried out, and Jez Moxey and his team were so impressed by what they'd seen, they intended to use the design of that ground as the template upon which to base their own ideas. Stoke had been given a date of February 1996 to submit the plans, or face the prospect of playing at a reduced capacity Victoria Ground. As time ticked on and supporters began to get concerned, all partners in the project eventually agreed a way forward and the project was given the green light.

The proposal certainly seemed exciting. An ebullient Moxey declared, 'It is fair to say that the new stadium will be one of the best in the country; certainly the best in the First Division.'

While that might have proved to be Moxey's usual hyperbole, the plans met approval with most supporters. A capacity of 28,000 was agreed, with the footings in place to develop another corner of the ground if needed, which could take the capacity to 30,000. The pitch would have undersoil heating and the corporate facilities would be at a different level than the 27 poorly constructed executive boxes that had been hastily added to the old Butler Street Stand. Moxey also talked about there being 50 boxes, banqueting suites for over 300 guests, executive concourses and a state-of-the-art media centre.

The project would cost a total of £15m, with £3m of that being provided by grants from the Football Trust. After initially mooting several favourable ideas for the name of the new ground such as the Stanley Matthews Stadium (which supporters would have loved), the club found it was unable to resist the windfall that commercial sponsorship would bring, and £1m from an eventual sponsorship deal with local building society Britannia would also go some way towards funding the move. There was also the sale of the Victoria Ground to developers St Modwen's, which raised an estimated £2m, coupled with the arrival on the board of St Modwen's owner Stan Clarke – the Burton-born self-made millionaire and owner of Uttoxeter Racecourse.

The support of the city council was also fundamental to the project, and 51 per cent of the stadium and surrounding land was purchased by the local authority. Peter Coates was particularly impressed by the tenacity and determination of former council leader Ted Smith in getting the project completed.

'I had a good relationship with Ted Smith,' remembers Coates. 'He was like an old Tammany Hall boss – I think they [the council workforce] were all a bit scared of him! He was a former trade union leader who liked to get his own way and get things done. The council wanted to develop that site, and I said to him that I was in favour of the move if they could make it work financially for us.'

Clearly, Stoke's share of the cost had to come from somewhere, and the outgoings from the playing staff that had prompted so much anger the previous season hinted at where the board planned to source most of their contribution from.

During the summer of 1996, Stoke had a clutch of first-team players out of contract, and four key players from the previous year would depart. Stalwarts Vince Overson and Nigel Gleghorn would leave on free transfers to join Burnley, both unhappy with the terms for renewal that had been offered. Lee Sandford eventually joined Sheffield United for £450,000 and Southampton paid £300,000 for the services of Graham Potter. Even Ian Clarkson, the epitome of unspectacular, left a gaping hole at right-back when he turned down a new contract to sign for Northampton Town instead – a sure-fire indicator of how dire the financial picture was behind the scenes.

Later on in the campaign, John Dreyer was allowed to join Bradford City for £25,000 based on the assumption that at 33, his legs were gone or at least about to do so. Three years later, Dreyer was playing as a regular for Bradford in the Premier League at 36 years of age! Funny old game, isn't it?

Macari Loses the Magic Touch

If the departures weren't bad enough, it wasn't long before Ian Cranson's knees finally gave up the ghost, while striker Simon Sturridge only made it to September before a serious injury put paid to his season. With Carl Beeston's ongoing fitness battles also limiting his appearances, Macari had effectively lost eight first-team players from his overachieving 1995/96 side.

Realising the enormity of the rebuild that was required, the board deflected some of the criticism that had come their way by at least making some cash available to Macari throughout the season to fund the acquisition of reinforcements. However, like Mick Mills before him, and to some extent Tony Pulis after him, Macari's golden touch seemed to desert him once he had a degree of spending power.

The manager's first mistake was to spend £250,000 on Ally Pickering as a replacement for Clarkson. Although the blame for Clarkson's departure probably lay elsewhere within the corridors of power, history shows that Stoke effectively paid a quarter of a million pounds to replace a mediocre player with someone who was even worse. Later in the season, the club threw another £120,000 down the toilet in signing right-back Mark McNally from Southend, who went on to make a grand total of seven starts for Stoke and was released on a free transfer 12 months later.

The decision to sign veteran left-back Nigel Worthington on a free transfer to replace Sandford didn't seem like a bad idea as a stop-gap, but it soon became apparent that not only did the former Sheffield Wednesday man look like Father Ted, he also played like him. Worthington's legs had clearly gone some time ago, and it was only the emergence of Andy Griffin from the under-18s that solved a considerable problem in this area.

Macari was clearly a big admirer of the young full-back. 'He was in the youth team,' he recalled. 'I'd always go and see them to keep an eye on the young lads. Griff was a warrior – no nonsense, willing to steam into people and was hard but fair. His enthusiasm boosted the team – he was a mature young man trying to make his way in the game.'

There have been far worse signings in Stoke's history than Richard Forsyth, who was a steady if unspectacular midfielder. However, £200,000 was a significant fee for such a limited player, although it constituted the deal of the century in comparison to the £450,000 that Macari was reported to have paid Tottenham for curly-haired winger Gerry McMahon. The Northern Irishman arrived with a reputation as a potential star of the future, but soon had the crowd on his back with a series of limp, heartless displays that saw him eventually shipped out to St Johnstone for a cut-price £85,000. Within three years, it was reported that McMahon had given up football to work as a postman.

A £25,000 gamble on winger Kofi Nyamah would have been better spent on a new chicken suit for Neil Baldwin, and the former Cambridge man was the cherry on top of a very depressing and wasteful cake. However, it could be argued that Macari's £250,000 deal for midfielder Graham Kavanagh in October, following a successful loan spell, pretty much wiped out his otherwise profligate spending that season.

The Irishman's impressive contribution immediately raised the spirits of the Stoke faithful and in years to come he'd go on to play in the Premier League with Wigan Athletic, following a spell at Cardiff City, and would also win 16 caps for the Republic of Ireland. Kavanagh was arguably the one permanent deal made in 1996/97 that came anywhere close to the kind of bargains that Macari had landed in the past.

Despite the sweeping changes to the first team, and a summer of poor transfers, Stoke were the league's surprise package in August, racing out of the traps with a 2-1 win at Oldham – a game that ended with Ian Cranson in goal following an injury to Mark Prudhoe. This was followed by a 2-1 win at home to Manchester City, managed – but not for much longer – by Alan Ball. Perhaps you could hardly blame him considering the abuse he suffered at Stoke, but Ball had no kind words for Stoke or Stoke-on-Trent, describing the people as 'insular' and stating that he didn't like us, didn't like the area and pretty much couldn't wait to see the back of our city!

Ever since his sacking he had continually trotted out excuse after excuse to explain away his failure in the Potteries. Failure was a recurring theme in his managerial career though, and other than his promotion with Portsmouth, he performed no better than averagely at any club he took charge of. Ball's spell at Manchester City was no different, and many felt that he'd only got the job based on his friendship with chairman Francis Lee. Ball's team looked just like ours did during the death throes of his 1990/91 nightmare – a team without belief or fight, despite having several good players in their ranks. In the case of Manchester City it was the East German Uwe Rosler and the brilliant Georgian Georgi Kinkladze who caught the eye, but they couldn't match the Stoke team for work ethic, and the Potters were good value for the win.

'It was a mad 15 minutes that cost us, otherwise we were the better team,' claimed Ball with the same delusional bluster he had exhibited so often during his spell at the Victoria Ground. It was no surprise when he was out of work again just three days later. As always, *The Oatcake* was quick to give a humorous take on proceedings, featuring a Spot the Ball competition in its next issue, which was simply a picture of the job centre!

By the time the calendars turned to September, Stoke were sitting top of the league – a quite unexpected position for them to be in. The ten points they had on the board though would prove to be more of a safety net against a relegation battle than a springboard for promotion, and as the season wore on it became more obvious that the side lacked the consistency of the 1995/96 play-off team. Gleghorn's playmaking ability in midfield hadn't really been replaced, and even though Larus Sigurdsson impressed in defence, the rest of the rearguard was poor. Up front, Mike Sheron was having to do the work of two men, but his 11 goals in just 16 games ensured that Stoke remained in a flattering top-half position, still in touch with the play-offs without ever convincing anyone that they were going to make a sustained promotion bid.

As autumn began to slip into winter and pockets of the crowd began to question his negative tactics, Macari pulled off his final masterstroke. He made a phone call to Chelsea and asked about the availability of a certain Mark Stein.

Steino: The Chelsea Years and a Second Spell in Red and White

A lot of people hate Chelsea. The commonly held assumption is that they fell into disfavour around the time that Roman Abramovich began to pump his roubles into the club, transforming them from one of the capital's many second-rate sides into the Premier League's brash and classless nouveau riche. Buying success was talked about like it was a new, unscrupulous concept, as though money and status had never before affected a football league table.

Personally I think it may simply be other teams' success that football fans find disagreeable. It's our job to hate whoever is top of the tree, whether that be a traditional superpower of the game or one that's awash with new money, but even the bowing of the shelves in the Stamford Bridge trophy room was not the reason I began to loathe Chelsea. No, my antipathy towards them developed much earlier, and not in a gradual way but overnight. It began on the day they offered £1.5m for Mark Stein.

I don't blame Stein himself for going. Nobody did. There were rumours doing the rounds at the time that Stein was on a measly £400 a week at Stoke, and the club had only offered him a small increase on that. If that was an attempt to keep him, it was as half-arsed as it gets. There were stories that Tottenham were interested, Liverpool were mentioned too; Stein's departure was always a matter of when, not if. But I was still always going to hate the team he went to, regardless. Seeing him in a Chelsea kit for the first time was like losing your woman and then watching her canoodle with a new lover in front of your eyes. It made me feel sick, and when Joe Jordan gave Stein's place to Gary Bannister it made me feel even worse!

Stein himself was obviously keen on testing himself at the highest level, and who can blame him?

'I had a fantastic time at Stoke but everyone wants to play in the Premier League and I had the chance to do that,' said Stein, when talking to Chelsea's official website about the move.

'Coming to Chelsea was phenomenal. You didn't realise until you got here the magnitude of the support and the club in general. I was fortunate Glenn Hoddle had the confidence in me to come and get me.'

Things didn't get off to the best of starts for our former hero. In fact he went seven games without scoring at all, leaving some fans wondering whether their new man had what it took to make the step up to the Premier League. After all, he had never quite made the grade at that level before in his earlier career at Luton Town and QPR, so the question was asked whether a man who had only really scored goals in the second and third tier could make the step up to the top flight.

Stein, however, still infused with the self-belief that Lou Macari had instilled into him, knew that his luck would eventually change.

'In training and games I was still doing the right things,' he recalled. 'The most important is to keep trying to get on the end of things but at the start we did not really create that many chances, and when we did the keeper blocked it, and that is the life of a striker, you go through streaks. Glenn [Hoddle] was superb through all that because when you come to a big London club the pressure is on. The Premier League is the best in the world and it is all about delivering the goods. He gave me the confidence to keep going, saying your luck will change. Fortunately it did.'

In a Boxing Day fixture at Southampton, Stein lobbed Dave Beasant to score Chelsea's consolation goal in a 3-1 defeat, and just as he had done at Stoke, once he'd broken his duck he couldn't stop scoring. In fact, he not only continued to find the net for his new side, but he broke the Premier League record for goals scored in consecutive games while he was at it. For seven games on the trot, Stein scored, notching nine in total during that run. While on one hand it still felt strange and rather nauseating to see him in the colours of another team, no one in Stoke begrudged him the success. In fact, I'm sure I wasn't the only one who celebrated a little bit every time he notched another. There was very little to cheer at Stoke that season, so taking vicarious pleasure in Stein's exploits was as good as it got!

Unfortunately, Stein's goalscoring was curtailed by an ankle injury in March 1994, leaving him with a race to be fit for the 1993/94 FA Cup Final. He eventually won it but the tight timescales of his recovery meant that he never truly regained match fitness and looked a shadow of his usual self during the final, which Chelsea lost 4-0 to Manchester United. The injury left him needing surgery. As a result he would miss the first few months of 1994/95, but still finished the season with a respectable eight goals from 24 appearances.

Although the Abramovich era was still some years away, Hoddle made a statement of intent in the summer of 1995 that would foreshadow the mega-money signings of later years, bringing in Dutch legend Ruud Gullit and former Manchester United striker Mark Hughes. Perhaps it was the first signs of age starting to creep in, or maybe just the increased competition for places, but Stein ended the 1995/96 season without a league goal from a mere eight outings.

One appearance he did make though was in that League Cup second round tie against Stoke, the first leg under the floodlights at the Victoria Ground ending 0-0 and the Potters springing a real surprise at Stamford Bridge by winning 1-0 thanks to Paul Peschisolido. What was really memorable about that second leg was that Steino missed an absolute sitter, which prompted many Stoke fans to jokingly speculate whether he'd done it on purpose due to him still loving his former club so much!

As 1996/97 began, and Chelsea increased the glamour factor of their squad even more with Italian superstars Gianluca Vialli and Gianfranco Zola, it would have been clear to Stein that his first-team chances at Chelsea were fading with each passing week. He would need to leave Stamford Bridge to seek first-team football, and that's when the glorious day arrived. Lou Macari was on red alert as to Stein's availability, as you'd expect, and in November 1996, the Prodigal Son returned home. It was only a three-month loan but no one was complaining. Once again we would see our hero wear a Stoke City shirt.

Partnering Mike Sheron in a strike force that sounds like the wet dream of someone compiling a Stoke City Best XI, Stein's second debut was against Southend at home. Even though we kept telling ourselves not to expect miracles and that he wouldn't be the same electric player we'd fallen in love with, it was still a disappointment to see him looking so off the pace in a damp squib 2-1 defeat. We knew he was 32 and he'd lost that bit of sharpness, so fans were supportive of Macari as he kept the faith through another couple of so-so performances.

By the time that Charlton came to town on 4 December though, Stein and Sheron were starting to combine. The little runs and interchanges of passes that the younger Stein had enjoyed with Wayne Biggins in his first spell looked like they might start to be replicated with Sheron. It was a Stein shot that set Sheron's winner up – the goalkeeper parrying an effort from Stein straight into his strike partner's path. A few days later and Tranmere were beaten 2-0 thanks to some more impressive combination play from the two strikers – this time Sheron cutting the ball across the box for Stein to tap in, which he surely would have done had a Tranmere defender not turned the ball into his own net. Another victory was recorded though, and we felt it would only be a matter of time before we got to see what we'd been praying for since the man we called 'The Golden One' had returned.

It was Macari's old team, Swindon, who were on the receiving end of a Stein masterclass. To be frank, the deadly finishing we always associated with Stein seemed to have deserted him in his first few games back, but the rustiness was falling away week by week, bit by bit, and as Graham Kavanagh's through ball sent Stein scampering through on goal, the clocks re-set to 1992 and the Boothen End roof lifted off as Stein's shot hit the net.

It was a moment we never thought we'd see again, but we enjoyed an encore just 20 minutes later as Sheron's slide-rule pass presented the returning hero with his second of the game. Only a few weeks before, Stein had looked devoid of fitness and completely lacking in confidence. Now history was repeating itself. Surely we had to bring him back permanently to the club where he truly belonged?

Alas, it wasn't to be. In total, Stein scored four times in 11 appearances during a spell when Stoke found their best period of form in what was otherwise a season of stagnation. A run of six wins from eight games around this time also saw Sheron enjoy a little purple patch, and by the time that Stein returned to Chelsea, the Potters had put themselves back into play-off contention.

The reasons that Stein didn't return permanently were surely financial as he'd been playing well and had visibly improved the team. It was a blow to see him go back to Chelsea, but not quite as crushing as his first departure had been. In truth we could all see that he wasn't quite the same mix of electric pace and laser-guided finishing as first time around. At 32, Stein would have perhaps only been able to make a contribution for another couple of years, but in hindsight even a fading Stein would have been a better option than the collection of duffers that Sheron had to try and forge partnerships with after The Golden One's departure.

Instead of the longed-for return to Stoke, Stein went on to sign for Bournemouth, where he bagged a very respectable 44 goals in 116 appearances – only seven fewer than he made for us. His professional career ended at Dagenham & Redbridge in the Conference, via a brief return to Luton. You won't be surprised to find out that Stein finished his career by banging in 40 goals in only 76 games at that level, despite being the ripe old age of 37. It clearly didn't matter to Stein what level he was playing at. Goals were in his blood.

It was a shame for us that he didn't stick around in 1993/94, as I suspect we might have reached the Promised Land a lot sooner had he done so. It was also regrettable that we didn't try harder to get him back permanently after his loan spell three years later as there was obviously still a fair bit of gas left in the tank.

These days, following several years working in football as a physio, Stein works at a school in the capital.

He says, 'I'm working in the special educational needs department, working with kids with difficult conditions and the fact I am giving something back into the community is really enjoyable. We are trying to get them more confident in little things that they do. Their health and well-being is the utmost concern and if I can help even one of the kids take the advice and have a bit more confidence in decision-making then it makes it all worthwhile.

'They talk about football all the time and they try to nutmeg me when I play football with them, but no one has yet. I am too long in the tooth for that one! But the kids are great fun.'

Despite living down south, Stein's links with Stoke are still strong and he's appeared in a number of charity games organised by the Stoke Old Boys Association – most recently playing alongside Ricardo Fuller in a match at Vale Park (there's another dream strike force!) and also appeared in Andy Wilkinson's testimonial game in 2016.

In the glittering history of Chelsea FC, Mark Stein will probably be something of a footnote. A man who scored goals and played his part when the club was nothing like the money-shitting juggernaut that it is today. To Stoke fans though, he'll forever be the man who scored goals that others can only dream of – the one and only Golden One.

Limping to the Line

Stein departed in January with the team in seventh position, but what should have been a celebratory five months to give the old ground a good send-off turned into one of the most depressing periods of the decade. The team looked devoid of ideas, the manager more so. Lou Macari talked a lot in the press about the team needing to play '100 miles an hour football', the idea being that we could just outwork teams to gain favourable results. Things didn't work out like that though, and the crowd soon began to tire of Stoke huffing and puffing every week without any craft or guile.

Macari was also forced to blood several youngsters in the team – the rangy midfielder Neil Mackenzie and his own son Mike Macari were promoted from the youth team to join fellow teenager Andy Griffin, who was already attracting some admiring glances from a number of top-flight suitors. Even though it was a mixed campaign for Stoke overall, Griffin still remembers that period of his career fondly. 'I felt a real sense of freedom,' he told *Duck* in 2017. 'I was like a full-back and a winger at the same time with bags of energy – it was like no one could stop me.'

The youngsters initially provided some excitement in a televised win over Oxford United on a Friday night, when Mackenzie and Mike Macari both scored in a 2-1 win. It was a brief moment of light in what was a depressing second half of the season, although Griffin also managed to score his first goal a few weeks later when Grimsby came to town. 'It was a midweek night game under the lights,' he recalled. 'I was moving towards the Boothen End with the ball – I played a one-two with someone then dragged it with a dummy on to my left and drove it into the far corner. I have a picture at home of the Boothen that night with my number three shirt, my back to the photographer.'

Stoke won that particular game 3-1, but there were fewer than 9,000 spectators in the ground. Stoke were doing just enough to avoid being sucked into the bottom half of the table, winning the odd home game against poor opposition, but barely even turning up in away games. Unbelievably, the team scored its last away goal of the season in February – failing to register at all on the road for seven consecutive games. Supporters, especially those who travelled to watch the team, were livid at the lack of attacking ambition that was being shown, and for the first time, sections of the crowd began to turn on Lou Macari.

Other than Griffin, the youngsters were struggling. Mackenzie looked a bit out of his depth, but would go on to forge a decent career in the lower leagues (and also appear on the Channel 4 show *Countdown!*) whereas Mike Macari dropped out of the game altogether following his time at Stoke. They were, however, being let down by some of the senior players in the team. Gerry McMahon, for example, was in awful form and didn't seem to beat a man after Christmas that year, while full-back Ally Pickering also became a target for supporters' frustrations.

Mike Sheron finally supplied some joy with a brace of goals in a rare 2-0 win over bogey side Port Vale, which was arguably the last game at the Victoria Ground to actually mean anything. Before the match, manager Lou Macari announced that he would be standing down at the end of the season to concentrate on his legal battle with Celtic, but some fans suspected that the financial situation at the club and the team's poor performance played a much bigger part in his decision than he let on publicly.

Macari himself hints that there were a number of factors in his decision.

'Well, I did have the legal battle with Celtic, which proved costly; £200,000 was a fortune back then – it still is now – and it was hard to see that go down the pan. I didn't have as much experience of the legal system back then, but you soon realise it's all a bit of a game and you're in the middle of that game and everyone's milking you.

'But I did know what the club's intentions were and I didn't see how it could possibly succeed. I was dead against the move at the time, but thinking about it now, maybe staying at the Victoria Ground wasn't achievable with the A500 being so close. But I was like a lot of managers – I knew that ground was worth so many points to us every season.

'I had a view that moving to the stadium was obviously the priority, so where are you going to get the money for the new ground? There's only one place really isn't there! Like all clubs that do it, if you think you can get away with selling players and keeping a competitive team on the pitch then you're probably going to be wrong, and so it proved at Stoke. You can't do it.'

Among those fans who still supported Macari, the feeling at the time was that no one would have begrudged our manager the time off to fight his court case, and that putting assistant Chic Bates in temporary charge would have been a workable solution. However, that Macari hadn't proposed that solution suggested that his heart simply wasn't in it like it used to be.

Immediately after the news about Macari's departure broke, Martin Smith wrote in *The Oatcake*, 'It is often said in football that it's folly to go back to a club for a second time, and maybe this proves the point. The Lou we got second time around was not the same ebullient and chirpy character we had lost to Celtic a year before. He was unable to carry on where he'd left off before and the aura surrounding his leadership slowly began to disappear.'

Peter Coates looks back on Macari's second departure regretfully. 'I still don't fully understand why he left that second time,' he states. 'Looking back I perhaps should have protected him from Jez Moxey a bit more. Jez was a good guy, very good at his job, but a strong personality. I think the two clashed a bit. That could have been sorted out though, basically. Lou didn't tell me at the time that there was an issue, but looking back, I think Lou had perhaps been badly affected by his experience at Celtic.

'My theory is, and it is only a theory, that here was a man who'd only ever known success. He'd been right to the very top, had played for Celtic and Manchester United, Scotland – an outstanding player and had always done well in management. His first failure – Celtic. He probably felt he hadn't been given a chance, that the media were undermining him all the time, and all this took its toll on him. He perhaps lost a bit of confidence.

'But I was more than satisfied with what he was doing at the time and there was no question that I was desperate for him to stay. I told him he was making a mistake, and the strange thing was he took us to court over it! It makes you wonder whether he was just going through a difficult time. He obviously couldn't win the case against us because he was on public record as saying he'd resigned – he certainly wasn't sacked. It was disappointing, but we're still friends now and I look back on those times with affection.'

Despite the sentiments expressed by some fans at the end of Macari's reign, history certainly frames his leadership in positive terms. Twenty years on, people remember the good times: the Autoglass Trophy win, the invincible 1992/93 team and the amazing run to the play-offs in 1995/96 more than they recall a final disappointing season. Overall, the 1996/97 campaign wasn't Macari's finest hour, but it did contain some memorable moments, and given the threadbare nature of a squad ravaged by age and injury and a board desperate to sell any saleable asset, a 12th-placed finish was by no means a disaster.

Goodbye Victoria

I was faced with a dilemma on 4 May 1997. My first year at university hadn't gone well and I'd missed numerous lectures after suffering with depression for a sizeable part of the year. I missed almost three months of my education and several Stoke matches too, unable to face even going outside some days. Through a combination of counselling and anti-depressants I was able to make at least a partial recovery and managed to drag myself in to enough seminars to avoid being kicked off my degree course. As much as I lacked the intrinsic motivation to study a subject I was no longer interested in, and as much as my post-graduation ambitions remained lost in a confused fog, I realised that being booted out would have left me in an even worse position.

My tutor had presented me with the ultimatum that unless my grades picked up, my improved attendance wouldn't make much difference as to whether I was allowed to take a second year. Therefore, I knew that my first end-of-year exam, scheduled for the first week in May, was crucial to my future. It may have been timetabled for the Monday or Tuesday after the football season ended, I can't remember exactly, but all I knew was that I had to use every available minute to revise (or, more accurately, learn) an entire term's work in one sleep-deprived, caffeine-fuelled weekend.

On the Sunday of the said weekend, Stoke were due to face West Bromwich Albion in the final game at the Victoria Ground, the fixture list providing a wonderful 119-year sense of symmetry as West Brom had also been the first visitors for a league fixture at the Victoria Ground back in 1888. Should I attend such a historic occasion and risk failing the most crucial exam of my life, or should I forego being there for the celebrations and the tears in order to get my head down and study like crazy? I felt sick at having to make the decision.

This was the first season in a while when I hadn't bought a season ticket, so I needed to make my mind up quickly as tickets surely wouldn't be on sale for long. They weren't. Almost instantly, the game was declared a 27,500 sell-out and the decision was made for me. For the final league game at the Victoria Ground, I'd be sitting in the loft conversion at my parents' house, neck deep in text books, all the while knowing that I was missing out on a piece of history.

In the end I passed the exam (just) and went on to complete a second and third year, eventually graduating with an upper second-class honours degree. Even though I've eventually stumbled into a graduate career after 15 years of drifting into various jobs and generally messing around, I still wonder to this day whether I made the right choice on that historic Sunday afternoon. Over the years, I might have gone through a few spells where my attendance at Stoke matches has been patchy, and my interest might have waned at times, but ever since my first game, I've been at every match that's really mattered. Cup finals, promotion and relegation deciders, all the big matches that we still talk about to this day – for all of them I was there. But the last ever game at the Victoria Ground, that one last chance to say goodbye to the old stadium – I missed it.

I've watched the video of the game since and heard the stories from people who were there about what a memorable day it was. In a carnival atmosphere, Stoke won 2-1 in the sunshine, Gerry McMahon and Graham Kavanagh scoring the goals – the latter forever etching his name in the record books as the last Stoke City goalscorer at the Vic. Prior to the kick-off there were parades of legends from decades before – a friendly match as well featuring the heroes of the 1970s team appearing on the pitch together one last time.

But it isn't the West Brom game itself that people still talk about, for that was nothing more than an insignificant mid-table clash – two sides with nothing to play for going through the motions. It was the hundreds of men, women and even children sitting on the terraces after the final whistle until they were forced to move, drinking in the experience one last time. Long lingering looks at all four stands: the Boothen End, the Boothen Stand and Paddock, the Butler Street (complete with the new roof after the old one blew off) and the Stoke End, or the Town End to people of a certain vintage. Names so familiar to us they were like old friends, and people felt the need to say a proper goodbye to all of them.

Former *Evening Sentinel* journalist Ian Bayley recalled the atmosphere after the final whistle had sounded for the last time: 'On that last day, even half an hour after the final whistle had gone, there were still lots of supporters inside the stadium. The club didn't just empty the ground as they normally do for health and safety reasons: they let people linger, and there were people just leaning over barriers on the Boothen End, literally not wanting to go and end it and say, "We're never coming back here again."'

Many fans took mementos with them. One, Dave White, recalls the compulsion that many fans felt – to take something of the Vic with them. 'After the match had finished and the lap of honour done, the crowd started to disperse. Something possessed me to nip back into the ground through a small open doorway not far from the corner of the Boothen where the Trent emerged from its culvert. I was after some sort of souvenir as a reminder of the old ground.

'Just inside this doorway there was a large, tired-looking wooden car park sign saying something like "Stoke City FC match day parking" about 5ft by 3ft, white paint background with presumably red lettering. I thought, I'll have that, who's going to complain? As I picked it up and took it outside I literally bumped into a copper who just laughed and said, "You're having that are you?" and carried on his way.'

Rob Eaton has similar recollections, 'People were saying goodbye to the Vic but also to each other. I often wonder how many stopped going once we'd moved. We'd stood next to the same people for years- those we recognised but didn't really know- but none of us would ever stand in "our" place again.

'I stood there a long time at the end, as did a lot of others, like they didn't want to leave as, maybe, subconsciously we knew it'd never be the same and we were leaving behind something we'd never get back – our youth. The atmosphere was subdued, glassy-eyed. I got a bit of stone off the side of the pitch for some silly reason just to keep *something*.'

Two hundred Stoke fans who'd hung around even longer got a surprise final tour from none other than Lou Macari, who took them around the ground a dozen at a time, conducting one final tour.

'It was the last example of the common touch which has figured so prominently in the Macari relation-ship with the people,' wrote Bayley in the *Sentinel*. It would be the following January when St Modwen's sent the bulldozers in to demolish the old ground, as they planned to construct a new housing estate on the location. Many Stoke fans immediately had visions of tree-lined streets named after former Stoke heroes, but even accounting for the slow pace of progress in Stoke-on-Trent, no one expected that the site would remain derelict for 21 years after we'd vacated the old place.

The area where the ground used to stand became a matter of local shame. A single flight of concrete steps, the ones we used to climb at the back of the Boothen End, was all that remained long after the four stands had been demolished. A once proud arena, the place where Matthews and Greenhoff weaved magic across the turf, became a waste ground of weeds, litter and used needles.

Mike Herbert, regional director of St Modwen's, pointed to the recession of 2007/08 as the main reason for the lack of development. 'The problem with the Victoria Ground was that inner urban sites can be more difficult and we had issues over potential flooding,' he stated. 'In 2007 the market changed dramatically and many developments came to a dead stop. It was very frustrating.'

For many fans it was depressing to walk past the old site as it became overgrown and infested by vermin. Former winger Terry

Conroy, speaking in 2013, was as affected as anyone at seeing the old site so neglected.

'I went there a few years ago just to visualise what it used to look like. It doesn't seem possible for it to be in the state that it is today. There should be a shrine there now for generations to come. It's desolate, it's gloomy, it's depressing. I try and blank out what it's like now compared to what it used to be.'

With the site being so visible from the A500, it was a grim, daily reminder for anyone using what's colloquially known as 'the D-Road' on their commute to and from work that there was now a loveless void in place of something that used to be held so dear. There was nothing left to do but hope that the future would bring news of a development, and all the while remember the good times the Victoria Ground had given us.

Defender Ian Cranson still speaks glowingly about the old place. 'It was a typical ground of that era really,' he recalls. 'The crowd was very close to you. There was only a little cinder track between the pitch and the terracing, and the Boothen End, when it was full, housed half of the overall capacity. The noise just reverberated around it, so it was an intimidating place to play.

'When you were driving through the area, past all the terraced houses, you felt the effect: you'd see the lights above the houses on evening games and the people flocking towards them – it was something special.'

Every Stoke fan old enough to have experienced the magic of the Victoria Ground will have stories to tell about it. Many will remember their first match more than any other.Mine was 27 December 1986 vs Sheffield United . I was taken to the game by my dad and my grandad. It's a match that's remained rooted in my psyche ever since. My grandad passed away in 2014. Not long after he died, I dreamt about that first game he took me to at the Victoria Ground, dreaming that I was walking through the day again as an adult – a ghost from the future, haunting his own past. The dream provided the inspiration for a short story, *Vivid Colours*, that I wrote soon after. What follows is an excerpt from that story:

> As an invisible entity, I was about to drift through the turnstile of the Boothen Stand when I caught sight of a

distant trio of familiar figures. I immediately recognised the taller man on the right as Grandad – his tweed trilby and purposeful stride contrasting with the shorter, stockier figure of my father, his grey hair restored to a youthful black. The adults flanked a small figure in a navy blue duffel coat.

'Dad!' I yelled. 'Grandad!' But of course they couldn't hear me, and before I knew it they were inside the ground and out of view. Determined to find them, I entered the Vic and ascended the old concrete steps.

I saw the pitch exactly as I'd seen it in 1986. Not a decaying football ground, holding 17,000 people for a Second Division fixture, but the San Siro, Bernabeu and Wembley all stacked on top of one another – a venue at which the entire world had arrived to watch the most important game ever played on earth. The swaying mass of the Boothen End looked dangerously enticing; an untamed beast with five thousand heads, primitive tribalism surging through its veins and violence never far from breaking through the skin. Not a place for eight-year-old boys.

One day I would be among them, surrounded by that earthy glamour of the profane insults, the hollered threats and the cruel but side-splitting chants. Back then, I had to be satisfied with the nursery slopes of the Boothen Stand – a sedate vantage point of thermos flasks and clanking wooden seats.

I turned to see the faces behind me.

Only there were none. Yes, there were people, but they were featureless, practically shapeless entities. A stand of shadows like a photograph, out of focus, distant and indistinguishable. I couldn't see Grandad, Dad or anyone else. I tried to picture the scene in my mind. The lady with the badges – not Mabel, but another survivor from the golden era – her memories of the good times pinned to her scarf. Where was she, or the man in the bowler hat – a dress sense that time forgot, but always a reliable source of half-time mints? If I could find them then I could find...no, it was hopeless. I sank to my knees. Somewhere in time and space, a whistle sounded.

The match was impressionistic. Water colour. No action or players formed, just flashes of half-remembered sound. The blurred colours eventually cleared to reveal Carl Saunders triumphantly pumping the air with both fists, his hat-trick having inspired Stoke to a thrilling 5-2 victory. A single vivid memory from a special day.

The ground was suddenly empty, the only movement on the pitch the litter that swirled in the breeze of the early evening. I was alone with my thoughts and the creaking of the rickety seats as the wind whistled through the stand. I took a final look at the old place – the paddocks where I would spend the glorious Macari years; the Butler Street clock; the Boothen End now empty and sad, as if drained of its life source. I said goodbye to these things all over again and rushed to the exit doors that welcomed me to the darkened street.

There was no one around at all, just three dimly-lit figures walking into the distance. I ran to catch them but never gained ground, sprinting past rows and rows of houses but all the while running on the spot. I fell to the floor exasperated and exhausted, screaming for my father to hear me. The end of the road was lit by a single streetlamp under which I could make out Grandad's old Fiesta, the only car visible under this dim and lonely spotlight.

I saw the young me climb into the back seat – smiling and clutching his programme. Dad got into the front passenger side, unable to hear my increasingly desperate cries. Grandad was the last to get into the car; he turned to face the street where I lay in the gutter, crying like a desperate child, not a grown man of 35. He watched me in silence for a time and raised his hand – a wave of valediction.

Season 1997/98

The Britannia Stadium

'**W**E are very proud of the stadium and we hope supporters will be too,' declared a buoyant Jez Moxey at the start of the 1997/98 campaign. 'Undoubtedly it gives us the foundation we need to progress and develop. We've created a Premier League stadium and we now need to get there.'

The 1997/98 campaign should have been one of celebration and progress – a club turning its vision into reality and embracing the future as it moved triumphantly towards a bright, new dawn A new stadium fit for the 21st century and the Premier League now overlooked the city like a gleaming white citadel. Within a matter of months, floodlights rising above terraced rooftops had become nostalgia. The world had moved on, transport had changed and supporters no longer all lived within a few miles of their team's ground. Progress meant an arena fit for the modern game and the modern world.

The stadium had risen from the ground piece by piece over the previous 12 months – a total of 46 weeks from start to finish – with each stage of its development being noted by any Stoke fans who travelled regularly along the A50. The enormous iron skeleton of the stadium began to take shape at the tail end of 1996 and progress was swift, the fleet of diggers and cranes working around the clock to complete the build ready for 1997/98. When the ground was finished it was indeed a magnificent sight. Many people thought it would never come to fruition, but to give him his due credit, Moxey delivered us a stadium to be proud of. However, those first few months in our new home exposed a number of fairly significant snags. The most obvious problem was the weight of traffic that blighted both access to and egress from the stadium's car parks. Access from the west was a nightmare as drivers had to travel past the stadium on the A50, get off at the next slip road and then double back on themselves at the next roundabout, joining the flow of traffic that was travelling from the east. The result was gridlock and the problem was reversed at the end of the match as everyone tried to get home. Leaving the south car park also seemed to take hours, with an insufficient number of exits and poor traffic management combining to leave drivers stuck on the car park for an hour or more after games.

If fans had, by and large, stopped fighting over the football, scuffles breaking out on the car park between frustrated motorists were becoming more commonplace. People felt compelled to leave the game ten minutes early to beat the weekly scramble, which led to the embarrassing sight of a constant stream of fans departing the ground. 'We can see you sneaking out' was a regular chant from the away end in those days.

Then there were the problems getting into the stadium. Fans who'd been used to leaving the pub at five to three, staggering up to the ground, handing over their cash and stumbling through the turnstile in time for kick-off were in for a shock. Fans were expected to queue beforehand at the small number of windows that fronted the ticket office and purchase their ticket. This involved handing over your money, choosing exactly where you were to sit, and if this was your first time at the ground, or you were taking a friend, you also needed to hand over your name and address, date of birth, inside leg measurement and three favourite Beatles albums in order.

You can imagine the sort of queues that developed. Many people were unaware of this system and began to queue, as they always had done, at the turnstiles, unaware that they'd first need to go to the ticket office. It wasn't rocket science, but it still confused enough people to cause disruption.

Various rumours had been flying around all summer that the development was running behind schedule, that the club had been denied a safety certificate and, quite laughably, that the foundations hadn't been laid correctly and the ground was sinking into the mud as a result. Antagonist-in-chief was local newspaper columnist Les Scott, a self-styled, supposedly hard-hitting 'voice of the people' reporter who never missed an opportunity to stick the boot into the club and write almost daily updates on imaginary problems and setbacks affecting the Britannia Stadium. It was all bullshit though. The ground opened for business on 12 August as planned for a midweek cup tie against Rochdale, although a number of people reported that they saw the carpets in the Legends Bar being stuck down only minutes before the doors opened to welcome the first customers!

In typical Stoke fashion though, organising the grand opening for the first actual match at the ground eluded the powers-that-be. Instead, Stoke took the option of ignoring that the Rochdale match was actually happening and instead arranged the opening ceremony for the league game against Swindon the following Saturday. Even this was beset by avoidable problems. Fans were understandably delighted that the city's most famous son, Sir Stanley Matthews, had been asked to officially open the ground, and he would do so by scoring a ceremonial 'goal' at the Boothen End.

However, somebody had neglected to consider that on a particularly blustery day, with the wind whipping into the ground through the three exposed corners, a frail octogenarian might need to stand a bit closer to the goal than 20 yards out. Sir Stan tried his best to muster enough power from his ancient legs, but couldn't avoid a Diana Ross USA 1994 moment as the ball trickled apologetically towards the six-yard line. 'I hope that's not an omen,' said one bloke behind me. Sadly, it would prove to be a fitting portent for what would follow.

Even with his diminished shooting power, Stoke might have still been better tempting the 82-year-old Wizard of the Dribble out of retirement, because the business they'd done in the transfer market was laughably poor. There was also the question of who was actually sanctioning the deals as Stoke didn't announce the new manager until late July – and there was a collective groan when it was announced that Lou Macari's erstwhile assistant Chic Bates would be the man to step into the hot seat.

When Macari had originally left to join Celtic, many people had felt that Bates would have been a good appointment then to continue the momentum that had been generated. The players liked him, he knew the squad and must have learnt a lot working so closely with Macari at several clubs. However, it wasn't to be and Bates had followed Macari up to Glasgow. This time was different though – fans weren't as enamoured with Macari's management as they had been in 1993/94, and a new man with new ideas – preferably someone to get the fans excited and shift a few season tickets – was the better option than a lazy, uninspiring appointment from within.

The board went for the easy, cheap option though and Bates took control of the side. At his disposal were the majority of Macari's players from the previous campaign, minus one noticeable departure. Mike Sheron had joined Queens Park Rangers for £2.75m, which was rumoured to be the exact amount that Stoke had to find to meet the funding requirements of the new ground. Sheron was quoted in the press as saying, 'It's every player's dream to be sold for £2m,' which raised a few eyebrows, and the club insisted that he had demanded a transfer and held the club to ransom.

Sheron's side of the story is somewhat different, 'I wanted to stay – of course I did. I'd had a difficult time at Norwich and in that Stoke team I felt like I was going places and I was at a club, with the new stadium, that was going places too. I'd moved back home and didn't want to leave.

'But I got the impression the club wanted to sell me. I think their priority was to pay for the new stadium, which I can understand now looking back and where Stoke have got to, but at the time it was frustrating.'

The supporters only heard the club's version of events and Sheron remembers the abuse he got when he returned to Stoke with his new club later in the season, 'It wasn't a nice day at all. Sometimes you want to come back and put on a bit of a performance in those circumstances, but I must admit, I was crap. I'd like to think that although it seemed like hatred from the supporters, it was actually a compliment because they were missing me!'

Whatever the circumstances, Stoke were left without their goalscorer and talisman. To replace him, Peter Thorne was signed from Swindon for £500,000 – a transfer that took a while to catch fire, but would prove another excellent piece of business over time. That was the only money spent though, and as the likes of Mark Prudhoe, Carl Beeston and Nigel Worthington also left the club, Bates was left to scour the free transfer market for reinforcements.

The summer of 1997 was the first when the Bosman ruling came into force, enabling players over the age of 24 to move to a new club for free if they were out of contract. The Stoke board, always amenable to anything that didn't involve spending money, were all over this like a rash and four 'freebie' players were quickly in through the doors.

First up was Paul Stewart, an England international and former Spurs player who was well past his best by the time we signed him. Stewart had been a decent player in his day, but was now 33 and about as fast as a man wading through a sea of treacle. Another striker joining was the familiar face of Zay Angola, who'd been staying with a friend in London when he heard the news that Chic Bates had taken over at Stoke. The opportunistic Portuguese thought he'd give him a call to ask, 'Remember me?'

Bates did indeed remember him, and based on the promise of one and a half games two years ago, before the striker had broken his leg, offered him a contract. He might have been better taking another look before he'd done so, as Angola looked a shadow of the player we'd had on loan.

Some people speculated whether the confusion over his name – was it Jose Andrade or Zay Angola? – was down to them being two different people. The joke was that we'd signed the good one a couple of years ago, but were now lumbered with his much shitter twin brother.

Then there was Jan Dirk Shreuder – a man who'd supposedly been the subject of a £600,000 bid the previous season, but was now a prize capture from the Dutch league on a Bosman. I didn't ever see Shreuder play, but a friend who watched him in the reserves said we'd been ripped off getting him for free. His Stoke career amounted to two unused substitute appearances.

Finally, Steven Tweed was the man chosen to replace the colossus that was Ian Cranson – who officially retired after one knee injury too many. Tweed had been at Hibs but landed in Stoke via a spell in Greece. I wouldn't say that Tweed was bad, but you wouldn't have trusted him to mark someone had he been stapled to them. In football, just like in life, you get what you pay for I'm afraid.

Despite signing the football equivalent of the dog-eared junk left over at a school fair, Stoke started the season in positive fashion. To give the builders extra time to put the finishing touches to the construction (and get those carpets in the bar stuck down), Stoke played their first three league games away from home and managed a very respectable four points.

The highlight was undoubtedly an unexpected 1-0 away win at Middlesbrough, who still boasted the likes of Fabrizio Ravanelli and Paul Merson in their side following relegation from the Premier League. After a classic smash and grab away performance, it was reported that Jez Moxey had got a little carried away and was telling everyone within earshot how his team would soon be in the Premier League! There's nothing like opening your big mouth too soon is there?

The grand opening of the stadium, complete with the Matthews miss and hundreds of confused fans wandering around outside looking for the ticket office and correct turnstile, ended in a 2-1 defeat at the hands of Swindon. That told us far more about the long-term prospects of this Stoke team than a slightly fortuitous win at an uncharacteristically off-colour Middlesbrough would do.

Yet still the results rolled in. During the opening three months of the season, Stoke managed a thrilling 3-2 win at Ipswich – their first there for 15 years – a rare 2-1 home success over Port Vale and another 'professional' 1-0 away victory at Manchester City. Although the team were flattering to deceive, and we all knew it wouldn't last, Stoke were as high as sixth following that triumph at Maine Road. The downturn in results that followed wasn't entirely unexpected, but the magnitude of the collapse certainly was. Within a matter of weeks, supporters would be invading the pitch, waving banners of protest and attempting to storm the boardroom.

Sack the Board

The rot started to set in with a 2-1 home defeat by Sunderland. Stoke were poor, but nobody really envisaged this as anything other than the kind of home defeat that happens from time to time throughout any season. Even a 3-1 reverse at bottom-placed Huddersfield the following week didn't set the alarm bells ringing too loudly. Eleven games later, with only one producing a victory (an uncharacteristically superb 3-0 win over Wolves), everyone was aware that Stoke were staring into a full-blown crisis. The players were terrible and were getting outplayed by pretty much every side they faced – even local rivals Crewe, punching well above their weight in the second tier, turned up at the Britannia Stadium and turned us over 2-0. With every passing week, the boos grew louder and anger at the board crept closer to the surface.

In January, the *Evening Sentinel* carried news of nine first-team squad players being transfer-listed. This was all well and good considering that most of the players affected were pretty hopeless, and no one would have argued that a good clearing of the decks was needed. However, it was alleged that no one at the club had told the players themselves. Finding out that you're transfer-listed through the press wouldn't do much for team spirit, and with the side already on a losing streak, if those stories were true, then morale must have plummeted through the floor.

No matter what the circumstances prior to the game though, to lose 7-0 at home, as Stoke did on 10 January to an average Birmingham City side, was unforgivable. The fans went berserk and over 1,000 of them poured on to the pitch, while 30 or so attempted to storm the Waddington Suite, trying to physically confront the board members who'd overseen this shambles. The scenes were similar to, if not worse than, those witnessed at West Ham in 2017/18 – an angry mob no longer demanding answers but action, namely, the removal of Peter Coates from power.

As I sit in front of Coates in 2018, in his office at bet365 HQ, listening to him talk with such warmth and knowledge about the great names of Stoke's past, I can't help but feel a twinge of guilt that I was part of that angry mob. In 2017, the Coates family sat 22nd on *The Times* Rich List with a net worth of £4.5bn. The vast majority of that wealth has been accumulated following the foresight of Denise Coates, Peter's daughter, to pay $25,000 to register the bet365 domain name in 2000, the family borrowing £15m from The Royal Bank of Scotland against their string of, in Denise's words, 'pretty rubbish' betting shops in order to set up what is now the largest online gambling company in the world. Back in 1998 though, the 'pretty rubbish' betting shops and Stadia Catering *were* the Coates empire. Coates was a typical parochial chairman of a provincial club – a supporter who had a bit more brass than the rest of us, but not the multi-millionaire who sits before me today.

During our conversation, I decide to keep the story about me being restrained by a steward as I attempted to force entry to the Waddington Suite to myself – others got in though, and corporate guests from the day spoke of the sight of fans rampaging through the room, looking for the board members who, probably sensing the way the day was going to end, had wisely managed to get themselves out of immediate danger.

'In all my years in football I've never seen anything like it,' commented matchday host Terry Conroy afterwards. 'It was one of the most frightening experiences of my life. It was mob fury – pure hatred. They tipped tables over and smashed glasses – there were children in there, it was disgusting.'

As police eventually managed to restore order and the ground was cleared, Stoke fans had no option but to conduct a temporary retreat, organise themselves and decide on their next move. For some, the anger took on a sinister form.

'I did get threats,' recalls Peter. 'The police were telling me I'd had death threats but I was quite light-hearted about it. I'm quite resilient. People don't frighten me and I'm not easily intimidated. I didn't take any notice of it – they said, "Look, we have to act on this and we have to make sure you're protected, otherwise we'll be culpable."'

You'd have thought that an experience like that would have forever discoloured Coates's opinion of Stoke fans, but he's remarkably forgiving about the whole episode.

'I don't hold a grudge,' he tells me. 'I know how people are with these things, even if they're wrong. Sometimes people haven't got their facts right, but they've got plenty of emotion. That's football supporters though – you've only got to switch on the television and listen to the stuff they come out with, and don't forget I'm as much of a supporter as anyone else is. If you listened to everyone though you'd have ten different managers. It's an emotional game, and I get all that. It's never been an issue for me.'

The dissatisfaction took on a less explosive form in the following home game against Bradford, which Stoke managed to win 2-1, as Stoke fans orchestrated a 'late arrival' protest. Supporters entered the ground 15 minutes into the game, in front of the Sky cameras, carrying placards and banners urging the board to sell up.

There was also a meeting at Kings Hall, orchestrated by the Stoke City Independent Supporters Association where it was decided that fans would boycott the club shop, season tickets and Stadia Catering in order to try and force the board out. The view from many supporters was that Coates was paying lip service to the idea of selling the club, and was either not making enough of an effort to attract outside investment, or was asking a ridiculously high price for his shares.

Coates insists that this simply wasn't true, 'It's frustrating because you know you've done all you can. I'd looked for new investment, in fact I'd spoken to many significant business people with local connections, all of whom had more money than I had, and I was more than happy for them to take over the club but we had no takers. There was a view out there that I was clinging on for grim death and wouldn't let anybody into the club, but it couldn't be further from the truth – there was no interest out there. You can't make people invest in something they don't want to invest in.

'It's different now with the Premier League money and the international money that's out there, but it was harder back then. It wasn't because of the asking price, and I wasn't preventing anything happening by being unreasonable, but supporters took a different view! It's part of the game though. You see it all the time in football. Mine wasn't a new experience and it wasn't a pleasant one, but it's the kind of thing you have to put up with and accept – it's not left any scars though.'

I'm sure that Peter didn't get to the position he's in today by acting as the charitable benefactor in every aspect of his professional life, but I can't help but feel that the money he's invested into the club in his second spell (Coates resumed control of the club in 2006) is as much, if not more, to do with wanting to leave a legacy to his home city as it is about profiting from the TV riches of the modern Premier League.

Born in Goldenhill, Stoke-on-Trent, the youngest of 14 children and the son of a miner, Coates, despite the clipped enunciation developed by elocution lessons as a young man, is of pure working class stock. A committed supporter of the Labour Party, financially and politically, his socialist principles are evident when he talks about Britain's education system – another of his passions – and in the fact that he sent all of his own children to the local comprehensive school in Sandbach where the family lived, foregoing the usual option of private education so often taken up by those with wealth. In fact, Coates partly attributes the success that his children have achieved in business to the experience they had during their school years, pointing out that in attending the school they did, each of them learned how to interact and empathise with people of varied backgrounds, rather than growing up in a bubble of privilege.

I also consider the bet365 office where I'm sat. It's an immaculately presented hive of activity – people buzzing in and out of doors – and everyone looks purposeful and busy. The company employs 3,000 people, most of its workforce being from Stoke-on-Trent. It's the largest private employer in the area, going some way to filling the enormous hole left by the closure of the mines and pot banks that formed the backbone of the city's economy for so long. Yet it would make more financial sense for a business this size to relocate; after all, there are many other gambling companies that base themselves offshore.

However, when asked why the company based itself in Stoke-on-Trent by *The Guardian* in 2012, Denise Coates gave a simple answer: 'It's where I'm from. As to why we have stayed here when every other major competitor is based in a lower tax jurisdiction, that's a more difficult question to answer logically.'

It's hard to admit that you were wrong about someone, but considering the contribution that the Coates family have made to Stoke City's success and the economic success of Stoke-on-Trent,

I'm more than willing to hold my hand up and admit that perhaps supporters should have given him an easier ride than they did. For a club the size of Stoke, funding a move to a new stadium in the days before the Sky money poured into football can't have been an easy task. Coates lists the move, as well as the 1992/93 promotion and reaching the Premier League in 2007/08, as his three finest achievements as chairman.

'I always put whatever money in that I could afford,' says Peter. 'But it was a difficult thing to do, keeping the show on the road and keeping things viable.'

Although nobody seemed keen to admit it at the time, the cost of the new stadium had undoubtedly had a crippling effect on the club's finances. There was no money available for new players, and maybe it would have been better all round had Coates taken the option of openly admitting that firstly, the club were flat broke, and secondly, he (at the time) hadn't got the personal wealth to plough into the club.

It's easy to spend other people's money, but maybe some fans would have been more understanding had Coates simply stated that he wasn't rich enough to invest in the team at the same time as meeting the club's financial obligations on the new ground. As Ian Bayley wrote in the *Evening Sentinel* at the time, 'A little honest self-appraisal would not go amiss now that Stoke have over-stretched themselves to the point where there is no money to buy new players.'

However, football fans aren't always the most patient and understanding characters when their team's not performing, and as Coates states, football's an emotional game. It's hard to accept that your team is absolute garbage for a lot of people because so much of their sense of identity is wrapped up in their club. It was hard for me, like it was for everybody, seeing the 11 men who represented us play so appallingly at times when every fibre of your being wanted to see a team you could be proud of, like previous generations had experienced, like the stories we'd been told about.

If they don't get a level of performance they're happy with, then fans quickly start to lash out – at the players, at the manager, at the board – whoever they deem responsible for the malaise that they might find themselves in. Whether it was justified or not, there's no doubt that Coates was the target for that frustration.

'Things got so bad that I did put the club on the market and up for sale simply because I thought the club would be better off having a new owner and seeing if somebody else could come in and turn things around,' he tells me.

Following the scenes after the Birmingham game, Coates resigned as chairman – but there was no one else immediately willing to take the club off his hands. Instead, his position was taken by long-term sidekick Keith Humphreys, so no one was under any illusions – the people in control were the same men who'd owned the club for the last 14 years; they'd literally just swapped chairs! At this point, it seemed like there was no hope whatsoever.

The Kamara Disaster

Following the Birmingham debacle, the board decided to remove Chic Bates from his position as manager. Bizarrely, they waited until after the team had beaten Bradford before wielding the axe, but there was never any doubt that the manager would pay with his job after losing a home game so heavily.

Looking to bring in a character who could lift the spirits of a demoralised dressing room, the board turned to former player and recently sacked Bradford manager Chris Kamara. Kamara had led the Bantams to promotion the previous season, but had allegedly fallen out with the chairman and lost his job as a result. That had been Kamara's only managerial job since his retirement as a player, so even though Stoke were appointing a man of little experience, the impression he'd made during his limited time as a manager was favourable. Fans liked his exuberance, although declaring that Stoke was 'a sleeping monster' that would soon be challenging near the top of the table had a worrying echo of Alan Ball-style 'Don't write us off for the play-offs/This'll be a piece of cake' type bluster about it.

It's hard to know exactly what went wrong for Kamara at Stoke, but I've never seen one man have such a dramatic impact in making what was already a poor team discover new levels of incompetence. It was as if every single player in that squad downed tools the moment that Kamara walked through the door. There were some games in which the side performed so badly, fans earnestly and openly suggested that the players were trying to lose on purpose in order to get Kamara the sack. What the hell was going on behind the doors of the Britannia Stadium?

'I took over when the club had just been beaten 0-7 by Birmingham under the previous manager and looking from the outside I thought it'd be OK,' recalls Kamara, Stoke a distant memory on his CV now following his rebirth as a popular *Soccer Saturday* reporter. 'I thought I could go in and change things around and do things my way.

'But the first week in charge as a manager I had to sell my best player [Andy Griffin] for £1.25m and then I'm on scraps. Obviously I made some mistakes, I'm not hiding from that at all.'

What were the mistakes? One change he made was to replace Mike Pejic with his former Bradford coach, Martin Hunter, but one can't imagine that the players stopped trying in protest at no longer having a character like Pejic barking at them in training every day. There were also some awful transfer deals – the most expensive of which was, for years, considered one of the worst pieces of business in Stoke's entire history.

At the time, Stoke were said to be weighing up a move for young Blackburn striker James Beattie, but eventually plumped for Walsall's Bermudan striker Kyle Lightbourne instead at a reported cost of £500,000. Backing the wrong horse springs to mind – although we'd have been better off signing an actual horse considering the limited contribution our new striker made. Lightbourne had a decent scoring record in the lower leagues, but played with the intensity of a man wandering around WH Smith on an extended lunch break. After an awful debut, people gave him the benefit of the doubt once it was discovered that Lightbourne had been suffering the after-effects of a bout of flu. Weeks later, fans were thumbing through their home medical dictionaries, because even a bloke with flu couldn't be as bad as Lightbourne was.

'By the way, we didn't pay £500,000 for Kyle Lightbourne like it says in the record books,' claimed Kamara in a recent interview with the *Sentinel*. 'I can guarantee you that!'

One imagines that Kamara is implying the fee was less, but knowing how badly Stoke was being run in 1998, he could just as easily mean we paid double.

There were other flops as well, most of whom lasted no more than one or two games. Not many fans will remember the likes of O'Neill Donaldson, Tosh McKinley, David Xausa, Paul Holsgrove, Jorg Sobiech or Tony Scully, and it's probably better it remains that way. No one really knew where any of them came from, they just seemed to turn up in the team one week then disappear out of it a couple of weeks later, never to be seen nor heard of again. There's always a chance that O'Neill Donaldson could still be wandering the corridors of the training ground following Mark Devlin around – who knows?

All in all though, Kamara's brief reign was a bizarre spell in Stoke's history. It may have lasted a bit longer than Brian Clough's infamous 44-day stint in charge of Leeds, but there are probably just as many stories to tell about what went on. The results were catastrophic. Only a single win in 14 games was recorded (2-1 at home to QPR. How bad must they have been?), five draws and eight defeats.

Kamara took over in January with the team 14th and left in April having guided Stoke to 24th. I'm not even sure whether guided is the correct word as this implies a level of control over events. What happened was more like watching a man attempt to stop the inexorable plummet of a heavy object from height, solely through the method of flapping his arms around and shouting a lot.

The board realised that this pantomime couldn't continue any longer and Kamara was relieved of his duties with only five games of the season remaining.

'I am disappointed that things have not worked out as I expected,' Kamara said at the time. 'I have enjoyed working with the board and under different circumstances and with a little bit of luck things could have been so much better.'

A little bit of luck was an understatement. Stoke would have needed some kind of divine miracle to stay up under Chris Kamara.

Relegation

With no one else to turn to, and little time left to rescue the situation, the board appointed assistant manager and former first-team boss Alan Durban on a short-term contract. Durban did a great job at Stoke in the early 1980s, taking the team to promotion and establishing them in the top flight, but he hadn't managed in the professional game for 12 years and clearly didn't want the hassle of a permanent managerial position. 'I'm here because I want to get this club out of their current situation,' Durban said at the time. But he also made it crystal clear that he didn't want the job on a full-time basis. Who the hell would?

Durban knew how to organise a team though. Now infamous for his, 'If you want entertainment, go to the circus and watch the clowns,' line after his team had defended their way to a particularly grim goalless draw at Arsenal, Durban was the sort of old-school pragmatist who might have been able to drag Stoke out of trouble had he been given longer to do so.

His first game in charge at least gave us hope. Stoke immediately looked more resolute and purposeful as Portsmouth came to town, and the team possessed the spirit to come back from a goal down and equalise with 12 minutes left thanks to Ally Pickering's thunderbolt shot. Just as supporters were drifting away to begin the mad dash to the car park, Lightbourne rose from his usual torpid state and planted an exquisite lob over the keeper's head and into the net. The ground erupted. From a position where we hadn't even dared to believe that escape was possible, three precious points had suddenly been presented to us.

A disappointing 2-0 defeat at Crewe followed, but the following week Stoke managed another good performance at home – this time comfortably seeing off Norwich 2-0 with an apparently rejuvenated Lightbourne once again on the scoresheet. For the first time in weeks, the club were outside the bottom three. However, with a game at runaway leaders Sunderland to come (which we lost 3-0), we knew that everything would end up resting on the final game at home to Manchester City.

It seems unthinkable now that City were in the bottom three of the First Division and also facing relegation to the third tier, but that was exactly the scenario. It was one of those situations where people try to work out the endless permutations that could have seen both clubs safe, one of us safe, or in the worst-case scenario, both of us relegated. Mathematically it was out of our hands, as if Bury, Port Vale and Portsmouth all won then neither City nor Stoke could catch them. That seemed unlikely though – all three of those sides were just as bad as us.

Whatever hopes we had of a great escape before 3pm were well and truly over by the time the second half kicked off. It was as if City had actually worked out that if they didn't get their shit together there and then, they were relegated, whereas we still seemed to be lost in some kind of deluded fantasy that the FA would let us stay in the First Division because we'd got a lovely new stadium full of nice, shiny red seats.

Manchester City weren't a good side, not back then, but they tore into us like a pack of jackals attacking a flock of particularly dozy sheep. By the 50th minute we were 2-0 down and the away end was bouncing. The only fight Stoke had was coming from the stands as interloping Mancunians were identified and given a traditional Stoke welcome. The law of the terraces still applied, even in all-seater stadiums.

Stoke offered token resistance when Peter Thorne pulled a goal back, but that just annoyed the visitors, who went straight up to the other end and made it 3-1. Those on the away end were no longer celebrating quite so jubilantly though as news filtered through that all of the sides above us were not only winning, but winning comfortably against sides who must have turned up in towels and flip-flops. The rest of the game played out in an atmosphere of shocked silence: shock from the Stoke fans that their team could turn up for such a crucial game and play so badly, and shock from the Manchester City faithful that their side could play so well and still end up getting relegated.

That's exactly what happened. The visitors won 5-2 and there were fights inside and outside the ground as everyone present took their frustrations out on one another. There were also numerous interruptions as fans spilled from the stands, particularly outed City fans making a break for it from the home areas of the ground and attempting to reach the safety of the away end. Peter Thorne remembers seeing a familiar face among the interlopers. 'I'm from Manchester myself and on one occasion someone I knew growing up actually ran past me on the pitch. I kept my head down. The last thing I wanted was for someone to shout out, "All right, Thorney!"'

The final game summed up the whole campaign – one long, sorry mess from start to finish. By 5pm both sets of supporters trooped home faced with the prospect of visiting Macclesfield Town in a league match the following season. I wonder if Pep Guardiola has ever been to the Moss Rose?

Season 1998/99
Brian Little

GETTING relegated again only five years after 1992/93 made it feel like all of the time and effort invested into building that squad was for nothing. All the blood and thunder battles against Port Vale, Stockport and West Brom – what was the point? We were back to square one.

Of course, there's no actual end goal in football, the game just keeps endlessly rolling in a cycle of promotions and relegations, but for teams like us, former top-flight mainstays who'd been out of the big league for so long the younger generation of fans (myself included) had never even seen us play a single game there, getting to the Premier League was our nirvana – the point where we could die peacefully in the knowledge that we'd seen it happen, if only for the briefest moment.

By the start of 1998/99 that dream felt further away than ever. Damn you, Lou Macari, for even giving us a fragile hope that soon shattered like a champagne flute. Damn you, Mark Stein, for giving us the belief that had now betrayed us. Damn you, Stoke, for taking us all the way to the edge of glory and then somehow finding a way to tip us back over the precipice of failure.

We'd been sent plummeting back into the same dark waters in which we thought we would never swim again and it was too much for some fans to take. At least the first time, it seemed like a novelty – we were relegated with a sense of delusional belief that we'd storm the division and that our stay in the Third Division would be like a 12-month holiday where we'd only have to turn up to win. Having been through the reality of how tough the division actually was to get out of so recently, this time we didn't even have any fantasies to cling on to. We had no money, no manager and no chance of a swift return. To say that the board surprised us with their managerial appointment would be an understatement though, for into the role stepped Brian Little – the former Aston Villa boss.

Little had managed to get Darlington promoted from the Conference and Fourth Division in successive seasons, he had led Leicester City to promotion to the Premier League and had then gone on to guide Aston Villa to fourth place and a League Cup victory at Wembley. Things had gone sour for him the previous year at Villa, and he'd left them in the bottom half of the table, but make no mistake, this was a guy whose CV stood up to anyone else's in the game at that point. It was an unbelievable coup to get him to agree to come to the Potteries, but maybe he saw Stoke, with our new stadium and passionate support, as a long-term project to build up gradually after becoming disillusioned with the goldfish bowl of Premier League management.

'Brian's pedigree was excellent,' recalls Peter Coates. 'His record was very impressive. You think you've done the right thing because the appointment was universally accepted and everyone seemed pleased that we'd got him.'

Little was also making the right noises that suggested this could be the perfect appointment for a club like Stoke – a man with a track record who wanted a long-term project. 'I've come to Stoke to be successful,' he told *The Oatcake* soon after taking the job. 'I haven't come here to work for one or two years while I decide what I want to do with my life. I've come to Stoke because I saw it, spoke to the people, quite liked the people, realised they wanted me to do it and didn't want to interfere with me doing the job.'

The supporters were delighted too, and suddenly those who had threatened never to go again while Coates, Humphreys and Moxey remained in charge decided they might just give the club one last chance after all. Little didn't have any money to spend, but was able to attract a few experienced campaigners in to bolster a squad that had shed a lot of the players who took the club down the previous year.

Full-backs Chris Short and Bryan Small joined from Sheffield United and Aston Villa respectively, and Little had them earmarked for the wing-back positions in a continental 5-3-2 system. Phil Robinson joined on a free from Notts County to play as one of the three centre-backs and joining the regular midfield of Keen, Kavanagh and Forsyth was the experienced David Oldfield, who was part of Little's promotion-winning squad at Leicester.

With Peter Thorne and youngster Dean Crowe (somewhat prematurely labelled 'The Michael Owen of Division Two!') up front, Stoke had what looked like a decent starting XI for the level they were playing at, and cautious optimism again began to creep into fans' thoughts.

The Blistering Start

Buoyed by the arrival of Little, Stoke flew out of the traps, winning eight of their opening nine league games to set a blistering pace at the top of the table ahead of promotion favourites Manchester City and big-spending Fulham, who were under the control of Harrods owner Mohammed Al Fayed and the management of Kevin Keegan.

A comfortable 3-1 opening-day victory at Northampton got Stoke off to the best possible start, and once we'd all got over the shock of seeing the name of Macclesfield Town on the match tickets, we were actually quite relieved to beat Sammy McIlroy's newly promoted team 2-0 in our first home game – especially as the Silkmen had dumped us out of the League Cup in the first round.

Jez Moxey was appalled by that particular result and announced that Stoke had budgeted for three rounds in the League Cup, so were set to be £125,000 short on their projected income for the season. For years, the business acumen of the Stoke board had been questioned by supporters, and this kind of statement just added fuel to the fire. For a team as awful as ours, and with such a laughable recent record in cup competitions, how on earth had anyone been able to forecast that we'd get to the third round? The only way that would have been a certainty is if we'd been given two byes or both of our opponents' team buses had got lost on their way to the Potteries.

A week later a thrilling comeback at Deepdale provided a welcome distraction from the permanent state of disillusionment with the board. Stoke were trailing Preston 2-0 at half-time, but inspired by superb performances from Dean Crowe and Graham Kavanagh they roared back to win a thrilling game 4-3.

'I can't pretend everything went as planned because it didn't,' admitted Brian Little. 'Our defending in the first-half was very poor at times and even in the second when we thought sorted it, one ball slaughtered us for their third goal.'

The next three games brought another three wins, but more of these sort of cracks were beginning to show. Perhaps learning something from the Preston game, Stoke looked fairly hard to break down, but were struggling to create chances and didn't really convince in any of the victories over Oldham (2-0), Colchester (1-0) or Bournemouth (2-0). Ironically, Stoke's best display of the season saw them lose 3-1 at home to Blackpool in a completely one-sided game!

Even Little's comments suggested that he knew the team were riding their luck. 'If you look at the games we've played [so far],' he said in September, 'you can see there are games where we might not have won, but where we have. Players have come in and scored for us at vital times, but yes, I am pleasantly surprised by how well it's gone so far.'

The start that the team had made though provided a considerable amount of leeway to lose the odd game and still retain a healthy lead at the top of the table. Fulham, after spending a significant chunk of Al Fayed's millions over the summer began to eat away into Stoke's lead, but Little's men managed to retain top spot all the way up to mid-December.

Losing my Religion

However passionate you are about your football team, and however committed to attending games and supporting the side you may be, sometimes life just unavoidably gets in the way. For some supporters a drastic life change may result in a permanent switch from the terrace to the armchair. For the rest of us, periods of football abstinence may only be temporary, but as a break becomes longer the urge to return can become ever weaker.

Any periods when finances and time become stretched are the danger zones. It doesn't take the wisdom of a sage to realise that periods of unemployment, living away from home and the years immediately following a marriage or the birth of children are times when pockets may not be deep enough, or days long enough, to accommodate the expense and time required to commit oneself fully to following a football team.

It's probably the latter of these life events that's responsible for most of our red and white brethren drifting from the flock and losing themselves. I've seen a number of once-fanatical Stoke fans reduced to sad-eyed shuffling figures, mournfully pushing shopping trolleys or prams around supermarkets, shell-shocked by their own descent into domesticity. They may offer an acknowledging nod of half-recognition and engage you with casual football small-talk, but there's nothing behind their eyes anymore other than a confused look that screams, 'How the hell has *this* happened to *me*?' Before long these men can't even escape their wives or their lives for even the occasional trip down memory lane to attend the odd match. There's always a fence panel to mend, a room that needs painting or a child that needs dropping off at a friend's house. Once a brother reaches that point they are gone forever, and are not ever likely to return to the fold.

I'm relieved that I've managed to navigate through that period of life completely unscathed. For this I'm thankful to an understanding wife, the financial resources to keep two children in clothes, shoes and Peppa Pig DVDs, and the foresight to establish very early on in my marriage that Saturday afternoon is a time of sanctity, not to be desecrated by shopping trips, family parties or statements like, 'I didn't realise they were playing and I've arranged coffee with the girls.'

However, 1998 was another period in my life when my relationship with Stoke City became rather fractured. Earlier in the year I moved into a rented house in Stoke with Louise. We didn't think it would change things, after all we practically lived together anyway is what we told ourselves. The changes that faced us came as a shock.

We lived in one of the small terrace houses on London Road – an eclectic street that sees pubs, fancy dress shops, barbers, takeaways and brothels sit happily alongside one another for the long stretch between Trent Vale and Stoke town. Our house was in what's known as West End, which really isn't as glamorous as it sounds. On a daily basis, I'd walk from this tiny terrace to attend university – often taking in the CD section of Woolworths (RIP) on the way, the newsagents next to The Wheatsheaf for a crafty read of *NME* (RIP) and sometimes The Glebe or The Fawn and Firkin (RIP) on the many days when I changed my mind about actually being present at the lectures. At the start of the season I went to the games as normal, usually on my own, which is a depressing experience at the best of times.

None of the lads I'd stood on the Boothen End with were around anymore. Big Dave had lost interest and even my dad preferred to stay at home watching the horse racing. Even when Stoke were winning games in August and September, I missed the social aspect of the match – meeting up for a pint somewhere beforehand, mates taking the piss out of each other, giving up on following the ball after about ten minutes to talk about something else instead. More than anything I missed the sense of camaraderie that grew out of a group of friends watching shit football together – all of you suffering the same crap week-in, week-out, but still turning up the next week because it's just what you *did*. When you're on your own, it's just you and the drivel on the pitch.

There's nothing to sugar-coat it, no social filter that makes even the bad games fun somehow – it's just plain, unadulterated misery. You try and replicate what you had by talking to the people around you, but you're always conscious of being 'that guy' – the lone weirdo with no mates who sits in a football ground because nowhere and no one else will tolerate him.

I tried to persuade Louise to come along, but football wasn't her thing. She did join me once when I managed to get a couple of complimentary tickets – a 2-1 win over Wigan on a wet Saturday in October – but I could tell she wasn't enjoying it. And why would she? The weather was foul; we were sat at the edge of the exposed Block 19; the rain was swirling through the open corner between the Boothen End and the main stand; it was fucking freezing; the ground was half-empty; the game was crap. On what level does any of that constitute entertainment? Durban was right – football's not about entertainment, it's about compulsion.

The mentality of the football die-hard is akin to the avid cult member, fervently trying to drag everyone else in their life into the madness, no matter how much they resist. Today, I still tell my wife off for referring to Stoke in the second person.

'You played well today,' she sometimes says.

'No, *we* played well,' I correct. 'You're a Stoke fan too,' I remind her.

'I suppose so. Whatever.'

She is though, I think. Her dad was, and she's been to about a dozen games over the years, so by my reasoning that brands her for life, as much as she might display a sense of ambivalence to all things red and white. Our kids, Isobel and Daniel, are a different matter. They had no chance – I got to them early!

Eventually though, realising I wasn't going to make a Potter of Louise, and bored of sitting alone, chuntering to the person next to me, or more often than not to no one in particular, I stopped going at all. There was also the worsening financial situation. Although I was lucky enough to get a student grant, and both Louise and I worked part-time around our studies, it really was hard going. We had even less money than Brian Little did in his transfer kitty, so most weeks it was a case of eating or going to the game. As the football was getting worse week-by-week, I was probably fortunate not to be wasting what precious little cash I had on watching such dire fare.

One man who wasn't losing his passion for the club though was Tim Gallimore, a Stoke fan since 1967. Disillusioned by what he was seeing on and off the pitch, Tim decided to take action and set-up the SOS (Save Our Stoke) campaign.

'Initially it wasn't a campaign,' he tells me. 'I was very down after the 3-1 home defeat to Wrexham in February and decided on the spur of the moment to do something in protest, to bring the plight of the club to the media's attention. The following week we were playing Blackpool away and the Matthews connection, as well as their own problems, presented an opportunity. My brother worked with the guy who ran their Progress pressure group and we got together for the original black balloon protest. I made it on to Alan Green's Friday night programme with a mention and was on live on Saturday morning on Radio 5 with Faye Clover and the late Alan Robb. They loved the story.'

The SOS campaign was one of the first of its type, certainly in Stoke's case, to gain members and mobilise support through the use of the internet.

'My brother and three of the Southern Supporters Club helped me dish out balloons – they got in touch through the first version of the *Oatcake* website,' Tim recalls. 'A couple of weeks later we played Fulham at home and I put out a message for people to meet in Delilah's to see if there was interest in forming a peaceful pressure group. SOS was born as about 25 people showed up. We grew to an active group of over 300 quickly with people from all over the world, connected by e-mail.'

The group had an active marketing campaign, contacting potential investors through a 'Stoke For Sale' web presence and mail shots to targeted individuals. There were protests such as marches from the site of the old Victoria Ground, a campaign for the issue of supporters' shares through the *Oatcake* fanzine, and the display of For Sale signs during televised games. 'We were well organised,' states Tim. 'We attended AGMs en masse, with Premier and Legends Club members letting us use their access [to the ground] so we had somewhere to meet.'

The group was a thorn in the side of the board, but Tim insists that the intention of SOS was to seek positive change. 'SOS was focused on getting new investors interested rather than a board out position. Coates and Humphries never got this. The board didn't like what we were doing. It was different and unpredictable, unlike SCISA [Stoke City Independent Supporters Association] which went before. We put them on the back foot.

'I remember getting Moxey on to Radio 5. I had a slot sorted with Ian Payne and offered it to Jez instead. He was cornered and Payne asked the question as to whether the club was for sale. Reluctantly he said they were always interested in investment. It was the turning point.'

Even after the club was eventually sold, the lasting legacy of SOS is that Stoke fans were given a voice. The SOS initiative led to the formation of the Fans' Forum and to a position of influence with the new owners. For the first time in years, supporters were being listened to again. Despite the years of relative success that Stoke have had under Peter Coates since his return, Tim's opinion remains different to mine in how history should now view the chairman.

'I never wanted him back in honesty. He did ask me to meet him the summer he took over and I didn't take him up on it. He spoke to me at the last AGM of the Icelandic era. He still seemed to think he hadn't done anything wrong in his first spell. That was it for me.'

Despite my own views on Coates being more conciliatory, Tim represents, to me, an essential part of any fan base – the activists who are always willing to punch upwards if they deem it necessary. It's people like Tim and fellow Stoke fans Malcolm Clarke, chair of the Football Supporters' Federation, and Angela Smith, chair of the Fans' Forum, who ensure that fans have a voice – in both good times and bad. While Stoke, despite relegation from the Premier League in 2017/18, have enjoyed a period of relative success in the last decade, other clubs – the likes of Blackpool, Coventry and Portsmouth for example – haven't been so fortunate. While I'm not aware of the Coates family having any plans to sell the club, things can change quickly in football, so when Tim says to me, 'I still think we need a supporters' trust – you never know when we might be needed,' I can't help but agree.

Sunday League Football

I wasn't watching much football at this point, but I was still playing it quite a lot – thankfully not as a non-backflipping left-winger. Looking for something to entertain ourselves with at the weekends, a few mates and I decided to form our own Sunday league football team. Sunday football is one of those things that sounds like a good idea until you actually have to drag your sorry, hungover arse out of bed on a rainy January morning to amble around in sub-zero temperatures.

It's even worse when you're the complete mug who's been landed with the responsibility of running the team, and therefore the person who ends up telephoning literally everyone he knows at 9am because five players have cried off with 'flu' (meaning they've looked outside and seen it's raining) and you know you'll face a fine from the Staffordshire FA if you can't fulfil your fixture.

Running a team teaches you a lot about human nature, and the harsh life lesson that people will always find a way to let you down. We started our first season in the unglamorous Marston's League with about 18 players registered and everyone was given their own strip to look after. Within a month we'd lost five kits, six players had gone off in a strop because they'd been picked as substitute or realised it was getting a bit cold, and our sponsors – a pub in the Newcastle-under-Lyme area – decided to drop us because only four people bothered to go for a drink after the matches!

To add to this, my dad was appointed manager to oversee all the in-game stuff like substitutions, but decided he was going to be the Marston's League's answer to Alex Ferguson and went on a recruitment drive, bringing in as many players as he could from all kinds of places. It was a bit like the Chris Kamara spell at Stoke – I half-expected O'Neill Donaldson to turn up at Knutton Recreation Centre one week with his boots and £2 subs!

We had some bloke my dad got talking to in a shoe shop turn up as the new striker, a mechanic who'd fixed his car was the new right-back, a former customer of his who was about 50 and used to play for Rhyl (he was pretty good actually!) and finally, his prize capture – a former Manchester United youth team player who played two games for us, took the piss completely then realised the rest of his team-mates were rubbish and didn't bother coming again (he's probably still got one of our kits).

This was all well and good, but by the end of the first season, a lot of the guys who'd been there at the start weren't getting a game and got fed up. I imagine most teams go through a similar crisis of wondering what they're actually turning up for on wet Sunday mornings: is it to win trophies or is it to enable a bunch of mates to play football together? You'd think that in a league where many of the players are overweight, over-the-hill or drunk, it would be the latter, but no – there were plenty of players strutting around, barking orders out thinking they were John Terry, grown men throwing hissy fits because they'd been substituted or, on occasion, team-mates brawling with each other over whose fault some random goal was. Absolutely ridiculous behaviour, but anyone who's played Sunday league football will be only too familiar with what I'm talking about.

You do come across all sorts on those muddy, turnip-field pitches though – the full spectrum of humanity, from nice, happy-go-lucky blokes like us to violent criminals who saw every game as a personal challenge to maim as many of the opposition as possible. Some of the tackles that used to go in should have warranted jail time. Against certain teams, you genuinely did take your life into your hands when you crossed that white line on a Sunday. To think we were actually paying money for this experience as well!

We had a few characters in our own team, thinking about it. Our goalkeeper was a complete lunatic who lived in a particular village in Staffordshire where the gene pool has always been more of a puddle. I won't mention it by name for fear of being lynched next time I visit there, but it's a place which I'm sure *The League of Gentlemen* is based on! Anyway, there was a story in the *Sentinel* at the time about someone in this village killing people's pet cats by bludgeoning them with a spade. We didn't dare to ask our goalie about it – we all suspected who the culprit was.

Then there was a guy whose claim to fame was that he had the Autoglass Trophy under his bed. Yes, the one Stoke City won at Wembley. I assumed he was bullshitting me about it, so when I popped round to his house on one occasion I asked if he'd still got the cup, fully expecting him to just say, 'Oh I was just having a laugh about that,' and admit it was a fib. No – he told me to follow him upstairs, which I did. Laughing, he pulled out one of the drawers of his divan and sure enough, there it was in all its silver, shiny glory. God knows how he'd got hold of it, but I'm guessing that whichever football club's shelf it should have been sitting on hadn't asked him to look after it for safe keeping (if there are any policemen reading this, I am pretty sure in hindsight that it was merely a replica).

There were also the regular trips to play Werrington Young Offenders' Institute, who unsurprisingly had to play all their games at home and bolstered their side with several wardens, all of whom looked more dangerous and unhinged than any of the prisoners. Then there was the time that someone rode a motorbike across the pitch mid-game. I can't remember where it was, but unless the bloke was Steve McQueen, I'm assuming it wasn't at Werrington!

The whole experience was crazy, but back then the Sunday leagues were thriving. There was the PDSL which had four divisions of ten or 12 sides, the Ansells League, which also had about 60 teams, the City Traders League (comprising of two or three divisions) and finally the Marston's League, which only had one division of about 14 clubs. The numbers seem to have reduced now – the PDSL has certainly shrunk in size and both the Marston's League and City Traders League disbanded some time ago.

My suspicion that Sunday league football has died a death since the 1990s is confirmed by Gareth Thomas, senior football services officer at the Staffs FA. Unfortunately, the FA only hold figures going back to 2005/06, but over the last 12 years there has been a gradual decrease in the number of adult teams registered, from 382 teams to 231 for the 2017/18 campaign. One can only imagine the fall in numbers would be even steeper from the 1990s.

'There are a lot of reasons for this,' Gareth tells me as we discuss the decline. 'People are leading busier lifestyles than ever, work commitments have increased with Saturdays and Sundays now being considered part of the working week for more people. People have less time to spare so more choose to spend it with their families rather than playing football. Plus with the rise of gyms and health clubs, there's also been an increase in the number of people choosing to exercise alone rather than through team sports like football.'

The professional game's also to blame I suppose. How many times do we see Stoke fixtures moved to Sundays to satisfy the demands of Sky? If games are kicking off at Sunday lunchtimes, there'll be plenty of people who'd rather watch football than play it, especially if they've got season tickets or have paid £40 a month for their Sky subscription.

It isn't just the case that cultural changes in society have had an impact though – the financial picture was also very different in the late 1990s to the economic state of the country in 2018.

'The pub trade's really been hit over the last 20 years,' agrees Gareth when I mention that only one of the pubs whose teams I played for is still in existence. 'But there's also the financial cuts that local authorities have suffered and the removal of the ring-fence that used to protect the budgets for sports facilities and pitches. Players don't want to be getting changed pitchside or in cars on cold January mornings, which you can fully understand.'

It's reassuring to know that the Staffordshire FA are fully involved in trying to get people playing football again and have a number of initiatives that have proven to be successful. There are now Friday night leagues on 3G pitches that seem to be proving popular, and the FA offer more support than ever to clubs and individuals involved in the amateur game to cut down the administration and bureaucracy that can also deter people from getting involved in grass roots football.

Gareth talks passionately about ensuring that the traditional form of Sunday league football is protected, but I suspect that it'll be an uphill battle. Even at the level of 22 hungover men kicking a ball around a park, in so many ways, the 1990s feels like a lifetime ago.

The Terrible Finish

Back to the main plot, and Christmas was the turning point for Brian Little's Stoke. After playing badly for weeks, or even months, and yet still hanging on to top spot, the team couldn't keep being lucky. Our fortune simply ran out and a tough run of fixtures against four of the top six (Gillingham, Walsall, Preston and Manchester City) ended with only one point being gained – a dismal 0-0 against Tony Pulis's Gillingham side. It was as if the belief drained out of the players at this point. A run of four straight defeats during February saw Stoke slip out of the play-offs for the first time and included one of the most embarrassing results in the club's history.

On 20 February 1999, Stoke travelled to ninth-placed Millwall and sensed a rare win on the cards when the home side went down to ten men as early as the third minute. By the 70th minute, our hosts were down to nine men. Surely Stoke had to win this game? Somehow, we lost 2-0.

'This is my worst result in 12 years of management,' said a clearly embarrassed Little afterwards.

Predictably, the season ended badly and so did my relationship with Louise. After a turbulent year of cohabiting, my girlfriend moved out – leaving me in an even bigger financial hole. A special £5 ticket offer against Bristol Rovers had offered respite for one afternoon at least, but ended with Jason Roberts and Jamie Cureton tearing Stoke to shreds, a 4-1 defeat at home and a sit-down protest on the pitch, which lasted an hour, and which, to my shame, I actually started. I'd watched one match in months and thought that gave me the right to lead the protests! That defeat at the start of April was pretty much the end of my 1998/99 season.

There were just too many other distractions at that time drawing my attention away from Stoke. I was getting into music in a big way, trying to form and join various bands and hanging around local indie club The Stage in Hanley in a long black overcoat, sporting a shock of bottle-black back-combed hair and thick eyeliner. It was a look that seduced a few impressionable art students but it certainly wouldn't have gone down well on the Boothen End.

Approaching graduation in the spring of 1999, there was the realisation that I would have to get some kind of job. Without realising quite how competitive the field was, and the level of drive and commitment one would need to actually succeed, I decided that I might as well attempt to use my degree and would become a clinical psychologist.

Naively, I thought that 12 months of care work would be enough experience to get me on to the necessary course (is that time machine still handy? I think another boot to the knackers might be in order). Before too long I'd been offered a part-time job in an old folks' home, wiping bottoms and dishing out cups of tea – usually at the same time given how short-staffed we always were.

One of the many drawbacks of this position was that I had to work on Saturdays, so my only contact with Stoke at the end of the 1998/99 season was quietly sneaking into what was known as 'the small lounge' where a couple of the old chaps would listen to match commentary on Radio Stoke and reminisce about better days. These men had been regular attendees back in the days of

Matthews, Franklin and Steele, had experienced the whole of the Waddington era and had probably only stopped attending in the 1980s when age and infirmity caught up with them.

I could tell they enjoyed having someone new and attentive to regale with their stories of the great Stoke teams, and even though neither had set foot in a football stadium for over a decade, they still followed the sport fairly closely. Their interest was probably greater than mine at that point, as most of my time away from work was still spent messing around with guitar effects pedals, getting wasted on cheap lager and wandering around Hanley in my black coat and make-up, pretending to be Robert Smith from The Cure.

The 4-1 defeat to Bristol Rovers had pretty much killed any slight chance of Stoke making the play-offs, and so we staggered through to the end of the season like a sad drunk at the end of the party, beyond help and receiving only distant pity as we did the footballing equivalent of puking all over our own clothes and shitting ourselves in public on a weekly basis. I lost track of the number of times we were thumped by four goals. Bournemouth did it to us, Reading, Burnley, Gillingham; it seemed that every week we were on the receiving end of a hiding. I was glad to be missing it.

Was this the lowest it could get? Probably, because even though statistically Alan Ball's team was worse, I genuinely think that Brian Little's side, especially towards the end of 1998/99, was the most pathetic, spineless bunch I've ever seen in the red and white. Somehow, despite all the miserable defeats, we hung on to eighth place, which was solely down to the number of points we'd amassed in August and September. Little looked a beaten man from Christmas onwards, and there was no surprise, only relief, when he announced his resignation at the end of the campaign.

'I have tried my best and the disappointment is very hard to take,' Little stated. 'I hope the supporters understand that it's best I leave.'

Never mind understanding, there would have been a queue all the way around the Britannia Stadium to drive Little to any club who'd take him off us.

'Sometimes you wonder why things don't work out with managers,' states Peter Coates, looking back on an appointment that seemed to promise so much, but deliver so little. 'But sometimes there are things in people's personal lives going on and they lose focus. Looking back, football's such a tough game that if you take your eye off the ball for a second, it can affect you. You've got to be fully focused and on the front foot all the time.'

If there were things going on in Little's personal life, and there were always rumours, then the situation wasn't going to help a team that needed dragging out of the torpid state they'd allowed themselves to get into. The final game of the season offered a bit of hope though and a window into the next century as players such as James O'Connor and Clive Clarke stepped up from the youth team to inspire Stoke to a rare 2-0 win over Walsall. However, it would need more than just a couple of promising kids to breathe life into the club.

We finished the decade in a worse position than we started it, even though those people who'd watched us flailing around under Mick Mills and Alan Ball would have struggled to believe that at the time. Supporters will put up with bad football and bad teams as long as they've got hope, but by the end of the 1998/99 season we were all out of that. All we'd got to live on were memories – the distant ones and the newer, more recent good times that seemed so much more painful to recall. They were so close, so recent; how the hell had it gone so wrong so quickly?

The club needed fresh investment, fresh ideas and fresh blood at all levels from the pitch to the boardroom. We didn't know it at the time, but somewhere in Reykjavik, Iceland, a group of businessmen were forming a plan to buy a particular football club in England.

Their compatriot and manager of the Icelandic national team, Gudjon Thordarson had been over to Stoke a few times to watch defender Larus Sigurdsson play and had noted the ground, the support and the potential that existed. By the time the calendar year was over, Stoke City would be in foreign hands for the first time and the seeds of progress that led to an eventual promotion to the Premier League would be planted.

I suppose all that's another story though. Another story for another decade.

Epilogue

A BRIEF word of explanation for any readers not hailing from the Potteries. Stoke-on-Trent isn't a city in the traditional sense, rather a federation of six towns that was granted city status in 1910. Confusingly, Stoke itself isn't the city centre, merely one of the towns – alongside Fenton, Longton, Burslem and Tunstall. Hanley is the town that became the city centre, and as such tends to be the area that receives the most investment, although you struggle to believe that whenever you look around the place. There's a lot more happening there though than in Stoke, which even more confusingly for visitors, is where the city's train station is located.

Winding the clock forward to (almost) the present day, and faced with the formidable task of entertaining Daniel during a school holiday, I decide to spend a few nostalgic hours seeing what's changed in the town of Stoke since the 1990s and my days of living on London Road, all the while selling this as some kind of 'exploring adventure' to the little man. That sounds far more appealing to a small child's ears than, 'Let's turn your cartoons off and go and look at some old buildings,' trust me!

So, filled with an admittedly limited sense of derring-do, we take wellies for jumping in puddles, a 12in high Spiderman figure (well, why wouldn't you?) and make no plans other than to park up and then see where the mood takes us. We start at the station, where the sight that greets visitors is as impressive as ever. Winton Square, constructed in the mid-19th century and consisting of the North Stafford Hotel and several other listed buildings, is a fine example of Victorian architecture and a superb backdrop to the iconic Wedgwood statue. I used to walk past it daily, and on the days when drunk students haven't adorned old Josiah with a traffic cone hat, you'd actually think you'd arrived somewhere quite magnificent until you turn the corner and walk under the bridge!

Before we reach the eyesores that await us though, Daniel and I walk down Glebe Street, past the new council offices and on to the impressive Town Hall and adjoining King's Hall. Spiderman seems quite impressed too as he briefly climbs the ashlar stone exterior of the latter, which, when you take a step back and actually look at it, is quite incredible. The largest municipal building in Stoke-on-Trent, the hall's been used for a variety of events over the years: boxing, a concert venue, and is probably most famous for hosting Northern Soul all-nighters, which are still sporadically being held there to this day. I took my A Level exams in there too, no doubt as an 18-year-old completely oblivious to the grandeur of my surroundings.

It's the sort of structure that you can easily take for granted when you're used to seeing it. As you drive along the one-way system though, the thing that really sticks in the mind isn't the glorious architecture of the Town Hall on your right, or the equally impressive Stoke Minster on your left, it's the long run of boarded-up shops and pubs that stretch the rest of the way down Glebe Street. Steel shutters, 'For Sale' boards and smashed windows are all that meets the eye, and there's the entire Potteries in microcosm: a few impressive blocks of history surrounded by neglect and urban decay.

Walking through the rest of town and the story is a similar one – hidden gems that are easy to miss. The original library building, the old banks and entrance arch of the Victorian market on Church Street are structures I must have walked past a thousand times during my student days in the late '90s. However, today is the first time I really notice the craft that must have gone into designing and building them. Sadly, their Victorian splendour only serves to highlight the surrounding mess. Campbell Place, the former home of Woolworths and Blockbuster, remains an atrocity to the eyes – a row of giant breeze blocks now housing nothing but charity shops, bookmakers and pound shops.

Further up the road, the statue of Colin Minton Campbell, former pottery manufacturer and town mayor, has the metallic grey panels of Sainsbury's as his backdrop rather than the dark brick and ivy of the historic Minton's building that I remember. That's Stoke all over – a mish-mash of 19th century grandness, glass-fronted modernity and architectural carbuncles from every decade thrown together with reckless abandon. Like a hundred different Lego sets scattered from their boxes then assembled by a drunk, it still lacks any sort of aesthetic consistency. For as long as I remember, it's never really changed.

I take the little one into the indoor market, which is as quiet as you'd expect on a wet Wednesday afternoon. We order two cheese oatcakes (no, son, Spiderman doesn't need one) and I try to eavesdrop on a group of pensioners drinking mugs of tea and chuntering among themselves. I imagine they come here quite often – probably keeping most of the traders here in business – and seem quite content in each other's company, putting the world to rights somewhere dry, and with tea coming back and forth to order. Eventually they shuffle off their separate ways and I notice that one has left a newspaper on the table. As Daniel's taking an age to finish his oatcake, I quickly relocate the paper to our table and scan through the headlines.

Would you believe it? On page four is the news that planning permission has finally been granted for the construction of 200 new homes on the Victoria Ground site. After all this time, we'll finally be able to see something of value sitting on the site of our former home. In the spirit of the day, I consider taking Daniel along to the old place and showing him where Daddy used to watch Stoke play, but I don't. It feels different than looking at the other old sites, monuments to a long-distant past, but all still proudly standing regardless of the squalor that now surrounds them. No, I'd rather remember the Vic for what it was, not for the mess it's sadly become.

Instead, we take in a puppet show at the old library then return to the car through the puddles of the King's Hall car park. As Daniel chatters away, I start to think about what we've lost. It's undeniable that Stoke City's relocation to Trentham Lakes has left a gap in the community, literally and figuratively. The practicalities of a Premier League stadium and 28,000 people and vehicles descending on those streets every other Saturday would have been unmanageable, but the romantic in me still misses the connection between our club and the residential area it served.

The Victoria Ground, Kings Hall, Winton Square, Stoke Minster – all iconic sites in Stoke, but one of them no longer there. So many pubs and shops have closed since the old ground was pulled down too. The skyline's very different to the pictures where floodlights rose up over the rooftops. The streets are just streets, not a route for Lowry-like men stooped low to beat the elements, all heading to the same, familiar shrine – the match.

One hundred and nineteen years. A place that existed in the souls of the men who stood there from the 19th century to the 1990s, generations of people from all manner of backgrounds: miners, middle managers, students, factory workers, soldiers, doctors and the millions who worked in the city's pot banks.

They dreamed then, like we dream now, of glory days when just for a mere hour or two they could be taken somewhere different than their own lives, spellbound by the artistry in front of them – the magic of Matthews or the working man's ballet of the Waddington years. The decades changed, the players changed, but when they got older, these men could close their eyes as they stood on those familiar terraces and listen to the chorus of voices. The Boothen End – it would still sound the same as it had done in their youth.

I think again of Grandad, standing on the old dirt heap of the Stoke End as a boy in the 1930s; I think about Dad as a young man in the '60s; I think about myself growing up and the friendships that were formed on those old terraces during the Macari years. There are thousands of us who are proud to be part of Stoke City, and it's our history that shapes us all. Not just what we've seen on the pitch over the years, but the faces in the crowd, the people we've loved and lost. The people who gave us this belonging, this passion that we carry on and then, in turn, that we'll inevitably pass on to others. *The people we shared all of that with.*

For as long as the old ground remained, something of them remained there too.